PEOPLES OF THE WORLD

Western Europeans

PEOPLES OF THE WORLD
Western Europeans

Joyce Moss • George Wilson

**The Culture, Geographical Setting,
and Historical Background of
38 Western European Peoples**

FIRST EDITION

 Gale Research Inc. • DETROIT • WASHINGTON, D.C. • LONDON

Joyce Moss
George Wilson

Gale Research Inc. staff

Coordinating Editors: Linda Metzger, Kenneth Estell

Production Manager: Mary Beth Trimper
Production Associate: Catherine Kemp

Art Director: Cindy Baldwin

Keyliner: Nicholas Jakubiak

The paper used in this publication meets the minimum requirements of American National Standard for Information Sciences—Permanence Paper for Printed Library Materials, ANSI Z39.48-1984. ∞ ™

Printed in the United States of America
Published in the United States by Gale Research Inc.
Published simultaneously in the United Kingdom
by Gale Research International Limited
(An affiliated company of Gale Research Inc.)
10 9 8 7 6 5 4 3 2

Contents

Preface

While ancient peoples were building city-states and great empires to take advantage of the Mediterranean Sea trade routes with the East and with Africa, Northern Europeans were living around the North and Baltic seas in small tribal units. Over the years, these people were joined, and sometimes overrun, by new immigrants from the east, who came across the mainland of Europe and through the Scandinavian peninsula. These northern peoples began to unite in more lasting political units, at first in tribal confederations.

The great Roman Empire spread its influence and cultural patterns (sprinkled with its own legacy from Greece) across Western Europe, meeting the emerging peoples from the east and north at the Rhine and Danube rivers. As that empire expired, its legacy merged with the tribal patterns to produce small duchies and kingdoms. In the northwest, a loose and temporary unity was provided first by the Holy Roman Empire of the Franks, and then by another Holy Roman Empire led by the Germans. However, the Roman Catholic Church became no real unifying influence on the various countries and eventually divided itself to further influence the separation within the various peoples.

North and east of the Danube, kingdoms rose and fell, and political units were redefined—often with little concern for the ethnicities of the people they included. One result has been a political makeup of Eastern Europe that overrides ethnic boundaries and has made, over the years, unhappy alliances and bitter land disputes. In contrast, strong national boundaries tended to define the ethnic groups in the West.

Within the kingdoms and empires of both East and West, dukes and princes ruled their small holdings with only the concern necessary for the kings they elected. Dukes presided over fortified estates surrounded by hosts of peasants dependent on and subservient to them. Even so, by the thirteenth century, the kings, often chosen by the dukes, had grown in stature so as to take some power from their electors. The chiefs of the smaller fiefdoms rebelled against their own kings, forcing statements of rights that, at first, only applied to the nobles. But as the nobles prospered and enjoyed these new rights, peasants became increasingly restless with their lot. Within the kingdoms defined by language and geography, and encouraged by the Roman governmental pattern, peasant uprisings gave rise to strong sentiments of nationalism.

The result is two Europes, almost diametrically opposed. Today, the east, formed into countries for convenience and not ethnic unity, is breaking up and reforming along ethnic lines. At the same time, with the assurance brought by a century or more of unity within national boundaries, Western Europe is moving to unite. Economic opportunities are bringing together peoples of differing languages and cultures in a new and potentially stronger Western European society.

This book is about the ever-changing peoples of Western Europe.

Acknowledgements

The authors are especially grateful to Dr. Michael Mann, Professor of Sociology, University of California at Los Angeles, who reviewed the entire manuscript for accuracy.

We also extend our gratitude to Colin Wells, Monica Gyulai, and Drew Digby, who contributed to the research and writing of various sections of the book. A "thank you" is extended to Rena Kleinfeld for her skillful word processing.

Finally, the authors express appreciation to Linda Metzger of Gale Research for careful editing of the complete manuscript and to Dana Huebler for her deft proofreading.

Introduction

The history of Western Europe is one of separation by language and geography and, at the same time, sporadic attempts to unite all of Europe under one government or as one society.

The ancient capital of Crete, Knossos, became a leading trade center and the center of a society with paved roads, running water, and great architecture. About 1500 B.C. the people of Mycena gained control of Knossos and nearby Greek land and a western society had begun to take shape. Interest in architecture, sports, religion, and philosophy grew with the new Greek empire that, through trade, influenced the lands bordering the Mediterranean Sea as far as present-day Morocco and Italy.

Greeks settled in the south of Italy and traded with Carthagians on Sicily and with Etruscans who had established cities in the north. In 509 B.C. nobles from one of these cities, in rebellion against the king, withdrew to a village to the south, Rome. Here the Etruscans took charge and built a new city-state that was to evolve into the great Roman Empire. Rome began to spread its influence around the Mediterranean Sea and on all the European continent south and west of the Danube River—finally reaching beyond the Danube into Dacia (now Romania). Over 1,000 years, Rome developed a system of rule and law and added to the culture of the Greeks.

Roman law gave stability to an emerging Europe as Roman governors supervised local governments. Thus, Greek and Roman empires served to provide the basis for government and cooperation among the peoples of Central and Southern Europe and among the Germanic northern peoples with whom they came in contact. But local governments were encouraged by the Romans, and with the demise of the empire the various peoples, who had kept their own languages while adopting Latin as a language of commerce, again divided into separate states.

A new force, Christianity, was to revitalize Rome for a time and then become a powerful force for unity in Europe. The Germanic tribes were settling along the rivers of Europe and establishing larger governmental areas. Between 481 and 511, the ruler of one Germanic group, the Franks, seized on the spread of Christianity to join that religion and use it as an ally as he expanded from the Rhine Valley to build a kingdom of most of present-day France. In 732 another Frankish leader, Pepin, defeated the Muslims and became ruler of the Franks with influence in Spain. A successor, Charlemagne (768–814), extended the Frankish empire into the lowlands along the northwest coast and northward through present-day Germany. Again, most of Europe was united under Charlemagne, who gave himself the title of Holy Roman Emperor and controlled both the land and the religion. While Charlemagne's influence was short-lived, the Holy Roman Empire lived on with power now vested in more northern Germanic groups. Christianity renewed the European ideas of unity for a time and then became a divisive force.

Much of Europe lapsed into feudal states in which the peasants served and sometimes lived at the whims of a local ruler. By the eleventh and twelfth centuries, these peasants were rebelling against their conditions and the nobles were uniting for self-defense. The Crusades that began in this period provided a rallying cause for the nobles but did little to remedy the conditions of the majority of Europeans. Neither were they helped by the division of Christianity that came with the Protestant movement of the sixteenth century. The nations of France, Germany, England, Spain, and finally Italy that arose out of the union of the various nobles had little meaning to the average peasant. In England and elsewhere, these peasants were demanding an increasing voice in their own government. Throughout Western Europe, language and customs became separated as the Germanic-Roman peoples became isolated in competing kingdoms.

Finally, in the late eighteenth century, peasants and small business operators rebelled against the noble-king rule of France. For the first time the loyalty to the dukes and kings, which still dominated Germany, was replaced by a sense of nationalism in France. With the empowering of Napoleon and his efforts to conquer and unite all of Europe, and then to divide it as kingdoms among his relatives, nationalism began to take form throughout the budding European states. Europe's people, who shared many common cultural patterns, were made distinct by geographic and linguistic barriers and by a common foe, Napoleon. The present-day configurations of states began to take shape. Other powers—Prussia, Austro-Hungary, and even Sweden—were to try to reunite large sections of the continent.

In the twentieth century, wars and their settlements have again divided Europe, sometimes on lines not in keeping with the older cultural separations. However, economic, defense, and justice considerations have served to draw Europeans together for various purposes. The year 1948 saw the establishment of the Organization for European Economic Cooperation, and 1949, NATO (North American Treaty Organization), with 15 European nations uniting for defense. A Court of Justice of the European Communities in which, on a voluntary basis, cases can be brought from any of the member countries, also came into being. In 1988, a Court of First Instance was added to this court.

The various sovereign states of Europe have come together in a new European Community. First established primarily to develop common marketing policies, the idea of a community has reached far beyond the original plan. In 1987, the European Community agreed to a "Single European Act" designed to create a single market— an area "without internal frontiers in which the free movement of goods, persons, services, and capital is ensured." This economic freedom has resulted in a commitment to a new common currency and free exchange of job opportunities.

With freedom of movement has come a dialog about government and free exploration of differences and similarities in cultures. A European parliament and council, a common court of justice, and a common European Investment Bank have already been established, along with consultative bodies on energy, industry, social policy, agriculture, fishing, education, culture, broadcasting, transportation, and the environment. The goals of the new Community, first established by the Treaty of Rome in January 1958, are rapidly being realized. But still to be dealt with are issues of a new ethnic diversity created by a need for workers in some areas (for example, the influx of Turks in Germany) and, in others, by changing configurations outside Europe (the Indians in England, for example).

Fear of domination by the strongest powers continues to separate Europeans. However, the inclination brought by common heritages and sometimes common languages (e.g., Latin and English) is, today, freeing Europeans to join economically and socially.

Members of the European Community

Original members (1958)

Belgium	Italy
France	Luxembourg
Germany	Netherlands

Newer members

United Kingdom (1973)	Greece (1981)
Denmark (1973)	Spain (1986)
Ireland (1973)	Portugal (1986)

About the Contents of This Book

This book capsulizes the cultural groups of Western Europe during a period of great turmoil. While the French and Italians remain stable at this moment, content with frequently changing governments, Spaniards are emerging from a long period of dictatorship and struggling to become part of the European economy. Meanwhile, two Germanies are reuniting after more than 40 years of separation under highly differing cultural influences. The authors have made every effort to adjust to these changes as they describe the European cultures today.

Format and Arrangement of Entries

Peoples of the World: Western Europeans is divided into two sections: The Old Cultures and Cultures Today. The entries in The Old Cultures provide a brief overview of the region's ancient peoples, which includes peoples who appeared in greatest strength in the past and influenced the societies known today.

Organized alphabetically by culture names, Cultures Today introduces the dominant cultures of the region today. The entry for each of the groups is arranged as follows:

A dictionary-style definition introduces the entry, providing a key to pronunciation of the people's name, describing the group in brief, and furnishing the key facts of population, location, and language. (Populations are estimates based on the best and most recent available data.)

Following this introduction are detailed descriptions under three main headings: Geographical Setting, Historical Background, and Culture Today.

For quick access to information, subheadings appear under main headings. The Culture Today section, for example, may include these categories: Food, clothing, and shelter; Religion; Education; Family life; The arts; Recreation; and Language. (Subheadings vary according to the unique experience of each group.)

Each entry in Cultures Today concludes with a section headed For More Information, which is a selective guide for readers who want to conduct further research on the society. This section lists reading materials and appropriate organizations to contact.

Western Europe has a longer history of national identity than was found in the *Peoples of the World* volume on Eastern Europeans;

therefore, in most cases, cultural identities and national identities have merged. The section containing country briefs is, therefore, a part of the general descriptions and the maps accompanying the entries in Cultures Today.

Other Helpful Features

To assist readers in understanding details, each entry includes a map that highlights the current geographical distribution of the featured society. Photographs illuminating cultural differences illustrate the entries. All quoted material is identified parenthetically within the text of the entry; for complete bibliographic identification, the reader should consult the Bibliography included in the book's back matter.

Although every effort has been made to explain foreign or difficult terms within the text, a Glossary has been compiled as a further aid to the reader. A comprehensive Subject Index provides another point of access to the information contained in the entries.

Comments and Suggestions

Your comments on this work, as well as your suggestions for future *Peoples of the World* volumes, are welcome. Please write to: Editors, *Peoples of the World*, Gale Research Inc., 835 Penobscot Bldg., Detroit, Michigan 48226-4094.

Western European Countries and the Cultures They Represent

Country	Cultures
Austria	Austrians, Germans
Belgium	Flemings, Walloons
Cyprus	Greek and Turkish Cypriots
Denmark	Danes
England	English, Welsh
Faroe Islands	Faroe Islanders
Finland	Finns, Lapps
France	Bretons, Normans, French
Germany	Germans
Greece	Greeks
Ireland	Irish, English
Italy	Italians, Sicilians
Netherlands	Dutch, Flemings
Norway	Lapps, Norwegians
Portugal	Portuguese
Scotland	Scots, English
Spain	Basques, Catalans, Spanish
Sweden	Swedes, Lapps

THE OLD CULTURES

ANGLES, SAXONS, AND JUTES

(an′ gles, sax′ uns, jewts)

Germanic peoples who settled in England after the Romans
abandoned the area.

Population: Unknown.
Location: England.
Language: Old English.

Geographical Setting

The present-day country of England is predominantly rolling hills
through which rivers have carved fertile basins. The land is divided
by indentations created as the rivers empty to the English Channel
and the Atlantic Ocean. A low mountain range cuts the northern part
of the country east and west, while the Cheviot Hills mark the boundary between England and Scotland. The indentations of the coastlines
made comfortable places for foreigners to land and settle. They also
encouraged these settlers to establish their own societies and governments.

Historical Background

By the time the leaders of the Roman Empire had discovered the
island of Great Britain, the land was discovered and inhabited by
Celts who had also moved from their German bases to inhabit parts
of what was to become France. Roman interest in these island people
came when the rulers of Rome discovered that aid was being sent
from the islands to help people in Gaul (France) resist Roman domination. The Romans sent expeditions to conquer the island people.
In 55 B.C. their armies penetrated as far inland as the site that is now

London but were unable to immediately subjugate the Celts. Over the next 100 years, Roman soldiers fought with the Celts, who distinguished themselves by entering the battles adorned in blue paint. (The Romans named them Britons after a Latin word for paint.) Gradually, the Celts were pushed back to Wales and Scotland and were held there with the help of a wall built by the Roman leader Hadrian across what is now northern England from the Atlantic Ocean to the North Sea.

Rome. For nearly five centuries from 55 B.C., England was under control of the Roman Empire. The inhabitants, Britons, lived under whatever Roman government was provided and held to their own customs and religion. However, the Scots (Celts) and Picts in the north were even more fierce and distant enemies of the Romans.

England was a distant and not-too-important outpost for the Roman Empire, so as the empire's strength declined in A.D. 410, the Roman administration withdrew from the island. The remaining Romans along with Britons and Celts in England and Wales were left to fend for themselves, and organized into small fiefdoms with no central rule. These groups were often at war with one another and were easy prey for the Picts and Scots of the north.

Teutonic peoples. One of the few stories of this period of disorganization tells how Britons appealed to Germanic peoples to come to their land as protection against the northern foes. According to this account, the Saxons of the Elbe River region, to whom this appeal was made, did send a force under Hengest and Horsa to defend the Britons in the year A.D. 442. These early Germanic visitors stayed among the Britons until 456 when they became upset over rations that had been promised them. Thereupon, according to the story, the Saxons rampaged through the south of England taking bounty and laying waste to the land, and then went back to their Elbe River homes.

The result was a British people completely disorganized and in need of unity. That unity was brought about by Ambrosius Aurelianus. (The legendary King Arthur may be based on this Roman-British leader.) Thus, when visitors again came to the island, led this time by Hengest and Aesc, they found a stronger force of Britons. However, the more warlike Saxons defeated the Britons and were ceded the southeast corner of present-day England, an area called

Kent, to the Saxons. This area would later be given to the Jutes, neighbors of the Saxons in the old country.

Cerdic, Cynric, and the Saxons. A stronger force of Saxons sailed to England in five ships in 495. In 508 the father and son team of Cerdic and Cynric battled with the Britons once more and reportedly killed 5,000 warriors. Once again war was initiated between Britons and their allies the Celts and the Saxons. From 514 to 560, the Saxons struggled to subdue the Britons. They were finally able to establish a powerful kingdom along the Thames River and to establish Ceawlin as king of this West Saxon nation. In these battles Cerdic and Cynric were aided by their nephews, Stuf and Withgar. As was common in those days, intermarriage between leading families had placed the nephews among the Jutes. When they were rewarded for their efforts with Kent and the Isle of Wight, the Jutes were able to establish their rule in the far south.

Angles. Meanwhile, in the fifth century neighbors of the Saxons in Germany, the Angles, had begun to establish themselves in the north of England. Three divisions quickly arose in this part of England—a group of Angles who were called Mercians, the middle Angles, and the east Angles. Shortly another group known as Benecians established themselves near the Mercians. In 547, Ida became the first king of the Benecians.

Kingdoms. The Saxon and Angle invaders of England were more adventurers than true royalty, so anyone who could support a claim of genealogical linkage with the Teutonic god Wodan could claim a right to rule in the new settlements. The result was conflict among the various factions and the eventual establishment of small kingdoms everywhere that indentations of the coast, or forests, or rising land provided a demarcation of the territory. At one time these small units were grouped into eight kingdoms, headed by eight different kings and controlled by overlords, called ealdormen, of lesser areas. The ealdormen were aided by enforcers in each shire, the sheriffs.

Merging societies. The new rulers of England had come from similar backgrounds in Europe, with organizations of nobles, freemen, and serfs, with common religious beliefs, and with related languages. Their kingdoms in England continued these patterns. However, the Angles who settled in the north found it easier to establish themselves and soon far outnumbered the Saxons of the south. Soon the Saxons had begun to merge their language with that of the Angles, and the whole of the land began to be known as Anglia, the land of the Angles. During the eighth and ninth centuries new waves of Danes raided along the coasts and attempted to settle England. Eventually, these Danes ruled most of the eastern half of England. Only the kingdoms of the south were able to withstand their invasions, and these because they had been unified by a great Anglo-Saxon king, Alfred.

Alfred. It was the powerful West Saxon kingdom that finally succeeded in binding all the kingdoms and claims to kingdoms into a single Anglo-Saxon country. In the early 800s, the West Saxon king, Æthelwulf, fathered four sons. Although Alfred was the youngest of these sons, he was treated as if he were heir apparent to the throne. At the age of five he was sent to Rome to receive the pope's blessings, which included taking Alfred as a bishop's son (a confirmation of Christianity) and hallowing him as king. However, when Æthelwulf died, the three older sons succeeded each other for short periods until Alfred finally became king in 871.

By that time, Alfred had gained experience helping his brothers repel Danish invasions. In his first year of reign, Alfred fought off nine attacks by the Danes. Fourteen years later, the battles resumed and Alfred succeeded in preserving the land south of the Thames River for the English. During his reign, the English army was strengthened as was the spirit of the English. Alfred encouraged the writing of English history and the general education of the people through sponsoring a compilation of the *Anglo-Saxon Chronicle* and through building libraries of the finest Latin books. Because of Alfred's strong leadership in the southern kingdom of Wessex, his successors were able to unite all of England under one rule. This rule was transferred to the Danish king, Canute, who conquered England early in the eleventh century, but was reestablished under English rule in 1042, when Edward became king.

Normans. In the year 1066, the Duke of Normandy, who had governed a section of the coastal land given to the Normans by the king at Paris, claimed that he had been promised the English throne by the king of England. But upon the king's death, another English noble, Harold, took the throne. At the one-day Battle of Hastings, William defeated Harold and became King of England and Duke of Normandy. However, after installing some Norman ways in England (replacing English landowners with Norman lords and building forts, for example) the Normans followed their traditional ways and blended with the English so that in the next several hundred years few signs of a distinct Norman population remained. William did, however, order a census of all landholdings in England as a basis for taxation (a necessary census because William had scattered the land-holdings of his nobles so that none of them could concentrate power in any one part of England). The census became known as the Doomesday Book. To ensure the accuracy of this census, William's tax collectors were empowered to force people to take oaths that they were telling the truth. This was the beginning of a jury system of justice ("jury" comes from a French word for oath).

English government and law. In 1154, William's great-grandson Henry II took the throne. He expanded the jury system, starting with every sheriff. (England had been divided into governmental units called *shires.* The enforcer of government in each shire was a sheriff.) The sheriff was to appoint a committee of 12 to determine what crimes were committed in the shire and who should be punished. After Henry's death, these grand juries were added to by establishing small juries to hear evidence and determine guilt or innocence. These English innovations were the beginning of today's judges and juries.

Even when England was composed of a half dozen or more separate kingdoms, the kings and their nobles and bishops gathered periodically in a Great Council to transact business. As the kings grew in strength and consolidated all of England, this organization of nobles was frequently at odds with the king over how much influence the nobles should have and how much taxes they should pay. In 1215 the nobles forced then King John to sign a document defining their rights—the Magna Carta. When John's successor, Henry III, tried to ignore this document, his brother-in-law organized the nobles and called them into a meeting to talk about what to do. This meeting became the "parliament" (again from a French word meaning "to talk"). Over the years, the parliament became the actual ruling body of England. The jury and its built-up body of Common Law and the parliament were patterns for governments and justice systems throughout the world.

England and France. Besides their strong government, Normans had brought a union with France. Many Norman nobles who were given land in England also owned land in France, and as subjects of the

English king this land was also thought to be property of the English throne. On one reign of a weak ruler, England lost its claim to most of this land. In the fourteenth century, when the country sought to reclaim French lands, a Hundred Years War resulted (1337–1453). As a result England lost nearly all its claim to French soil.

Rebellion. While the Hundred Years' War was going on, nobles in England had resumed squabbling among themselves. Eventually this bickering developed into a struggle between two noble houses, Lancaster and York, for the ruling power. Following this "War of Roses," Henry VII became the recognized king of England. His son, Henry VIII, broke away from Rome and made himself head of the English Protestant church. Henry VIII's successor, Elizabeth I, became one of the most powerful of the English rulers. Her forces fought with the forces of the Catholic king of Spain. The powerful Spanish fleet, the Armada, was defeated by English "sea pirates" in 1688 and England began its rise toward becoming a world power.

By the 1680s, England's people had accepted the Magna Carta and a later Petition of Rights as a sort of constitution under which they were governed. When James II refused to abide by these rules, and because he was a Catholic who threatened to destroy the Protestant church, he was forced out of rule by the Parliament, which then developed conditions under which it would allow a new king to rule. King William (of Orange) agreed to these terms, and England began to be ruled by a parliamentary government.

The Empire. With the countries of the British Islands (Ireland, Scotland, England) as a base, the great British fleets of the eighteenth century sailed all the seas, and British soldiers took possession of far-flung lands—among them, India, South Africa, Pakistan, and Canada. So widespread did the Empire become that it was said that the sun never set on it. Aided by raw materials from its empire, the economy of England began to change. Between 1750 and 1850 the country changed from an agricultural nation into an industrial one. In the nineteenth century, Great Britain, with England at its center, became a dominant force in world economics. But in the twentieth century, the empire began to crumble, and the economy of England was dealt severe blows by the two World Wars, in which Great Britain was the staunchest defender against aggressive forces from Germany. Over the years, Great Britain (England, Scotland, Wales, and the northern part of Ireland) was forced to grant independence to its former colonies. Since World War II, the island nations have been struggling to regain their sound economic bases.

Culture

A merging of societies. Having been always distant from Roman influence, the Angles and Saxons developed their own language and customs. At first they organized themselves into city-states in which some sort of castle was the center of government. The "castles" of the early English were crude wooden affairs, the use of stone in building mostly coming from the takeover by the Normans in 1066. The Normans also introduced the French language, which contributed many words to the emerging English language.

Government. Each castle had its own rules of government, often borrowing from older Roman regulations. These rules, codes of conduct, lists of penalties, and prescriptions of government set a pattern for today's English government, in which a formal constitution has never been prepared, but that remains a collection of separate edicts and contracts developed through the last 600 years. Each city-state was headed by a person who called himself king. The land around the city was apportioned to nobles, and under them freemen. Land was worked by landless serfs and slaves. The present English society evolved from these various peoples—Celts, Romans, Normans, Danes, Angles, Saxons, and Jutes.

Arts and literature. The English were internationally known for their gold work and for their fine embroidery. They also were excellent makers of iron tools and fine weavers.

During most of the period before the Norman invasion, there was no common language among the people of England. Rather there were three variations of the old Germanic languages the people had used on the continent: Anglian in the midlands, West-Saxon south of the Thames River, and Kentish. Literature was first produced in the Anglian language and that became the most powerful spoken language. However, as West Saxon became more influential under Egbert, Alfred, and Eadweard (802–924), much of the early Anglian literature (mostly poetry) was translated into the West Saxon language. In that language, Anglo-Saxon poetry has been preserved in the Vercelli Book (now in the cathedral of Vercelli, Italy), the Exeter Book (Exeter, England cathedral), and in two manuscripts now in the

British Museum. One of these contains an old copy of one of the most famous West Saxon works, *Beowulf.* This story of a mythical hero was probably written in the 700s.

For More Information

Stenton, F. M. *Anglo-Saxon England.* Oxford: The Clarendon Press, 1971.

Whitelock, Dorothy, translator and revisor, with David C. Douglas and Susie I. Tucker. *The Anglo-Saxon Chronicle.* New Brunswick, New Jersey: Rutgers University Press, 1962.

CELTS
(kelts)

Migrants from Teutonic lands who settled in Ireland, Scotland, Wales, Cornwall, and Brittany.

Population: 4,000,000 descendants of Celts in France and the British Isles today.
Location: Ireland, Scotland, England, France.
Language: Celtic.

Geographical Setting

The Celts who were forced out of present-day Germany took up residence in Ireland, then Scotland, Wales, Cornwall, and finally Britanny, France. In all these places, they chose to settle along rugged seacoasts. The climate varied according to the latitude on which the land lay, but all Celtic settlements were on land strewn with rocks and with the poorest of soils—as if the early Celts took pride in their ability to overcome the land.

Historical Background

Origin. Before 300 B.C. the original Celtic people lived along the northwest coast of Europe, west of land occupied by other Teutonic tribes. As the Teutonic groups and later invaders from the Roman Empire moved into the area, the Celts were pushed toward the sea. Eventually, Celts moved across the channel to England, and then to Ireland. In Ireland and the Cornish section of England, Celts managed to maintain their identity in spite of Roman attempts to assimilate them. Romans pushed many Celts westward in England and destroyed those who remained in the east. Then as the Roman Empire loosened its grasp, some Celts returned eastward, setting up villages in Scotland by A.D. 500.

Celts in Scotland. There Celts merged with other residents, the Picts, giving rise to today's Scots. This union was not complete, especially in the north of Scotland. Here the Celts remained relatively isolated in the most difficult of Scottish lands. Meanwhile Celts from Cornwall in England moved back across the channel to the coast of France. While contact with other peoples in the four Celtic regions–Ireland, northern Scotland, Cornwall, and Britanny–has created differences in the cultures, there remains strong traditional bonds among the Celts.

King Kenneth had organized a Celtic kingdom in Scotland by A.D. 844. Successive Scottish kings sought to unify all of the people of the British Isles. They fell short of their goal, but the Celts and Norse in Scotland were at least able to ward off assimilation by the English. The Scottish Celts remained free and mostly unthreatened until 1286, when they found themselves under mounting pressure from the English. Between 1329 and 1513 the Scots aligned themselves with France and thus avoided a takeover by England until marriage between members of the Scot and English royal families finally brought them under English rule. At first, the peoples of Scotland and England remained separated, but in 1707 they were formally joined to one another by the Act of Union. Contact first with the Norse, then the French, and finally the English, have influenced the Celts of Scotland.

Celts in Ireland. In Ireland the Celts moved into land that before 300 B.C. was occupied by a people called the Pretani. Once there Celts found a rugged land in which small groups of Celts became isolated from each other. Contact among Celts was largely at a few marketing places. These market centers eventually grew into separate Celtic states and then into five kingdoms. The kingdoms fought among themselves for supremacy until Comac, king of Connaught, succeeded in organizing a government. That government ruled over a weakly united Ireland until about A.D. 275. The union was short-lived, and Ireland soon broke into seven kingdoms. About the year 400 the man who became known as Saint Patrick moved from England to become a Catholic bishop among the Celts. He was kidnapped by one of the kingdoms and enslaved. Escaping after six years, Patrick became a great unifying influence on the island. The Celts of this time were renowned marauders, frequently raiding England and bringing back English slaves. However, the Celts themselves became victims of raids in the 700s and 800s, as Norse people swept across Scotland and Ireland, and again in the 1100s when the English invaded Ireland. By 1172 King Henry II of England had grown strong enough to pay a personal visit to Ireland, bringing English rule and church to the Celts. In 1297 a viceroy named John Wogan succeeded in organizing a legislative assembly with representatives from every town. This English-Irish assembly lasted until the 1800s but excluded the original Celtic inhabitants of Ireland. Through the movements of people in and out of Ireland (in the 1800s half the population of Ireland migrated to avoid great famines) the Celts have continued to live in accordance with their traditions on the most difficult Irish land.

Celts in Wales and Cornwall. From the 1500s until today the land of the Celts in Wales and Cornwall has been part of England. The Cornish (Cornwall Celts) live on the west coast of England, where they have occupied rugged land similar to the coastal areas of Ireland and Scotland since the last century B.C. As with Celtic groups of other areas, they have been frequently subjected to incursion by different groups: the Romans in the first century A.D., then the Angles and Saxons, the Scandinavians in the 700s and 800s, and finally the Normans and the English. As with the Celts of Ireland and Scotland, those in Wales were caught in disputes over the emerging forms of Christianity. In the 1700s, emigrations from Ireland added to the preference of Protestantism over Catholicism among Celts in Wales.

Celts in Brittany. In the fifth century A.D. people who spoke the old Celtic language and lived in the traditions of the Celts migrated to some of the most rugged areas of the French coast in the region of Brittany. They earned their livelihood there by fishing and farming in the manner that was common among Celts of Cornwall, Wales, Ireland, and Scotland.

Culture

Shelter and economy. Everywhere the Celts settled in rocky, windswept coastal regions of the countries. They subsisted by farming small plots of land, often supplementing the farm produce by fishing. The Irish Celts lived and still live in stone and brick houses that often consist of only one room and lay near farms that might be as small as ten acres. French Celts also farmed small pieces of land, but preferred to live in village cottages of all-white plaster and slate or tile roofs. The dependence on small parcels of land is the same in parts of Scotland where hills and bogs limit the holdings and where the Scottish Celts, too, build small homes of stone.

Religion and folklore. Celts in different areas clung to common bonds; for example, the Filids of Ireland and the Druids of Wales had similar roles as wise men who served as religious leaders and administrators. The *vatis* or *filidh,* who became the subjects of many folktales, were experts in magic and in divining the future. Bards were and are guardians of the people's oral literature. A tradition of storytelling has been passed from generation to generation, stories of a fighting and pioneering people. Scottish Celts tell of battles with the Sassenacks (Saxons). Irish Celts tell of struggles with the Norsemen and the English. French Celts tell of courage at sea. Celtic mythology developed into stories of deities and heroes (e.g., Lug—god of magic and warfare) to explain the history of the Celts. In Ireland folk stories tell of the warrior-heroes Culchulain and Finn MacCumhail.

Language. The original language of the Celts gave way early to many quite different dialects. One Celtic language, Cornish, has disappeared, giving way to English. English has also become the language of the cities, but in the rural areas old Celtic languages survive and, since the twentieth century, government programs have encouraged their maintenance. Welsh, Irish, and, in France, Breton are examples of living Celtic languages.

Arts. As early as the third century B.C., Celts had begun to develop distinctive art forms, creating tankards with ornamental handles and bronze mirrors with elaborate backings. Brooches and hanging bowls were later additions to Celtic art, and religious manuscripts elaborately decorated with abstract geometric shapes and stylized animal heads were created after the people's conversion to Christianity.

Holidays. Celts in the various countries they inhabit today celebrate common holidays centered around seasonal changes and harvest times. All Hallows Day, November 1, and St. Bridget's Day on February 1 are typical holidays and are celebrated among the Celts with music, games, and dance. In Wales, an Eisteddfod festival has been conducted in the same fashion since the twelfth century. Poets and singers compete for prizes in reading, choral singing, and other musical performances. The bagpipe, a traditional instrument of Celtic music is played at the different celebrations in both Ireland and Scotland.

Celts prize strength. Highland games in Scotland and similar games among the Welsh feature such contests as the shotput, caber toss, and hurling, a team game played with hockey-like sticks. The heritage of the past is remembered at these games in events such as the traditional sword dance.

Family life. Among the early Celts, roles of family members were once clearly defined. Families were self-sufficient. Mothers took care of the home, and fathers farmed and fished. The fathers wielded authority in the family. Outside the family, the men gathered in small groups to tell stories and share wine or ale. The men wore homespun suits woven by the women. Sometimes the women created unique Celtic clothes such as the high lace hats worn by the women in Britanny even today. The old ways centered around the family unit and religion. Celtic lands bear signs of the ancient times in great monasteries built along the coasts and great stone and earthen forts on the hills.

Celts today. Traditions of the past have not been forgotten. Older people in Britanny and along the rocky shores of Wales, Ireland, and Scotland still gather to exchange stories, still wear the old costumes, and still practice the combination of fishing and farming the harsh land. Celts seem to be attracted to the land that is most difficult to farm. However, today's younger Celts have been exposed to an easier life seen on television. Rather than remaining on the land, they are leaving behind the ways of the ancient Celts and entering into industry and the cities. The result is that traditional Celtic culture is disappearing. Strong examples exist in Britanny, France where Paris industry offers an easier life, and in Ireland, where one-third of the Celts have gathered in the city of Dublin.

For More Information

Cunliffe, Barry. *The Celtic World.* New York: McGraw-Hill, 1979.

Herm, Gerhard. *The Celts: The People Who Came Out of the Darkness.* New York: St. Martin's Press, 1975.

Powell, Terence. *The Celts.* New York: Frederick A. Praeger, 1958.

ETRUSCANS

(eh trus' kans)

An early people of Italy who once ruled Rome.

Population: Unknown.
Location: Etruria, now the Italian region of Tuscany and part of Umbria.
Language: Etruscan.

Geographical Setting

Ancient Etruria spanned an area between present-day Florence and Rome, 350 miles north to south and 95 miles from the coast of Tyrrhenian Sea on the west to the Tiber River on the east. The coast of Etruria (present-day Tuscany) is rugged, with promontories jutting up above the jagged coast. Several river mouths have formed small ports along the coast. It is from these city-ports, sheltered by the carved coast and with rising land for great visibility and defense, that the ancient Etruscans carried on trade throughout the Mediterranean.

Historical Background

Beginnings. The Etruscans (people of the coastal cities of Etruria) probably migrated to the coast of Italy before 900 B.C. There is much mystery about their origin. Some claim that the Etruscan culture grew with local people as they traded around Italy and its islands. More popularly it is believed that the Etruscans came by sea from somewhere in Asia Minor. Their exact origin is lost in history. At any rate, by 900 B.C. groups of people with similar cultures had settled in villages along the western coast of the Italian peninsula. There they developed a dozen city-states, each with its own government and style, and each controlling land and villages around it.

Trade. Ships from these city-states traded up and down the coast and with the people of Sicily and eventually extended their trade as far as Greece. Between the seventh and third century B.C., these city-states grew to their greatest strength. At their peak around 500 B.C. one of the Etruscan cities was in control of the bordering city of Rome. In fact the last three kings of the ancient Roman city-state were Etruscans.

About 700 B.C. Etruscan traders had reached the Orient, having already established trade with Greek cities. At home they continued to expand their sphere of influence to include Campania and Salermo by 600. By 535 Etruscans had trade agreements with the African city of Carthage and joined the Carthagians in their battle against the Phoenicians. Ten years later the Greeks established trade in Campania, resulting in a battle with the Etruscans. Although this was the beginning of the fall of the Etruscans, one Etruscan city-state, Tarquinia, had expanded its influence to Rome. Before this city ceased to be a kingdom, three Tarquinian kings had ruled Rome. In 509, the last Tarquinian king, Tarquinius Superbus, was expelled from Rome and that city established a republican government.

Decline. The Etruscans had never been able to unite the 12 Etruscan cities into a unified defense force. The demise of the Etruscan trade dynasty was, nevertheless, lengthy. In 474 Greek and Syracuse (Sicily) seamen defeated the Etruscan fleet. The year 435 saw the beginning of Etruscan-Roman wars. At last the Etruscans were alarmed. One of their cities, Veii, was only 11 miles from Rome. The nearness of this threat resulted in a weak attempt at Etruscan union, hindered in 423 when their influence in Campania gave way to an invasion by eastern Sammites. Meanwhile the war with Rome dragged on. In 405 Romans began a siege of Veii that was to last ten years and result in the submission of the first Etruscan city to Rome.

Fall of the Etruscans. Everywhere, the Etruscans were pressured—from the north by the forces of the Gauls, at sea by the fleet of Syracuse, and from the south by Rome, which by 358 was in battle with its old overseer, Tarquinia. That battle resulted in Rome forming a 40-year peace treaty with the other Etruscan cities. Peace gave Etruscans time to unite, but also gave Rome time to increase its strength.

It was followed by 50 years of war between the two states. After unsuccessfully supporting raids by other groups on Rome, the Etruscans finally were controlled by Rome in 241 B.C.

Culture

Etruscan building. Twelve large cities and many villages were formed by the Etruscans in the following manner: A group desiring the new home had a pit dug in the center of a desired location in which an offering was given to the gods by the group's leader. The leader then decided the breadth and width of the new city and the outside walls of stone were erected, the site being oriented to the points of the compass. The town wall contained three gates, from which extended three streets to three temples to the principal gods—Jupiter, Juno, and Minerva. Inside the walls streets were laid out to form blocks of building land. Houses of stone and wood were erected irregularly in the blocks. Popular building materials were stone walls capped by wooden beams over which tile roofs were laid. The homes had low walls, cut stone foundations, a central supporting beam, and tile or thatched roofs. Major Etruscan cities had stone drainage canals covered with stone slabs and water supplies from nearby streams carried to the homes in terra cotta pipes.

Etruscan cities. Twelve city-states erected after this style have been identified: Volterra, Arezzo, Cortona, Perugia, Vetalonia, Populonia, Rosalle, Vula, Tarquinia, Cerveteri, Veii, and Bolsena. Each was an independent state with its own customs and located to take advantage of local resources. The city of Cerveteri, for example, was erected near the metals that could be mined from the Tofa Hills and established a metal trade with Greece. The hills also allowed the citizens of Cerveteri to inter their dead in tombs cut from the rocks of the cliff walls. The city of Veii, located near rock and clay deposits, used these deposits to create sculptures and to build cumuli, rock-cut passages for water to the city. The Veii citizens decorated their tombs with painted designs. Volterra citizens believed in cremating the dead, while Tarquinians believed in divination, the art of foretelling the future. Thus, each Etruscan city-state was separate in trade and in customs. Some cities were built without walls, some with strong walls. This separatism encouraged persecution from all sides. In spite of this, the Etruscan society grew to produce fine products for trade.

Country life. Outside the cities, peasants lived on the land like their predecessors—in round-shaped huts erected around a central pole, with mud and wattle walls and thatched roofs. These people planted and harvested grain, flax, olives, and grapes for the kingdom's use, or worked as lumbermen in the nearby forests. Berries, pomegranates, chickens, ducks, pigs, goats, cattle, and sheep were among the farm products, along with milk products and wool.

Family life. The names of parents of a dead person were often used as decorations for the tomb. These tombs reflect the importance of the family as the basic structure of society. Among the living, women in a family enjoyed freedom that was exceptional for their time. The family, if it could afford the expense, owned slaves (who ranked below freemen and nobles in Etruscan society). Slaves served meals outdoors at tables near which the diners reclined on couches. Food was served in dishes and pots from which the Etruscans ate with their fingers.

Clothing. Early in their history, Etruscan men dressed mostly in loincloths of wool or flax. Later this was replaced by a long tunic with sleeves and often a scarf or shawl. Women wore draped dresses with high domed hats and shoes with turned up toes. Women wore their hair in long ringlets while men kept their hair short and were clean shaven. Those men who practiced sea raiding carried short swords and spears of bronze.

Industry. The Etruscans were traders and raiders. In their cities, they created pottery, jewelry and tools of gold, bronze, and iron, fine wooden furniture, leather goods, and cloth, which they used or traded with people around the Mediterranean Sea.

Language. By the seventh century B.C., Etruscans had developed a unique written language. This language consisted of 22 letters and allowed such ease of writing that the Etruscans were among the best-educated people of Italy by the sixth century.

Arts. Etruscan artisans were skilled with clay and metal. Among the artifacts found in Etruscan ruins are urns, terra cotta figures, pottery modeled after the Greek creations, bronze statues, bronze cups, metal and stone effigies and stone reliefs, silver bowls, painted clay pots, and fine works in bronze—wine servers, candelabra, fire tools, and mirrors.

Murals and pottery painting indicate that the Etruscans enjoyed music and dance. Their most important musical instrument was the flute, which was accompanied by a lyre and war trumpet.

Religion. Etruscans believed that all events occurred for a reason, and that reason was to be found among the gods. The Etruscan sky was divided into 16 sections, each presided over by a god. Over all these gods stood Voltumna, assisted by Jupiter, Juno, and Minerva. Priests, who held noble rank and were identified by a fringed mantle and conical hat, could forecast the future from the signs of these gods—thunder and lightning—and also by examining the entrails of animals, particularly the liver.

Sports. Only nobles were allowed to hunt, and they hunted with nets and dogs. But the average Etruscan was not without interest in sports. Wrestling and boxing (possibly borrowed from the Greeks) were popular, as were track and field events. An armed dance, the Troy dance, was a popular spectator event.

Contributions to Rome. Aside from lending their own government to Rome, Etruscan culture contributed to that of the Romans. By 364 B.C., the Etruscans had introduced their music to Rome, as well as rites related to kingships. Etruscan writing presented ideas of trade and government to Rome. Because of their trade routes, Etruscans were able to influence Roman culture by bringing Greek ideas to the Italian peninsula.

For More Information

Scullard, H. H. *The Etruscan Cities and Rome.* London: Thames and Hudson, 1989.

FRANKS
(franks)

A Germanic tribe that expanded throughout Europe to form the Holy Roman Empire.

Population: Unknown.
Location: Present-day France, Belgium, and Germany.
Language: Germanic.

Geographical Setting

The land of the Franks is a low land bordering the Atlantic Ocean and North Sea. It is mostly a flat, fertile land through which great rivers flow from southern and eastern mountains to the sea—the Rhine, Meuse, Seine, Loire, Garonne, and Rhone. It is in the northeast along the Rhine River that the first records of Frankish tribes begin.

Historical Background

Beginnings. By the third century A.D. Germanic tribes were known by the Roman Empire to inhabit the northern half of the Rhine River valley. These tribes were first called Franks about the year 240, and were shortly thereafter thought to have divided into two sections— those living on the lower Rhine River, the Salinians, and those on the middle Rhine, the Ripaurians (River Franks). By the year 241, the Roman leader Aurelian had defeated some of the Salinian Franks, and within a hundred years most of the Frankish tribes had been subjugated by the Romans. Many of them then served in the armed forces of their conquerors.

Independence. In the next century, the Franks again became independent. When in 406 skirmishes elsewhere demanded the attention of the Roman troops, Frankish tribesmen united under Chlodio and marched south along the coast. Although unable to defeat the remaining Romans, this excursion moved the Franks southward to establish a capital at Tournai by 431. Shortly, ambassadors of the Franks were traveling eastward to enlist the aid of Attila, leader of the Huns, and, at the same time, southward to befriend the Romans. The later trek was successful, and in 451 Franks joined with Romans to repel Attila and his army.

The beginnings of empire. In 481, a powerful leader arose among the Franks. This leader, Clovis, united the Frankish nobles, defeated the Romans, then turned toward the center of Europe. In short order, his troops subjugated the Ripaurian Franks on the middle Rhine, the Allemani, a tribe west of the upper Rhine River, the Visigoths, who controlled southern France and part of Spain, and the people of Burgundy. By the time of Clovis's death in 511, the empire of the Franks stretched from the Main River in present-day Germany to the Atlantic Ocean. Before he died, however, Clovis divided this kingdom among his four sons, who established four kingdoms with capitals at Metz, Orleans, Paris, and Soissons. That began the disintegration of the first Frankish empire and, in another generation, the Franks had reverted to a collection of independent nobles ruling over a peasant work force, but with no central organization. From these nobles, arose a new powerful unifier, Clotair II. Upon his death in 613, there followed a succession of great Frankish leaders known as the Carolingians. The last of these was the most feared and the most respected—Charlemagne. In his reign, the Franks conquered the Saxons, another powerful Germanic tribe, defeated the Avars who were advancing southward through central Europe, and forced Bavarian nobles to submit to his rule. In 800 Charlemagne became Holy Roman Emperor with the blessings of Pope Leo III.

After the reign of Charlemagne's son Louis, the empire was again divided—this time among three sons. The great Frankish empire began to fade, and with it the identity of the Frankish people. However, the empire had left its mark in a beginning of an identity for French people and in its passing of Christian civilization to the peoples of Central Europe.

France. Following the rule of Louis and Charles the Bald, the old Frankish empire broke under pressure of invasions by Germanic tribes and contentions of various dukes over different parts of the land. The rebirth of the empire as the present-day country of France may have begun with the excursions of the Vikings, who reached as far as Paris. Always the center of information and direction of the area, Paris established itself as the center of the new France when its chief, Odo, led a successful defense against a Viking seige in 885. Odo was succeeded by his brother Robert. This ruler's grandson, Hugh Capet, strengthened the position of Paris and demanded allegiance of the dukes who controlled France. Hugh began a tradition of hereditary claim to the throne that was to last until the 1400s and provide France with a stability unmatched in the rest of Europe.

Culture

Early Franks. Little is known of the ways of the early Frankish tribes. They lived by hunting and by some agriculture and probably spoke related tongues so that they were able to communicate among themselves. But by the time the Franks had moved into Roman territory, they had become a system of nobles and serfs in which the nobles, in fact, owned the people who worked and fought for them. There were some freemen, living somctimes in separate communities, who were made free in order to focus their attentions solely on protection and war.

The Leaders of the Franks

Pepin, died 639.

Grimwald, died 656.

Pepin, the first of the Carolingian rulers who was mayor of the palace in Burgundy, Nuestria, and Austrasia (princes often left the actual management of their realms to "mayors"), died 714.

Charles Martel, son of Pepin, who conquered Germanic tribes and repelled the Saracens in southern France in 732, died 741.

Pepin II, a king who cultivated literature and arts, died 752.

Charlemagne, one of two sons of Pepin II, who took the empire from his brother and began 30 years of campaigning to unify Europe. He also began reforms of the noble-serf relationship to establish a society governed locally by freemen, died 814.

Louis, son of Charlemagne, who divided the kingdom among his own sons, died 840. The last of the Carolingians.

Clothing. Dress among the Franks was simple—a linen shirt and pants were common. Where there was sufficient wealth, this was covered with a silk tunic and accompanied by hose that were held in place by bands of leather. In winter, those who could afford such extravagances also wore otter- or marten-skin coats.

Civilization under Charlemagne. Under Charlemagne, conditions improved considerably. The constant war excursions yielded much wealth and permitted Charlemagne to press for a greater number of freemen—not necessarily restricted to fighters. He also demanded that his followers show greater respect for women.

In order to control the conquered people, Charlemagne organized governing units of local people. His rule was guided by a national assembly of free men. This assembly was repeated in smaller units of government, with local assemblies having much rule over local disputes and needs.

Charlemagne expanded the Frankish interest in agriculture. One of his plans, never completed, was to build an irrigation canal from the Rhine to the Danube to ensure water for crops in Central Europe.

Although universal education was not then more than an idea held by a few, Charlemagne pushed for greater education, and the Frank noble houses were among the best-educated Europeans of their day.

For More Information

James, Edward. *The Franks*. London: David Blackwell, 1988.

Rivers, Theodore, editor. *Laws of Salian and Ripaurian Franks*. New York: Ams Press, 1986.

GOTHS
(goths)

A Teutonic people who settled near the Black Sea and spread from there across Europe, bringing the downfall of the Roman Empire.

Population: The real population of the Goths is unknown. One estimate of the Gothic population of one area, Toulouse, is 10,000,000.
Location: North and west of the Black Sea; later spread throughout Europe.
Languages: Gothic, an old Germanic language; later the languages of the countries they settled.

Geographical Setting

The range of the Goths between 7 B.C. and A.D. 711 spans Europe from the Black Sea to the Atlantic coast of France and Spain, and from the Danube River to Constantinople. They were an agricultural people who turned to fighting on horseback, therefore ranging over much of the fertile farmland of Europe.

Historical Background

Origin. The earliest Gothic people, the Gutones, appear to have come from an area of present-day Sweden known as Gotland and the region south of the Baltic Sea between the Oder River and the Vistula River. From there they made their way in several tribes to the north shore of the Baltic Sea between the Dnieper and Dniester Rivers. In this region, they were early identified as Scythians. Here they established several tribal kingdoms and took up raiding as a supplement to their agricultural income. These tribes gradually united enough to seriously threaten the Romans across the Danube River. Their raiding grew into battles. In the year 250, one Gothic king, Cniva, led an army against the Romans, and by 251 had exacted a promise of tribute from them. When in 253 the governors of the Roman region of Moesia refused to pay this tribute, the Goths moved around the shores of the Black Sea through Moesia toward Thrace. Winning some battles and losing others, the Goths advanced so that in 272 the Romans ceded Dacia (present-day Romania) to them. However, the Goths by this time had begun to divide among themselves. By 291, there was a clearly defined separation between the more western Tervingi-Vesi people (perhaps the ancestors of the Visigoths) and the eastern Greutungi-Ostrogoths. By 332, the Tervingi-Vesi had spread west and south so as to threaten the Byzantine capital of Constantinople. In that year, a treaty was arranged with the emperor Constantine the Great. Some of the Tervingi-Vesi then espoused Christianity and one of them, Ulfilas, was made a bishop. Still the Goths quarreled with the Romans and in 367 were at war with the Romans under Valens. By the end of this war in 369, the separation between eastern and western Goths was fixed.

Huns. A more feared people, the Asiatic Huns, were also moving westward across the northern shores of the Baltic Sea and threatened to overrun the settled Goths. By 375 the Huns had pressed into the territory of the eastern Goths. Fighters who lived by looting and ravaging the land, the Huns encouraged a large migration of Goths to the west and south.

Romans. In 376 the Goths crossed the Danube River into Roman territory. Some of the Goths united with the Huns and their allies, the Alans, to battle the Romans at Adrianople. The Roman emperor Valens died in this battle and Huns, Alans, and Goths settled in Pannonia (mostly today's Hungary and Yugoslavia). These people would later become known as Ostrogoths. Meanwhile other Goths accepted a peace treaty with the Romans that allowed them to settle under Theodosius in Thrace. After 376, the Goths were allowed to settle on Roman land in return for forming an army to defend the empire. Under the Romans, the Goths gradually acquired military strength that would eventually allow them to take over the Roman Empire.

In the Balkans. Even though the leadership was then strong, progress in acquiring more land was slow. The Goths met with a serious setback when they fought among themselves in the year 394. A year later, Theodosius died and Alaric became king of the western Goths (the Visigoths). Five years later, these Goths were at the doors of Constantinople, where they suffered a harsh defeat. Thereupon, Alaric moved his army toward Italy. He was followed in 405 by Radagaisus, a leader of the eastern Goths (Ostrogoths). In 408 Alaric invaded Italy, and in 410 captured Rome. From there this group under Alaric's successor, Athaulf, sent expeditions into present-day France (then Gaul) and into Spain.

By 459, the Ostrogoths had also moved south to the Balkans and had made an alliance with the government at Constantinople that was sealed with the assigning of a Gothic prince, Theodoric (the Great), as hostage there.

Meanwhile, the Visigoths began a series of wars in Spain and Gaul. In 475, these battles resulted in a treaty with Rome recognizing the conquests of the Visigoths—one year after Theodoric, now the Ostrogoth king, was named by the government at Constantinople to be king of Macedonia. From 484 to 507, the Visigoths in Spain and Gaul were led by King Alaric II, who paid allegiance to the government at Rome. He would reign until his death in 507. In this period Theodoric became a counsel of the eastern Roman Empire, led an army to defeat the people of Ravenna, and killed his rival, Odovacar, for power. By 497 Theodoric the Great had become king of Italy.

Following the death of Alaric II, Theodoric the Great became king of the Visigoths (511) in addition to his leadership of the Ostrogoths. The union was short-lived, however. Theodoric died in 526 and the two Goth groups again divided: Visigoths led by Amalric and Ostrogoths by Athalaric. The Ostrogoths went on to disastrous wars with Constantinople, then with the Franks, and finally with Rome. After some successes, their leader, Totila, was killed in battle, and in 552, the next Ostrogoth ruler, Teja, also died in battle. By 555 the last Goths in Italy had surrendered and the Ostrogoths as a force in the region had disappeared.

Visigoth kingdom. In order to preserve peace and to protect themselves from the onrushing forces of Western Europe, the government of Rome recognized a Visigoth kingdom with a capital at Toulouse and later at Toledo. This kingdom would endure for nearly a century and a half, with the Visigoth kings affirming the Catholic religion before the Arab invasion of Spain ended the reign of the Visigoths, and they, too, ceased to be a power in Europe.

Culture

Early Goths. For much of their history, both Visigoths and Ostrogoths borrowed the clothing, housing, and governmental styles of those in whose lands they lived. Fairly early in their history, they abandoned their own language in favor of that of their overlords. The few writings in their original language suggest the Gothic lifestyle. For example, in the 380s, Bishop Ulfilas translated the Bible into Gothic but, fearing that some passages would add to the Goth's already strong penchant for battle, eliminated many biblical passages dealing with war.

War. The Goths were, indeed, fierce warriors. Relying primarily on a horse cavalry backed by foot soldiers, they were skilled at the hit-and-run tactics of raids. But their will to die in glory and therefore their earnestness in fighting for their cause, made them formidable even against more organized military units. The early Gothic warriors wore long pelted coats and kept long flowing hair worn under a bowl-shaped helmet. Each warrior carried a sword and spear, made by the skilled ironworkers among them. A favorite ornament for weapons and for saddles was the eagle.

Food, clothing, and shelter. The Goths produced woolen and leather goods. Women wore woolen skirts and hip-length shirts that were fastened at the shoulders with straight but ornately carved pins. Other metal jewelry was worn as decorations on both shirts and skirts, and necklaces were common. The men, too, wore long shirts fastened usually at the right shoulder by a pin. As time passed, gold armbands became a symbol of might among the warriors.

These goods were produced by craftspeople and were traded in markets in the Gothic villages. There were no large cities in the early Gothic patterns. Instead, family units built collections of huts that formed a loose village. Frequently, these huts were gathered around the house of a leader, the *reik*, who lived in a larger house fortified by a wooden stockade. These rulers also provided *gards* (houses) for servants and armed retainers. Wealthy Goth families included slaves and freemen who owed allegiance to the reiks but lived in small huts near the fortification. Another type of village, the *haims*, was a collection of huts and small single-room houses in a communal farming community.

Since war was nearly a way of life, and other peoples, especially the Romans, were always nearby, much of the Gothic population lived along *limes*, the frontier limits of their lands. Here they exchanged ideas and styles between Romans and the other Germanic groups. Rye bread and ale, for example, sometimes gave way to the wheat bread and wine of the Romans. A typical meal of bread, meat, fruits, and vegetables in a noble house would be served to diners sitting on couches, as in the Roman style, and eaten with fingers.

Religion. Until the Visigoths espoused the Christian religion of the Romans in the late fourth century, the religion of the Goths was one of several gods, ritual sacrificial meals, and veneration of ancestors. One important god was Wodan, the god of warriors. Wodan's symbol was often carried on the armbands of the fighters.

The reik was also the religious head of the community and directed a group of priests who attended to shrines to the various gods that were important to a particular community. The priests were of great power in the early religious cults. They alone could punish warriors, sometimes by flogging or imprisonment. Even the reiks and army commanders did not have this authority over their men.

Belief in witchcraft was an important part of Gothic religious practice. One story tells how Gothic witches were once rounded up and exiled, only to mate with evil spirits from the east and give birth to the feared neighbors, the Huns.

Some Goths early swore allegiance to Christianity, but for others this change was difficult. Early conquerors were known to ride through the Christian communities carrying wooden symbols of their own religions and demanding veneration of these idols under threat of punishment. The belief in several gods led by a single god who was the inspiration for warriors continued even after the Goths recognized or joined Christianity. Pacts made with Christians often recognized and accepted that religion on condition that certain older beliefs could also be held.

Economy. The Goths were primarily farmers and warriors. However, the significance of trade among them and with the Greeks, Turks, and Romans is marked by their use of money. Their coinage also serves as an example of the interaction between Goths and others. Frequently, coins were minted with Roman symbols on one side and Gothic symbols on the other. Mostly, though, the early Goths were consumed with the daily need for food and security. These needs forced them into village units and eventually into kingdoms.

Government. The earliest Goths were independent, loosely governed by tribal chiefs. As these chiefs saw the need to unite, they eventually set up kingdoms headed by an elected king. The role of king became hereditary but still needed the approval of the nobles who would serve the king. For the protection of everyone, laws were established governing the behavior of tribesmen and subjects and defining the penalties for violating the law. Thus, the Goths from the north country, as the Vikings and Normans farther west, contributed to European ideas of law and government, and their interaction with others over such a widespread area allowed Gothic ideas to be shared with the communities they encountered.

For More Information

Burns, Thomas. *A History of the Ostrogoths*. Bloomington, Indiana: Indiana University Press, 1984.

Wolfram, Herwig. Translated by Thomas J. Dunlap. *History of the Goths*. Berkeley, California: University of California Press, 1988.

LOMBARDS

(lom' bards)

People of the lower Elbe River who became conquerors of Italy.

Population: Unknown.
Location: Hungary, northern Italy.
Language: Lombard.

Geographical Setting

The land on which the Lombards settled in northern Italy rises to the Alps Mountains. The climate in this region is Mediterranean but modified by the altitude of the mountain slopes. Lombards found the grass-covered hills rising to the mountains good land for their herds and left the valleys and sea plains to their neighbors who were farmers.

Historical Background

Origin. The Lombards, although they were not originally known by that name (they appear to have come from Scandinavia, where they were known as Winnil), first became known as herders of sheep and cattle as well as fierce warriors along the lower Elbe River. From this position they pressed southward into present-day Hungary and were, by A.D. 166, testing the strength of the Roman protectors of the Danube River. From that time of battle with the Romans, the Lombards were insignificant for several hundred years. In this period, another tribal group, the Gepids, had settled southward in present-day Hungary and had chosen to remain there in face of growing threats by the Huns. In all this early life, the Lombards were warriors, sometimes raiding other groups and sometimes enlisting to help Romans defend their Danube River border.

Heruls. Their movements had brought them to Bohemia and Moravia by the year 500. Fresh from defeating the Rugi, another group living near the Danube River, the Lombards fell to still another kingdom, the Heruls. At first subject to the Heruls, the Lombards later organized and fought against them. By 512, the Heruls had been divided and scattered, some choosing to live among the Gepids, who themselves chose to live as peaceful farmers among the oncoming Huns.

Territorial expansion. The year 526 found the Lombards occupying land abandoned by still another tribe, the Suebians, along the north bank of the Danube River. In 568, the Lombards abandoned their homes to the Avars, and moved into present-day northern Italy. Here they managed their first great union, under the caliph Autharis. By 692 Agilulf had become king and gathered support to help the Roman ruler, Gregory the Great. From that time, the Lombards were an organized kingdom, and were trying to expand their territory westward toward Italy and the land of the Franks. The great King Rothair (636–652) solidified the kingdom by creating a set of laws followed by all the Lombards. The efforts to expand Lombard boundaries were intensified under King Liutprant between 713 and 744. By the end of this period, Liutprant dominated most of Italy.

Franks. In the years 754–756 the Franks led by Peppin defeated the Lombards and subjugated them, capturing the stronghold at Pavia. Some of the Lombard land was given to the pope to secure his blessings on the Franks. The kings of the Lombards were vassals of the Franks under Charlemagne until 774, when the Lombard king, Desiderius, was imprisoned. Charlemagne then named himself king of the Franks and Lombards. The Lombards found themselves incorporated with other people of Italy who, in the tenth century, broke into new tribal systems.

Culture

Early life. The Lombards, or Longobardi, were originally a Teutonic people whose religion was derived from that of the Norse. Wherever they moved, Lombards disdained agriculture, feeling that tilling the land was slave work. Instead, they preferred to live on the fringes of hill country and among swamps where their animals could find suitable grazing. Lombard herders raised horses, cows, sheep, and chickens. They lived among other peoples who preferred agriculture and depended upon these people for trade.

Appearance and clothing. The Lombards were a distinctive people. They are reported to have been generally tall for their time (men averaged about five feet nine inches in height) and long-legged. Lombard women were often heavy. Both men and women wore loose linen garments. As a rule, women's dresses had high necks. The women tied this dress at the waist with a belt from which hung a mantle, or strip of cloth, frequently decorated with pins and knives. For accessories, the women wore necklaces of glass beads, bronze hairpins, and bronze or iron armlets. Their robe-like dresses were accompanied by shoes open at the toe and laced with leather laces that crossed up the leg to the knee.

Men wore tight-fitting linen trousers and tunics along with war gear—a suit of armor for mounted soldiers and a long heavy coat for foot soldiers. Lombard warriors parted their hair in the center and wore it nape-length and combed toward the mouth.

Home life. At first located along the Elbe River, Lombards lived in scattered homes partly sunken into the earth and sheltered by thatched roofs supported on six poles. As they migrated south, these people took up residences in sites abandoned earlier by the Romans. On these sites the Lombards built houses of timber. They preferred sites in the hill country or near swamps—lands with abundant greenery on which to graze their livestock. In Italy, the Lombards raised cattle, horses, sheep, oxen, and chickens. Their diets concentrated on dairy products supplemented with chicken and with the vegetables and fruits they purchased in trade with their neighbors. As they became more established in northern Italy, Lombards increased their interest in agriculture, which before had been restricted mostly to raising flax, to include grains (particularly millet) and vegetables.

Women. A Lombard woman was given property early in life, and this became the property of her husband's family when she married. The result was that, although respected, the Lombard woman was never completely free. In fact, one law of the Lombards gave a man the right to kill his wife should she be unfaithful.

Social structure. Families of Lombards lived near relatives in loosely knit villages. Several related villages formed a clan, and several clans formed a tribe after the pattern set by their predecessors in the movement westward, the Visigoths. Until Athanaric persuaded the tribes to unite in 364, there was no higher central government than the king of a tribe. From Athanaric forward the Lombards were united under a military leader who was also king. This king was subject to advice from a collection of nobles and freemen, in an assembly called the *Thing*. The assembly also determined the social rank of people in the kingdom.

The early Lombard society included several classes: arms-bearing freemen (*arimanni*, females were *frea*); half-free men (*aldii* or *aldia*), who had bought freedom with some restrictions by paying launegild at the Thing or who became freemen by virtue of their commitment to bear arms (bows and arrows); a lower class of servants; and prisoners of war. As society grew more organized, a class of nobles and a military class of duces (dukes) were imposed over the freemen.

Religion. Before 564, the year in which King Albion accepted Christianity, the Lombards were frequently in conflict with the Catholic Church. Their religion was one of many gods and of the rituals and icons of northern religions. A popular icon among them was a gold snake. In 488 the Lombards found themselves in the land of another people, the Rugi, and were introduced to eastern Christianity. They began to incorporate some of the Christian ideas into their own religion nearly 100 years before Albion became a convert.

That the Lombards, like most of their neighbors, believed in an afterlife can be seen in the arrangement of their graves. Lombard people were often buried with the tools to pursue their occupations in the next world. Scythes, shears, anvils, tongs, and hammers have been found in Lombard graves along with the horses and hunting dogs of nobles. Nobles were buried in more substantial graves, sometimes in enlarged stone coffers that would accommodate the favorite horse.

Laws. The laws of the Lombards were applied to the people according to their apparent value to the society. These laws varied among the tribes until they were formalized by King Rothair during his reign, 636–652. The formal *Edictus Ruthari* reflected some of the earlier laws. For example, the penalties for taking the little finger of a person varied according to occupation: freeman, 16 *solidi*; half-free man, 4 solidi; and slave, 2 solidi. There were 363 articles in the Edictus Ruthari dealing with penal law, family law, and additional laws regarding politics and economy. The Lombards are distinguished from other peoples moving west into Roman territory for the uniqueness of their code of laws, few of which show any relation to Roman law.

Arts. Early in their migration, the Lombards had mastered the lost wax method for casting jewelry. In silver and iron, the craftspeople cast silver pins, animal figurines for baskets and harnesses, jewelry inlaid with red almadine stones and garnets. In these designs, the Lombards were not unique, sharing their crafts with the Gepids, with whom they also shared the land that the Romans called Pannonia II. By 540, however, the arts of the two groups were distinct. Lombard art then began to feature garnets in oval pendants, eagle-head buckles, and iron straps inlaid with silver designs.

For More Information

Bóna, István. *The Dawn of the Dark Ages: The Gepids and the Lombards in the Carpathian Basin.* Budapest: Corvina Press, 1976.

Butler, William F. *Lombard Communes.* World History Series #48. London: Haskell, 1969.

Ogg, David. *Europe of the Ancient Regime.* New York: Harper, 1965.

NORMANS
(nor' mans)

Viking settlers of the coast of France.

Population: Unknown.
Location: Normandy, England, Italy, Sicily.
Languages: Danish and the languages of the countries invaded.

Geographical Setting

The original Normans were pirates and sea kings from the northern countries of Sweden and Denmark who earned their living by raiding and plundering seaports in quick strikes from their unusual military ships. In Europe, they settled at the mouth of the Seine River and used this river to plunder the towns of the French. Wherever the Normans traveled, they searched for good ports and navigable waterways for their raids.

Historical Background

Origin. The original people who gave rise to those who came to be known as Normans were hunters and warriors who moved westward across Scandinavia. Here they became shipbuilders and developed their military skills as they raided nearby people for food and wealth. Their ships were designed to navigate the rough seas and to put fear into the hearts of their prey. Ships at least 80-feet long carried a square sail amidship and pairs of long oars spaced at distances along the sides. They were decorated with rising hulls fore and aft. The masthead of many of the warships was decorated with a dragon carved in wood.

Attacks in Europe. Before A.D. 800, these "Vikings," or pirates, had raided villages along the coast of Sweden and Norway and among the islands of the North Sea, and had begun to raid the coastal towns of present-day Poland and Germany. In 810, the northmen made their first attempt to establish a settlement in Europe at Friesland— an attempt repelled by the forces of Charlemagne.

Charlemagne died in 814, leaving the Frankish empire so shaken that the northmen were able to sail up the Seine River in their pillaging excursions. In 845, they sailed as far as Paris.

First northmen in France. In 885 one sea king of the northmen, Siegfried, led 700 skilled warriors to plunder Paris. To escape the total destruction of the city, the king of France ceded land in Burgundy to Siegfried. Settling in this region, the northmen indicated their adaptability by becoming settled landowners and were soon assimilated into the general population. About this same time, Harold Haarfager had succeeded in unifying the northmen in Scandinavia and began to modify their behavior by refusing to allow raiding from one port to another within his kingdom. According to legends, one Viking, Rollo (or Rolf), chose to ignore this edict and was banished from the country.

Rollo. Gathering some followers, Rollo sailed down the coast of Europe to the Seine and up this river to Rouen. Choosing to appease the Vikings, the people of Rouen invited them into the city. Rollo and his men liked the city and decided to stay and rule there. From this vantage point, the northmen were able to control the Seine and presented such a threat to the French that King Charles ("the simple") offered Rollo coastal territory of his own. Rollo accepted, and the bargain was sealed by the marriage of Rollo to the king's daughter. The land given to Rollo was named Normandy. It became a separate political unit, subject at first to the king of France, but remaining independent until 1204. The ruler was given the title of Duke of Normandy. With few men and a great deal of land, it is probable that the Vikings soon adapted to the French noble-serf customs and replaced the French noblemen as the large landowners, who in those days also owned the people who lived on the land.

England. In the second half of the eleventh century, the land that is now England was divided into six kingdoms. One of these, in the south of England, was ruled by Harold. In 1066, Duke William of

Normandy, claiming to have been promised the kingdom of England by a former king and to have been assured of Harold's support in this claim, invaded the English kingdom. In a one-day battle, the Battle of Hastings, Harold and many of his nobles were killed and William was proclaimed king of England. That one-day war changed the course of history, giving William a base from which to wage battles against the other kings, all of whom were defeated between 1068 and 1070. And, since William, as Duke of Normandy, was subject to the king of France, the war had changed the relationship between France and England.

The Normans immediately began to apply the methods learned from the French. Great forts (castles) were built throughout the new land, at first of wood and later of stone, using architectural designs borrowed from the French and improved by the Normans. Normans began to replace the English nobles as rulers of the king's lands. The church was made a part of the government as heads of abbeys were moved and the abbeys themselves began to take on the appearances of fortifications. By 1086, the landholdings of the king (at that time, Alfred) had become so vast and required such a large number of feifs to control it, that a book was assembled documenting all the land-holdings and their overlords. This book, the Doomesday Book, has left records of the early Normans in England.

Italy. Other Normans sailed to Italy and Greece. Between 1030 and 1072 Normans had settled in Avena, Apalia, and Calabria in the south of Italy and on Sicily. Here, as elsewhere, the Normans showed great military skill and equally great skill in adapting to local ways and improving upon them. The great Norman-built churches of Italy added architectural features learned by the Normans in experiences with Arabic and Greek peoples (Normans had briefly fought with Greeks in Greece between 1082 and 1084). Very early in their European experience, Normans had accepted Christianity. From Italy, Normans took part in the first crusade, fighting against Muslim forces in Antioch under Bohemond ("the giant") in 1098.

Disappearance. Everywhere, the Normans were excellent not only in warfare but in government and in assimilating the best of the society they conquered. In France, the Norman language was soon abandoned in favor of French. Norman warriors took French wives, and Norman nobles conducted themselves much like the French nobles they had displaced. This pattern repeated itself with slight variations in England and Italy. In England, for example, Normans adopted English ways, but preferred the French language to English. Everywhere the Normans built upon the civilization that was already in existence and brought the native populations into an improved system of laws and customs.

This pattern may have been the undoing of the Normans as a distinct people. By 1154, England's Normans had become firmly integrated with the English. By 1194, the Italian Normans had been assimilated into a Germanic culture, and by 1204 Normandy was once again firmly a French land.

Culture

Vikings. The ancestors of the Normans were shipbuilders, raiders, and warriors. In their native land they built large wooden houses—as long as 200 feet on a side—to house the members of a ship crew and their families. Beds along three sides of the building were often separated by tapestries. Alongside the bed, a seat was provided for the man. On the north and bedless side, a higher seat was provided for the master. The ceilings were high and the walls had few windows, which were covered with animal skins. More wealthy ship owners built compounds for their crews and families and included a great hall for dining and entertaining. Entertainment among the northmen consisted mostly of telling and listening to sagas of great adventures.

In this atmosphere, some became skilled at ironwork, others at manufacturing rope, and still others at weaving. They set up systems of rules and laws, created poetry, and initiated special customs for treatment of others. Theirs was a society based on wealth and heredity. Any man could become a "viking," a pirate seaman, but only a few nobly-born could be called sea kings.

The northern religion included many gods. Odin was the chief god, Frigga his wife, and Thor the god of war. The Vikings believed in an afterlife, with valiant ones ascending into Valhalla. In some accounts, only those who lived carefully enough to die of old age were consigned to hell.

Vikings. When the Vikings came to Normandy and then to England and Italy, they brought with them their religion, customs, and skills. But they soon blended these skills with those of their neighbors. Upon receiving a grant to Normandy and marrying into the French royal family, Rollo, the first Norman leader, quickly abandoned the ancient religion in favor of Christianity. The resettled Vikings gave up their own language for French, perhaps to better manage the French peasants who worked their land. Also, they traded the fur clothing of the north for the linen, cotton, and silk of the French.

The storytelling art continued, but, with French as the language, sagas were now written in both verse and prose. In architecture, too, the Normans kept some old ideas while adding arches and designs borrowed from Greeks and Arabs as well as from the French with their Roman influence. The castles built by the Normans retained the high walls, narrow windows, and great rooms of their northern ancestors.

Food. Food changed with the move south. The early northmen found little productive soil in which to grow crops, choosing instead to hunt for food and to fish. The French in Normandy had long planted and harvested crops. While assuming noble positions and refraining from work other than war, the Normans were introduced to fruits and vegetables to supplement their diets of meat and fish.

Arts and architecture. The major Norman contributions to humanity sprung from their adaptability and their widespread travels. They were able to bring ideas of art and architecture from Arabs, Greeks, French, Italians, and others together in innovative syntheses. The Normans left their own legacy of government and record keeping. Besides the massive record of the Doomesday Book, similar records of land tenancy were kept in Italy in the Catalogus Baronum, completed in 1175.

Education. One great contribution of the Normans resulted from their deep interest in education. Schools were established in many of the abbeys. The Norman abbey at Bec was a leading educational institution in the French area from 1044–1093. Monks associated with these abbeys became scribes, documenting events of the day. History became a popular theme, and dozens of histories of the Normans were written, although most of them portrayed Norman history in glorified terms—this in spite of the Norman habit of heading the abbeys with experienced people of other societies.

In the end it may have been their own ability to adapt to other cultures that resulted in the disappearance of Normans as a separate people.

For More Information

Brown, Reginald Allen. *The Normans.* New York: St. Martin's Press, 1984.

Haskins, Charles Homer. *The Normans in European History.* London: F. Ungar, 1959.

ROMANS
(ro′ muns)

Citizens of the early city-state that became an empire—Rome.

Population: 1,000,000 (one estimate of the population of the city of Rome at the peak of the Roman Empire).
Location: The city of Rome, in west-central Italy.
Language: Latin.

Geographical Setting

The ancient city of Rome began as a walled village on Palatine Hill and grew to include other villages on the cluster of seven hills rising above the Tiber River in present-day west-central Italy. It is surrounded by fertile fields that served as the granary and grazing country for the ancient villagers. Here the climate is mild, soothed by breezes from the Mediterranean Sea 16 miles to the southwest and the Sabine Mountains about 55 miles inland. Colder winds sometimes blow south from the Alps, and warmer "sirocco" winds from Africa, across the Mediterranean.

Historical Background

Origin. According to legend, the capture of Troy by the Greeks in 1184 B.C. resulted in Æneas fleeing the ancient city. Guided by the goddess Venus, he traveled to Latium, where he established another kingdom, Alba Longa. Here Æneas and his descendants ruled over much of southern Italy for 300 years. But then, King Procas of Alba died, and his two sons quarreled about rule. A granddaughter gave birth to twins fathered by Mars. The new king, Amulius, ordered the twins thrown into the Tiber River, but they were rescued and nursed to maturity by a wolf. Finally, the two young men left Alba to establish a new kingdom on seven hills above the Tiber. The men, Romulus and Remus, decided to leave the decision about who should rule to the gods. Seeing 12 vultures when his brother saw only six, Romulus claimed the right to rule and named the new kingdom after himself.

Whatever the origin, settlers of Indo-European descent moved into the Italian peninsula sometime between 2000 and 1000 B.C. Early immigrants settled in the Po Valley in the age of copper and bronze. Later settlers, with iron tools, settled on hills in the lower valley of the Tiber River, a region known as the Plain of Latium. Rome arose from one of the farming villages on the seven hills inland from the mouth of the Tiber River and south of the 12 prosperous trading cities of the Etruscans (see ETRUSCANS). By the eighth century B.C. the small villages had united to form one city, while Greek immigrants had settled trading centers throughout southern Italy. By the sixth century B.C., disgruntled Etruscans had moved south to invade Rome and take command of the city. The early rulers of Rome came from leaders among the Etruscans.

The early kingdom was ruled by imperium—the power of life and death—symbolized by a scepter with an eagle head and an axe in a bundle of rods. The imperium was granted by a popular assembly of all the citizens of Rome. However, the king soon came to rely on a senate for advice. Senators held tenure for life and set themselves apart from the mass of citizens, the plebians.

Republic. In 509 B.C., Roman nobles rose up against a treacherous king and changed the form of government. The power of imperium was now placed in the hands of two consuls—leaders chosen by the senate to rule for one year. In that year, each consul headed an army, acted as high priests, and formed the supreme court. In this "republic" the plebians were left out of the ruling circle. For 200 years these citizens would struggle for a voice in government. In time they succeeded in dividing the senate into two bodies: a Comitia Centuriata, made up of landholders qualified to serve in the army, and a Comitia Tribuna, made up of plebians. Officials of the Tribuna were a dozen tribunes who took up the citizens' causes at any time, day or night. Over the years the tribunes guarded the rights of the landless citizens of Rome and gradually expanded their voice in the government. Part of their efforts resulted in a Roman committee being sent to Greek cities in the south of Italy to study law. In 454 B.C. this committee drafted the Laws of the Twelve Tables, which were set up in the Forum for all to observe. These laws became the basis for Roman law and themselves gained a great advance for the plebians—the right to appeal an oppressive sentence imposed by a consul.

Gradually the plebians obtained rights of government: the right to pass their own laws, the right for tribunes to veto legislation, and finally in 367 B.C. the right to elect one of the consuls.

Control of the Mediterranean. Meanwhile Greece, Carthage, and the Etruscans were warring over control of Italy, with the Greeks finally emerging victorious. However, Rome continued to expand into neighboring territories, and other Italian cities formed a Latin League to combat the expansion. Eventually the two foes—Rome and the Latin League—united to combat the Greeks, later to disagree and war among themselves. In this war, in which the Latin League was defeated, Rome became ruler of most of Italy. The various tribes that made up the Latin League had made separate agreements to live under Roman rule by 338 B.C. Fifty years later Rome was at war with Pyrrhus and his Greek army in the south of Italy. At first defeated, Rome joined with Carthage to destroy the Greek fleet and army. Now only Carthage and Sicily stood in the way of Roman control of the Mediterranean Sea trade routes. In a series of wars beginning in 264 B.C. (Punic Wars) Rome and Carthage fought over control of Sicily. After losing 200,000 soldiers in the first battle, Romans recognized the need to build a strong naval force. With this they destroyed the forces of Carthage, and then withstood the overland invasion of the great Carthagean general Hannibal. Rome gained Spain in the terms of surrender, and then pursued Hannibal into Asia Minor.

The Roman Legions. The Roman army was well organized and fast moving. Units of 3,000 soldiers formed a Roman Legion that was supported by 1,200 lightly armed and mobile soldiers and a cavalry of 300. This legion was divided into companies of 120 for additional mobility. By force of arms, and by reputation, Romans quickly came to control the European shores of the Mediterranean and to force allies of the kingdoms in present-day Tunisia and Egypt. One ruler in Asia Minor, seeing the inevitable victory of Rome, even willed his kingdom to that rule.

Wherever they conquered, Romans tended to treat their victims kindly, to gain allies rather than to plunder enemies. Thus their armies grew through alliances. By 131 B.C. Rome ruled the Mediterranean.

Aristocrats and plebians. At home in Rome, however, the wealthy citizens, aided by the consuls and the senate, were becoming owners of vast plots of land. Great plantations became the landmark of the Roman plains. These lands demanded a great many laborers, and slavery became the solution to this labor need. At Rome's peak, one-third of the residents of Rome were slaves. In the process small landowners were displaced and found themselves living in squalid apartments and performing menial tasks for the aristocracy in Rome. The government added to these woes of the masses by leasing conquered lands in Italy to those wealthy enough to work them and pay a percentage of the crops to the benefit of the high-living aristocracy. The wars with Carthage and Hannibal had made it necessary to give control of the government to the senate and consuls. The plebians began to lose their hard-earned rights. The result was a decline in the Roman republic (by now really a rule of the rich), which ended in civil wars. A great land reform, planned to restore small plots to the plebians, was begun by the tribune Tiberius and carried on by his brother Gaius. Their work weakened the senate, whose members then began to hire mercenaries to combat the changes. Three thousand of Gaius' followers were killed and he committed suicide. The issue of reform subsided, but reappeared when Rome was threatened by the king of Pontus (in Asia Minor). The need to defend Roman interests gave the plebians a new rallying point. The senate had, as was tradition, appointed a consul, Sulla, to lead the army against Pontus. The tribunal countered by appointing Marius to lead the defense. Civil war broke out between the two factions. Eventually Sulla emerged victorious and declared himself emperor (81 B.C.). Before he resigned four years later, the senate had been restored to its greatest power and the tribunal reduced to near uselessness.

Julius Caesar. But now the seeds of discontent had grown even among the wealthy. A powerful general, Pompey, and a powerful politician, Julius Caesar, vied for power through conquest. Pompey turned his army to the east and subdued much of Asia Minor. Caesar gathered an army and invaded Gaul (now France), where he took control of the various peoples of Europe as far as the Rhine River and even into the British Islands. Wise in politics, Caesar kept the people at home aware of his accomplishments through written essays, titled *Commentaries on the Gallic War.* However, a jealous Pompey convinced the senate to turn against Caesar, and that body ordered Caesar to disband his troops and return to Rome. Caesar defied this order by crossing with his troops across the Rubicon River in a declaration of war against Pompey. The victorious Julius Caesar transformed Rome from a republic to a benevolent dictatorship, even establishing that his successor in a blood line would be his grandnephew Octavian. Neither the wealth-seekers nor the champions of the old republic approved. On the Ides of March, 44 B.C., Julius Caesar was assassinated.

Dictatorship. Octavian, 18 years old at the time, found an ally in Antony, and the two controlled Rome absolutely for more than 10 years. The partnership dissolved when Antony fell in love with and married Cleopatra, queen of Egypt. More fighting occurred. Eventually Antony deserted a losing battle and committed suicide. One outcome of these events was the capture of Alexandria by Rome. Now Rome became proprietor of Egyptian culture as well as that of Greece and was soon to become the conveyor of these cultures throughout Europe. Octavian consolidated his power in the senate while holding his position as tribune. Retitled Augustus by the senate, he began a long line of rulers (princeps) who ruled Rome with an ever-declining senate. Four descendants of Augustus succeeded him as princeps, and these were followed by the ruling family of Flavius Vespasianus.

Some Emperors of Rome and Notable Accomplishments

Julio-Claudian family

Augustus 23 B.C.–14 A.D.	Allowed unemployed landless to join the army, forming the Praetorians, who eventually came to control Rome

Tiberius (14–31)
Caius Caligula (37–41)
Claudius (41–54)
Nero (54–68)

Flavian family

Flavius Vespasianus (69–79)	Took Jerusalem and began conquest of Britain

Titus (79–81)
Domitian (81–96)

The Antoines
Nerva (96–98)

Trajan (98–117)	Expanded Roman rule across the Danube into Dacia. Conquered Armenia and Mesopotamia
Hadrian (117–138)	Consolidated Roman holdings
Marcus Aurelius (161–180)	Ruler of a welfare state

Emperors during Rome's decline

Comodus (180–192)	
Pertinax (192–193)	Appointed by senate but deposed by the Praetorian guard, who appointed the emperor . . .
Didius Julianus (193)	who was deposed by the army and replaced by . . .
Septimus Severus (193–211)	
Caracalla (211–217)	A violent tyrant under whose rule all freemen of Rome gained citizenship; he was then killed
Heliogabalus (218–222)	A priest of the sun who brought oriental religions to Rome
Severus (222–235)	Was killed by German legions
Maximinus (235–238)	A Thracian soldier of fortune
Gordianus III (238–244)	Chosen by the Praetorians
Gallus (251–254)	His reign began 15 years in which Rome was really ruled by provincial rulers, and Germanic peoples and Persians invaded Rome and enslaved nearly half the population
Claudius (268–270)	Began revival of empire after 15 years of destruction
Probus (276–282)	Held the Rhine River against invaders
Diocletian (285–305)	Changed government to an absolute monarchy
Constantine (324–337)	Moved seat of government to Constantinople and adopted Christianity; finally abandoned the rule
Julian (361–363)	Fell to Persians
Valens (in east 364–379)	Defeated by Goths
Honorius (west) and Arcadius (east)	Honorius died in 423 after surviving a Gothic invasion of the city of Rome and after losing Spain to other Germanic groups
Valentinian III (423–455)	Valentinian's widow sought aid from the Vandals of Africa, who sacked Rome and ended the Roman Empire

Through this succession Roman culture, and consequently that of Greece and Egypt, spread throughout Europe. Roman forms of government merged with Germanic ideas to establish the rules of government and justice that shaped modern-day societies, and the Latin language influenced in various degrees the languages of today's Europe. A major contribution to the eventual unifying of the tribal units of Europe was the Roman need for and ability to construct major highways on which the Roman legions and government agents could travel quickly into the provinces.

Culture

Roman buildings. Beginning as a village of mud and wattle farm homes, the city of Rome, center of the empire, became a city of contrasts. Homes for the rich and monuments of government were made of brick and marble and lavishly furnished with luxurious drapery, ornate carvings, brass fixtures, and comfortable couches. Water was drawn from wells lined with marble. Most homes were built around courts and included beautiful gardens cared for by slaves. Frequently, carved fountains enhanced the courts.

Roman aristocracy was favored with large meeting places made of brick, stone, and marble—for example, the Forum as a seat of government, the Pantheon, dedicated to the gods, and the Colosseum, where 45,000 spectators could sit to view athletic and other contests. There were about 800 public baths to be enjoyed by both rich and poor.

However, Rome was a city of contrasts. As the rich acquired more and more of the land, peasant farmers moved in droves to the city, where some became artisans but most became welfare recipients. To accommodate these new city dwellers, narrow streets were constructed around the hills and lined with shabby apartments in such disarray that a writer of the time, Juvenal, described a walk through a city street:

> I am blocked by a surging crowd in front, while a vast mass of people crushes onto me from behind . . . . One . . . punches me with a hard litter-pole: one bangs a beam against my head, a wine cask someone else.
> . . . that roof, from which a tile may crash down on my skull, how high it seems above us.
>
> Trevelyan 1941, pp. 129–130

Social structure. At first, Roman society consisted of an aristocracy, peasants who owned small bits of land, and slaves who worked in the homes of the aristocrats. As the aristocrats gained strength, they took control of the land, creating a large landless, unemployed rural group. These people migrated to Rome and became artisans or remained unemployed. The craftspeople organized into guilds according to their occupations, built meeting halls, and developed systems for helping the sick and needy among them. However, a large part of the population of Rome were slaves who were treated variously depending on whether they were plantation workers or more favored house servants. Sometimes these slaves were allowed by their owners to work their way out of slavery. A large part of the population of

Rome was dependent on government welfare, which in turn was dependent on taxes and booty gathered by the Roman Legions.

At first these legions were made up only of men who owned land. However, as the population increased, unemployed farm men were encouraged to become legionnaires. Eventually these recruits, feeling new strength, became the Praetorians and were able to dictate who would be chosen emperor. The Praetorians were one example of the struggle of average Roman citizens to gain a voice in the government—a voice never fully realized.

Recreation. The city of Rome was one of trade, government, and pleasure for the wealthy. Large dinners were common events, with the guests and hosts reclining on couches while being served a series of fruit, vegetable, and meat courses along with wine by the servants. Races on foot or in chariots were popular events, as were gladiatorial contests in which men fought against men or animals, often to the death. The public baths, ingeniously heated by Roman invention, were open to all citizens. Each year, Romans celebrated 159 holidays during which they were able to attend and enjoy 93 special games (races and other contests).

Government. While the Roman political system changed, and seemed never to reach its own designs, Roman government began many ideas that helped to shape future governments. Roman scholars considered government to originate through voluntary agreements among the citizens. They held that all power ultimately was in the people. Believed, but not always practiced, was the idea of separation of state functions. Romans believed in government by law. To properly collect taxes from the peoples they overwhelmed, Romans divided areas into provinces, and until the World Wars of this century, boundaries of some European states varied little from those defined by the Romans. German kings borrowed ideas of law and political organization to add to their own Scandinavian-influenced concepts to develop principles of government used today.

Roman law began with the Laws of the Twelve Tables and grew as the prosperity of Rome advanced and its population increased. Over a thousand years, Roman law evolved into a system administered by a judicial system that came to rely on a *praetor*—a position roughly equivalent to an attorney general. Gradually, the laws changed from divine law to civil law and the separation of church and state began.

Architecture. Romans took the architectural ideas of Greece and Egypt and added their own. They built temples and other public buildings with massive columns similar to those found in Athens. Series of arches of stone and brick supported bridges and aqueducts. At some point Roman architects discovered how to construct large concrete domes to shelter their buildings. But of all their architectural accomplishments, perhaps the greatest were the Roman roads. The Appian Way connected Rome with southeastern trading centers. The Flaminian Way crossed Italy to the Adriatic Sea. Such highways allowed rapid troop movement and trade.

Art. In art as in architecture, Romans borrowed from Greece and built upon this base. Where Greeks specialized in sculpture and reliefs stylized to portray ideal images, Romans became experts in creating lifelike figures of emperors, warriors, and public figures. Roman artists also developed a wide array of decorations, from cupids to garlands of flowers, to scrolls. Roman artists excelled in painting frescos—wall paintings of realistic scenes with accurately portrayed humans and with some sense of perspective.

Literature. More moralistic than the imaginative Greeks, Roman poetry still echoed that of their early rivals. Both Romans and Greeks excelled in drama; Romans preferred comedies. Plays were part of holiday festivals and were acted by men only. Suspicion of actors developed in Rome and lasted for centuries afterward. Roman men who became actors lost their rights to participate in civic decisions. Plautus and Terence were popular playwrights, the former specializing in ribald humor and the latter in subtle works written in polished Latin.

Roman histories contribute to our understanding of the Europe of that day. Caesar wrote *Commentaries on the Gallic War*. Later Livy developed the *History of Rome*. Plutarch, a Greek, wrote 46 biographies of famous Greeks and Romans.

Famous names in Roman literature included Cicero, a philosopher, literary critic, and political theorist who left a legacy of more than 900 letters. Lucretius used the atomic theory proposed by Democritus to write about evolution, natural selection, and the movement of atoms in *On the Nature of Things*.

Virgil has been claimed to be the greatest of Roman poets. His *Aeneid* glorified Augustus and the Roman divine destiny to conquer the world. In this work, he was influenced by Homer's *Iliad* and *Odyssey*, drawing from the Greek literary traditions.

Juvenal and Martial were humorists and critics of the conditions in Rome. Martial wrote more than 1,500 brief poems making fun of Roman conditions and customs. One example of these witty notes is:

> The golden hair that Galla wears
> Is hers: who would have thought it?
> She swears 'tis hers, and true she swears,
> For I know where she bought it.
>
> Harrington 1904, p. 268

Science. Romans were doers with little patience for theoretical matters. They preferred to take Greek, Persian, and Egyptian ideas and convert them into practical actions. The Romans built the first known hospitals, developed the idea of taking mineral baths for health, and created a public medical service. They built great aqueducts capable of delivering 50 gallons of fresh water to each citizen of the city daily.

To use the scientific ideas and other knowledge gathered from all the regions they visited, Romans became encyclopedists. Pliny the Elder (A.D. 23–79) produced the most important work, *Natural History*. During Roman rule, the Greek scholar Ptolemy developed ideas in cartography (although his concept of the world was distorted) and astronomy. Galen, another Greek, gathered important concepts in anatomy through his work as surgeon to the gladiators. His encyclopedia of anatomy was the accepted work until the Renaissance.

In art, government, literature, science, and language, Rome contributed to the current state of Europe through its blending of ideas with Germanic tribes, its innovations in architecture and construction, its transmittal of the cultures of Greece, Persia, and Egypt, its definition of political boundaries, and its development of a system of laws.

For More Information

Harrington, Sir J. *The Epigrams of Martial.* London: G. Bell and Sons, 1904.

Trevelyan, R. C. *Translations from Horace, Juvenal and Montaigne.* New York: Cambridge University Press, 1941.

Wallbank, T. Walter, Alastair M. Taylor, and Nels M. Bailkey. *Civilization Past and Present*, Volume 1, fifth edition. Chicago: Scott, Foresman and Company, 1965.

VIKINGS

(vi′ kings)

Early people of the seacoast of Scandinavia.

Population: Unknown.
Location: The Baltic and North Sea coasts of Scandinavia, Iceland, Greenland, Ireland, Scotland, Russia, and Western Europe.
Language: A Norse language related to present-day Swedish, Danish, and Icelandic.

Geographical Setting

The earliest settlements of the Vikings were along the coasts of Sweden and Norway. Here the land is rocky and indented with many fjords and rocky inlets, partly protected from the sea by small islands that ring the mainland. In this region, growing seasons are short, and fertile, easily worked soil is scarce. Much of the land is forested. The combination of abundant lumber and scarce farmland, along with good fishing possibilities, caused some of the early Scandinavians to turn from farming to shipbuilding and trade.

Historical Background

Long before the eighth century A.D., the Scandinavian countries had been widely inhabited by hunters and farmers. Beginning in the east, these settlers moved farther and farther west in search of suitable farmland for their growing numbers. Finding a suitable farmland, a family held it forever, passing it from one generation either through the eldest son or by division of the land among the heirs. In the first case, those disinherited found a need to relocate, and in the second, land parcels eventually grew too small to accommodate a family, resulting in an unending need to find new land.

Coastal settlers. Traveling in small groups or family units, and with little other organization, some of the farmers eventually reached the coast. Here they became shipbuilders and added fishing to their farm skills in order to earn a livelihood. Their skill as shipbuilders and the protection of the offshore islands permitted some to become master sailors even though they had only a knowledge of some fixed stars and were not accustomed to charts and maps. Ironworking and carpentry skills improved and the Norse ships became larger and more efficient. Large for their day, and with shallow drafts, the ships were capable of sailing in the ocean and also navigating some of the rivers of the north. Their success encouraged another means of livelihood— raiding.

Vikings. The name Viking may have its base in the Norse word *vik* for creek or fjord, where the early seamen built camps or villages. The name for a camp, *wick*, might also be the source of the name of the Viking, as might *vig*, the Norse term for fighting. At any rate, the name Viking soon became synonymous with pirating. At first, this pirating involved sailing along the coast to make sudden strikes on other Norse coastal villages. But as sailing skills improved and ships grew larger and more diversified, the Vikings, the noblest of whom were known as sea kings, began to raid and to settle farther from their bases.

Island excursions. Early in the eighth century, Vikings had sailed as far as the Shetland Islands and on to the Orkney Islands. From these bases it was an easier venture to raid Ireland and Scotland. In the north and west of these countries, people had lived free of interference from outside and were unprepared for sudden raids by fierce-looking warriors in high-bowed boats decorated with carved dragon heads, especially when it appeared that the invaders were better organized and more accustomed to rule than those they preyed upon. Viking settlements appeared in both Ireland and Scotland. By the 790s, Viking raiders were striking England. In 798 Vikings settled on the Isle of Man just off the English coast. By 853 Olaf the White had established a kingdom in Ireland. By 880 Viking seamen and settlers had arrived in Iceland, and by 900 Eric the Red had established settlers in Greenland. His son, Leif Ericson is reputed to have reached a land, Vinland (now the Americas). Support for this idea has been seen in Viking remains unearthed in Newfoundland and New England.

In England, Viking raiders struck York (866), East Anglia (869), and Wessex (871). Never in great numbers, Viking raiders and settlers searched for victims unable to sufficiently organize to resist them. In 871 Vikings from Denmark based in France sought to establish colonies in England but had miscalculated the strength of the kingdom and were rebuffed by the forces of King Alfred.

In 911 a renegade Viking named Rolf, who had been exiled for violating the newly organized Swedish kingdom's rule against local raiding, sailed up the Seine River to Paris. Other Vikings had raided this city earlier, but this time, the king of France bought peace with Rolf by ceding him and his followers a section of land along the coast of present-day France. The land became known as Normandy, and its Viking settlers, Normans (see NORMANS). By 892 new and stronger raids were being made in England. A hundred years later, a Viking invasion of the kingdom of King Ethelred resulted in a settlement of Vikings in England. From this base, Vikings expanded their hold on the land and by 1016, their King Cnut ruled much of England. Fifty years later, and 31 years after the death of Cnut, Normans were to invade and, in a one-day war, become rulers of England.

Russia. The rivers of Russia were attractive sailing routes for the Vikings based in Sweden and Denmark. Along these rivers, farmers had settled with little association with others nearby, and no organization to combat the raiders. In fact, these peaceful farmers had been subject to raids by so many of their neighbors that they were often willing to be or even hopeful of being ruled by the Vikings. The Viking excursions made known that a strong people with sound governmental skills lived in the north. Later, these northmen were to be invited to come to Russia and rule the people there, establishing a great kingdom based at Kiev.

Disappearance. Vikings, like their subgroup, the Normans, were quick to take on favorable aspects of the peoples they conquered, adapting to the new languages and customs, and improving on the governmental organizations. Their adaptability led to their assimilation into the cultures of the people they conquered. By 980, for example, Vikings had become vassals of the Irish, and soon became part of the general Irish population. The same melting into the general society occurred in France and England. As landowning became more important than shipbuilding and raiding, the Vikings disappeared into the masses of Europeans.

Culture

Economy. The early northmen were farmers and hunters. Along the coasts, they became skilled ironsmiths and carpenters. The attractions of fishing and trade led to the development of skills in building distinctive ships. Eventually, for a segment of the north population, shipbuilding, trading, and raiding became the bases for their economy. The ships were unusual for their time—large (the longest yet discovered is 160 feet), shallow, and moved both by oarsmen and square sails. Two types of vessels soon became standards—the longship, used primarily for war and raiding, and the knaar, a shorter, stouter, and deeper vessel used for trade and moving settlers. Their earliest sea ventures were for trade—northern furs and amber for other necessities. Vikings became so attached to their ships that they were sometimes buried with them. Examination of these ship burials has given modern investigators much information about the Vikings.

Government. Although they did not have a central organization until late (Denmark became a kingdom in 950), Vikings had strict rules of conduct. For example, they early devised sets of compensation laws under which wrongdoers, even murderers, were required to pay in gold and goods for their errors. In their excursions, Vikings experimented with democratic rule. In Iceland, for example, the colonies were ruled by a gathering of all the people. Once a year or more, the people gathered in a group called an Althing to decide on land distribution and other matters of general concern. In England, the Norman descendants of Vikings established systems of noble landowners, who protected their interests by hiring workers and defenders and giving them portions of land, fiefs, for their services so long as the services were properly rendered.

Food, clothing, and shelter. Vikings adapted to the ways of life of the people they encountered, so food and housing took the forms of those people with modifications from earlier northern times. The Scandinavian houses were at first single rooms, although sometimes quite large. A central fireplace served for warmth and cooking. Beds lined the walls and benches sat near the beds. Tools and weapons were hung along walls that were made of wood, often supporting a roof of thatch. One end of the room usually held a seat for the leader of the house. The other end was used as work space and might contain a loom. Vikings were capable weavers of coarse woolen cloth, from which they sewed the trousers, skirts, and simple shirts worn by everyone, supplemented by furs and leather vests (jerkins) in winter or in time of war.

Wild game, vegetables from their gardens, fish, and the abundant wild berries provided food for the family.

Religion. The Vikings venerated many gods, as did other Norsemen. Odin was the chief god, but Thor, the god of war, held a special place with the Vikings. For these people believed that fighting was of primary importance. Their religion held that after this life, some would ascend to Valhalla, to continue the battle between good and evil. Valhalla was a place of endless fighting by day and feasting by night. Only those who died in courageous acts would eventually reach Valhalla—Vikings believed that those who led peaceful lives and died of old age were doomed to hell. This religion faded as Vikings came into contact with Christians and adopted the Christian beliefs.

War. Raiding and war were part of every Viking life. A goal of men in a Viking village was to become a raider, a Viking. Some aspired to be sea kings, if their lineage included noble ancestry. This Viking life was hard, ships were designed to carry few luxuries and not even cots or beds for long trips. A Viking must endure the hardships of the voyage and be prepared to turn warrior at its end. Skilled ironworkers, the Vikings made long swords (or traded for them in France), spears, and two-edged battle axes. Each warrior carried a round wooden shield, decorated and protected by ironwork. Some went into battle in chain mail, while others donned stout leather jerkins. The Viking warriors wore conical helmets, frequently with a long nose-protector added.

Literature and arts. Before the 700s, Norsemen had adopted a written alphabet borrowed from the Goths using straight line symbols for the letters (*runes*). They carved words and signs into their wooden ships and burial sites. However, no other records were written in this language. It was not until the people of Iceland began to document the rich folklore in the *Edda* that the stories and poetry of the Vikings were recorded. Vikings were accomplished storytellers and creators of poetry. A Viking house was entertained in the evenings by stories of the great adventures of the past.

Beside this skill in literature, Vikings were master woodcarvers and stonecutters. Stone symbols of their religion and of death mark their graves. Perhaps the most well-known woodcarvings are parts of their ships. Each ship rose fore and aft to wood-carved pieces that often included displays of dragons.

Even though their adaptability led to the eventual disappearance of the Vikings, they left a legacy of government and law, and of belief in heroes and heroics that carried into the other societies and heavily influenced the people of England.

For More Information

Sellman, R. R. *The Vikings*. London: Methuen and Co. Ltd., 1957.

Wilson, David M. *The Vikings and Their Origins*. London: Thames and Hudson, 1970.

Rosedahl, Else. *The Vikings*. London: Allen Lane, 1991.

Simpson, Jacqueline. *The Viking World*. New York: St. Martin's Press, 1980.

CULTURES TODAY

AUSTRIANS

(aws' tree uns)

People of German, Slav, Italian, and Magyar ancestry living in the present country of Austria.

Population: 7,700,000 (1990 estimate).
Location: Central Europe; bounded by Germany, Czechoslovakia, Hungary, Yugoslavia (Croatia), and Italy.
Language: German.

Geographical Setting

Austria is a small country, three-fourths of which is mountainous. The various Alps mountain ranges cross the southern part of the country, separating it from Italy and Yugoslavia. Only in the north is the land lowered and level, a broad plain carved by the Danube River that passes through the capital city of Vienna on its way toward Hungary. Large tributaries to this river, principally the Inn, Traun, Ems, Mur, and Drava rivers, carve valleys in the Alps in which much of the population resides. The mountains and rivers separate the land of the Austrians into eight well-defined states—each with its own characteristics and distinctive cultural patterns. The divisions complete a country shaped like a bag with its bound neck drawn westward. The climate varies according to altitude but is generally cool.

Historical Background

Origins. The land of the Austrians is a relatively modern creation. At one time, the great Habsburg empire, centered on Austria, stretched through some of present-day Hungary, Yugoslavia, and Germany and vied with the Prussians, Turks, and Russians for con-

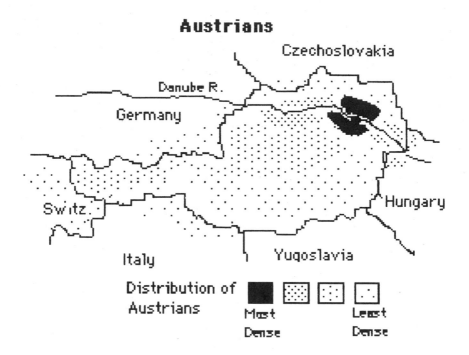

Austrians

Czechoslovakia

Danube R.

Germany

Switz.

Italy

Hungary

Yugoslavia

Distribution of Austrians

Most Dense

Least Dense

trol of most of Central Europe. Only after World War I were the present boundaries set, and the name Austrians became identified with the people in this smaller area.

Beginnings. The plains of northern Austria and the mountains of the Alps were first settled before 2000 B.C. by Illyrians, a Balkan people. In the mountains these people mined copper and salt for their own use and for trade. In the protected river valleys, particularly along the Danube in the north, the first settlers established an agricultural economy.

A mixing spot. Between 500 and 200 B.C., the land of the Illyrians was settled by immigrants from the north, south, and west. Germans followed the Danube to settle in what is now Austria. Scandinavians followed them and were joined by travelers from Spain. About 400 B.C. Celts from northwest France and west Germany crashed into the region on the strength of their weaponry—coats of mail, large shields, and swords of iron. The Celts established a capital at Noria, south of the Danube River, and began to build towns along the river.

Romans. Celts and Romans clashed as the Romans claimed the land as far north as the Danube in 14 B.C. This was to be the northernmost expansion of the Roman Empire. Romans built forts along the southern banks of the river to protect against the northern and eastern hordes that were moving toward Rome. For 400 years, the Danube River served to define the border of Roman civilization. In the early part of this period, the elite Roman Legions of perhaps a third of a million well-paid soldiers held and expanded the borders of the empire. But as the Roman civilization consumed its wealth and expanded its territory, the government sought ways to increase the size of the army and at the same time reduce its costs. The result was an army doubled or tripled in size with the addition of fighters from the very tribes they were to defend against. With this less-dedicated soldiery, the Romans were constantly challenged along its borders, and an eastern tribe, the Huns, overran what is now Austria about A.D. 433. The Huns were not settlers, however; rather they were raiders who left the land to be settled by Germanic Bavarians and Slavs. For a while the land was divided—a Roman west and tribal east inhabited by Slavic and Germanic tribes. Part of the eastern region fell to the kingdom of the Avars.

Franks. Christianity further divided the land, coming to the west in the seventh century. Charlemagne, leader of the Franks, claimed the region in 811 and established an "eastern province" of his empire. The province was called Ostmark—the beginnings of an identification of the region as Austria. With the collapse of the Frank's Holy Roman Empire, much of this area fell to the Magyars and, after their defeat by the Germans at the Battle of Lechfield, to Otto, the German emperor of the new Holy Roman Empire. Again the region was placed under separate rule, this time by Leopold I, ruler of the duchy of Oesterreich. The region remained part of the Holy Roman Empire until the breakup of this rule in 1254. There followed 20 years of rule by a collection of nobles, who in 1273 finally elected Rudolph of the family of Habsburg to be king of all Germany. Although challenged by Ottokar II, a Slavic ruler, the Habsburgs were to control central Europe and reach as far as the Netherlands and Spain during the next 600 years.

Expansion. During this period, the Habsburg family expanded its area of influence by war and by marriage.

Albert II (about 1438)	Married the daughter of the king of Hungary and Bohemia
Albert's son, Frederick III	Married Leonora, daughter of the king of Portugal, and was succeeded by his son
Maximilian I (1493)	Married Mary, daughter of Charles the Bold, king of Burgundy and the Netherlands
Philip	Married Joanna, daughter of Frederick and Isabella of Spain

Catholics and Protestants. The expansion of the influence of the Habsburgs was not without challenge, however. By the middle of the sixteenth century, German nobles were dissenting—driven by religious differences between the Protestant Germans and the Catholic Austrians. The Peace of Augsburg (1555) established the rights of ruling nobles to decide the religious affiliations of their own realms. Still threatened by this privilege, Ferdinand II, the Habsburg ruler of Bohemia, was chosen Emperor in 1619. This set off a long brewing dissent by the Protestant German nobles of the Evangelic League, who elected their own candidate, Frederic V, for Emperor of Bohemia. Ferdinand II and the Catholic Union opposed this selection and there followed the Thirty Years' War, which devastated the region. Maximilian of Bavaria defeated the Protestants, but the harsh terms imposed by Ferdinand again inspired war, this time with Denmark and England and then Sweden (supported by France) participating on the side of the Protestants. The Protestant alliance was weakened when some German princes refused to support the Swedish king Gustavus Adolphus. The war dragged on until two peace treaties, known as the Peace of Westphalia, that had been five years in the making were finally signed.

The end result of this war was the reduction of the peasantry to poverty, the cessation for a time of the growing literary and musical heritage of the Habsburg empire, and serious weakening of the rule of the Habsburgs. Their holding in Alsace was given to the French. Sweden gained control of some northern German region, and Spain and Switzerland gained independence. Within the remaining empire of the Habsburgs, German nobles gained power. The emperor could no longer place one of them under bans without consent of the others, and the nobles won the right to make their own treaties with other nations.

France and Spain. Again marriage strengthened the empire. In 1700, Philip married into the French royal family and inherited Spain and its possessions. Following a war that saw France opposed by a "Grand Alliance" of England, Holland, and Austria, the 1713 Treaty of Utrect divided Spain and gave Austria rule over the Netherlands, Naples, and Milan.

Maria Theresa. In 1740, Charles VI died without a male heir and the Habsburg male rule ended. Charles' daughter Maria Theresa inherited the crown and immediately was challenged by Frederick the Great of Prussia. Great Britain sided with Austria, and France with Prussia in the ensuing short conflict that resulted in Frederick claiming a part of Austria, Silesia, and then abandoning the conflict and its ally, France. Maria Theresa and the French did not forget this action and seized on the invitation of Russia to join in a new battle to regain Silesia (1756). The battle went on for seven years. But political winds changed and in 1772 Frederick invited Maria Theresa and Catherine the Great of Russia to join him in dividing Poland among them. The total dismemberment of Poland was concluded in three steps in the remaining years of the century.

The declining empire. Wars with France at the end of the 1700s and beginning of the 1800s weakened Austria and so reduced its influence that the monarch Francis II renamed his rule to coincide with the restricted territorial rights—Emperor of Austria and King of Hungary. Not until the defeat of Napoleon in 1815 was Austria, under its chancellor Prince Metternich, able to regain some of its lost territory. Even so, in 1867 Austria and Hungary each agreed to establish some autonomy under a dual rule, forming the Austro-Hungarian dual monarchy that survived and even grew until World War I. The acquisition of Bosnia and Herzegovina from the Turks and the long-standing ambition of Austro-Hungary to annex Serbia angered Germans and Serbs in the region and led to the assassination of the heir to the Austro-Hungarian throne, Archduke Francis Ferdinand, and his wife. This resulted in a declaration of war between that country and Serbia, which was followed by a German declaration of war against Russia and the involvement of all Europe in World War I.

Post-war Austria. With the defeat of Germany and Austria-Hungary in 1918, Europe was rearranged into a pattern of states that lasted more than 70 years. Austria and Hungary were separated and each reduced in size. Czechoslovakia was formed, Poland was reestablished as a separate country, and Yugoslavia was formed as a southern Slavic state.

World War II. Formed from eight distinctly different regions bound by industrial development, language, and the culture of the Habsburg empire, centered at Vienna, Austria, became weakened by the burden of its largest city. Vienna, with two million citizens, was no longer the empire center of trade and politics. It now had to depend on building an industrial base in smaller Austria and meanwhile to support the more than 25 percent of the Austrians living in Vienna. Under this strain, some Austrians hoped to join the growing strength of Germany. In 1938, without much opposition, Germany invaded the country. Following the defeat of Germany, Austrians set up a provisional government in 1945 under Dr. Karl Renner, who became the first elected president of a new republic in 1950. Since 1986 this republic has been under the presidency of Dr. Kurt Waldheim, a former United Nations leader whose rule has been clouded by accusations of Nazi war crimes during the war.

The long history of a larger empire and the merging peoples under it has resulted in a present-day Austria that is decidedly German in the west, but has a mixed German-Celtic-Slavic population in the east.

Culture Today

United Austrians. Austrians are bound by their German language, even though this language takes on flavors of Italy and other adjacent territories, giving it distinct dialects. They are also united by their success in recovering from the economic disaster that followed World War I, and in their rich heritage of music once centered at Vienna. Austrians, too, are united by their position as the heart of the old Habsburg Empire, an empire that is still reflected in the buildings of Vienna and in the people's reputation for courtesy and politeness.

Divided Austria. While nearly all Austrians are proud to claim Austrian ancestry and loyalty, Austrians are divided by a geography that results in eight distinctive administrative regions and the separate quality of Vienna.

In the southwest is the sparsely settled state of Vorarlberg. The area was inhabited by Alemanics (people who were once part of a province of France) and Celts when it fell to the Habsburgs in the fourteenth century. Distanced from the rest of the Austria by the mountains, the Vorarlbergers once chose to be annexed to Switzerland, but failing that, united strongly under Austria and strengthened their own bonds by refusing to allow foreigners to purchase land while they built small industries in textiles and agriculture. Most farms here contain about 25 acres of farmland and 50 acres of forest.

East of Vorarlberg in the Alps Mountains is the state of Tyrol, perhaps the image of Austrian land known best to outsiders. It has been part of Austria since the time of Napoleon. Germans influenced the north and Italians influenced the south. The southern mountain area is a land of resorts and of the distinctive leather jackets and lederhosen others associate mistakenly with all of Austria. Once this area was most famous for its logging industry and the Inn River, down which the logs could be floated all the way to the processing centers along the Danube River. The word *tyrol* means "crossing." Early Alemanic and Bavarian settlers here found travel through the Tyrolean passes an easy route from Germany to Italy. After World War I part of Tyrol beyond the peaks of the Alps was given to Italy even though the people continue to speak German and wanted to unite with the rest of Tyrol.

The state of Carinthia, east of Tryol, is the home of about a half million Austrians. A mixture of descendants of Slavs, Bavarians, Germans, and Italians live in this southernmost of the Austrian states, where lumber is still the major product.

The southeastern state of Austria is Styria. The settlement of World War I split this region, with part of the old Styria going to Yugoslavia. More than one million Austrians live in Styria, where they are fond of a costume consisting of a grey suit with green lapels and green stripes on the trousers, the *steirergewand*, which Austrians consider to be the traditional dress of the people.

North of Styria, Burgenland abuts Hungary, of which it was a part until the present boundaries were established. About 30,000 Croats live in Burgenland along with 250,000 people of German and Hungarian ancestry. Not so mountainous as its southern neighbors, Burgenland supplies Austria with much of its wine.

In the northeast the Danube River separates the states of Upper Austria and Lower Austria. Both regions are heavily populated, with Lower Austria containing the separate governmental unit that is Vienna. It is in these populated areas with larger towns and cities that the Austrians are most noted for their courtesy, good manners, and free-spiritedness.

Salzburg lies in the west at the base of Tyrol, where roads and rails begin the climb to the passes in the Alps toward Italy. This region, too, was acquired by Austria after the defeat of Napoleon and has become a center of tourism, one of Austria's major industries.

Housing. Before the move to industrialization after World War I more than half the Austrians lived in small single- or two-family homes. These houses were built of different materials depending on the section of Austria, with most made of lumber from Austria's abundant forests. About one-fifth of the people live in these homes now. Others have moved to the larger towns and cities to work in a wide variety of small industries. Consequently, there has been little need for new homes in rural Austria and the cost of housing, like most other costs, is low. Austrians spend about one-twentieth of their income on housing—less than is spent for recreation. In the cities, housing remains economical but now consists of one- or two-room flats with a separate kitchen. Fewer than one-fourth of the Austrian city dwellers live in homes that have four or more rooms.

Salzburg, Austria, is the gateway to the Alpine resort region. *Courtesy of Amy A. Trenkle.*

Clothing. Along the Danube River Austrians dress in Western-style clothing, but in the mountain areas, older Austrian styles such as lederhosen and the stierergewand are still popular. Only on holidays do Austrian men wear the more traditional costume of knee pants, colorful cumberbund, bright vest, long-tailed coat, and high top hat. Rural women of Austria are frequently seen in a long skirt and an apron.

Food. Everywhere Austrians enjoy snacking. The most popular snacks are hot sausages and beer. At dinner time, Austrians rely heavily on meat. A typical meal might include a thick soup served with dumplings or meat (pork, beef, and veal are most popular) and salad. Bread is often served with fat bacon. Some Austrian foods are world-famous—the small cakes called *torten*, for example, *weiner schnitzel*, or breaded veal, and *goulash* (beef, potatoes, and papryka). *Naturrschnitzel* is veal cutlet cooked with butter. A well-known dessert is *apfelstrudel* (apple strudel).

Recreation. If Austrians differ culturally from the Germans farther north, it is in their spirit of lightheartedness. Austrians work long hours and work hard as illustrated by their recovery from economic disaster since World War I. They also play hard and take time for pleasure. At almost any time Austrians can be found in the town and village cafés, places similar to coffee houses, where they can sit and talk for as long as they desire. Seven or eight forms of coffee drinks are served in these cafés—from mocca, a small very black drink, to coffee with milk.

Music is a pervasive interest in Austria, the homeland of such great composers as Mozart. The Salzburg Festival each year celebrates classical music in the town where Mozart's opera, "The Magic Flute," was originally performed. Another great music festival is held in the opera houses of Vienna. In this city, too, religious festivals are celebrated with such activities as burning the "demon" of winter. Along with conversation and music, Austrians take pleasure in all sports, but particularly water sports. Swimming, ice skating, sailing, and fishing are universally enjoyed, while such sports as football (soccer) are played for fun and for audiences in the cities and larger towns.

Economy. Vienna is one of the few major cities in the world with a declining population. One-and-one-half million people now live in the city, which housed two million before World War I. Meanwhile the rural areas have increased in population, and Austrian industry (which includes textile factories, copper and iron works, and magnesium mines) has been distributed through the towns in such a way as to make Austria a model of industry with a minimum of pollution. At the same time mechanization has decreased the need for farm workers and increased agricultural productivity—raising such crops as wheat, barley, maize, and sugar beets. Woven fabrics, fertilizers, aluminum products, and motorcycles are among the largest industries. These are supplied with abundant electrical energy generated by the large and fast-flowing rivers.

Austrian laws carefully balance human values with industrial ones. In many ways, Austria may be described as a strong welfare state. For example, families are paid an allowance for children by the government. The laws require that a working wife be given six weeks off work before and after a baby is born. Another law requires that an industry hire one disabled veteran for every 20 able-bodied workers.

Religion. The influence of the old empire has shown itself in religion. Even though religious freedom and separation of church and state are national policies, 89 percent of all Austrians are Roman Catholic. Others are Protestant—mostly Baptists, Methodists, and members of the Protestant Church of the Augsburgian Confession and the Protestant Church of the Helvetic Confession. There are about 10,000 Jews in Austria.

Holidays. Most of the public holidays in Austria are religious holidays celebrated at first by the Catholic Church. In December, Austrians celebrate the Immaculate Conception (Dec. 8), Christmas, and St. Steven's Day (Dec. 26). In the spring and early summer the religious holidays mark Easter, Ascension Day, Whit Monday, and Corpus Christi (a holiday remembering the Last Supper). Labor Day in Austria is marked with work shutdowns and parades, and falls on May 1. Another day of no work is the National Holiday, October 26.

Education. The rectors of universities in Austria are called *magnifizenz*, a word that indicates the high respect for educators and education in Austria. Elementary education is required of all students between the ages of six and 15. The education includes four years of primary schooling in a *Volksschule*. After that some students attend a *Haptschule* for four more years and then go on to vocational training, while some attend the *Allgemeinbildende böhere Schule* for an eight-year program leading to examinations for entry into the universities. The University of Vienna, the largest in the country, was the first German-language university founded in Europe (1365). Austrian education has produced such prominent scientists as Karl Landsteiner, the discoverer of blood grouping, and Victor Hess, a pioneer in the study of cosmic radiation.

Music. However grand the accomplishments of its scientists and politicians, Austrians are most noted for their fondness of and contributions to music. World-famous Austrian musicians include Wolfgang Amadeus Mozart, Franz Schubert, Franz Joseph Haydn, and Johann Strauss. These composers of the 1700s were preceded by equally popular artists, such as Gluck, who worked in Austria but created operas in Italian.

Born in 1756 at Salzburg, Mozart began composing music at age five and toured Europe as a harpsichordist at age six. Compelled by the Archbishop of Salzburg to write an oratorio (a religious story for both voices and instruments), Mozart accomplished the feat in a single week. By 12 he was composing operas for the emperor of Austria. Later, Mozart moved to Italy, where he, like Gluck, composed some of his works in Italian, then to Germany and France. Mozart

The old Schonbrunn Castle has been converted into a college. *From the Library of Congress.*

Wolfgang Amadeus Mozart, the famous composer, lived and worked here in Salzburg. *Courtesy of Amy A. Trenkle.*

composed operas such as "The Magic Flute," symphonies, concertos, and six quartets that he dedicated to his friend Franz Joseph Haydn.

Joseph Haydn was 24 years old when Mozart was born and is said to be the first master of the symphony. He developed the string choir, which is the heart of the symphony orchestra today. After working in Austria, then England, he returned to Austria to created his great oratorio, "The Creation."

At the end of the eighteenth century, Franz Schubert was one of Vienna's best-known composers. He wrote more than 1,200 musical pieces, but none were published until 1821—seven years before the man called the most poetic musician that ever lived died.

Johann Strauss was a musician in Vienna at the same time as Schubert. Born in 1804, he had become an orchestra conductor by age 19. A master of the waltz, he is best known for his "Songs of the Danube." The family fame in music was continued in the last half of the nineteenth century by his son Johann Jr. This Johann Strauss was known as the king of the waltz because of such works as "Tales from the Vienna Woods."

These great musical composers and the popular performers of today are recognized each year at the famous musical festivals in Vienna and Salzburg.

Art. The art of Austrians is nearly as well-known as their music. Austrians have long been recognized for their fine woodcarvings and intricate wrought-iron works. Recent Austrian fame in painting began with Gustav Klimt, born in 1898. In more recent years Ernst Fuchs, Wolfgang Hutter, and Anton Lehmdan have produced popular works in a style that is called fantastic realism, which exaggerates real forms. In the twentieth century, Anton Hansk has become internationally known for his extremely large sculptures and Fritz Wotruba has become a recognized master for sculpting human forms.

For More Information

Briion, Marcel. *Daily Life in the Vienna of Mozart and Schubert.* New York: The Macmillan Company, 1962.

The Europa World Yearbook 1991, Vol. I. London: Europa Publications Limited, 1991.

Janik, Allan and Stephen Toulmin. *Wittgenstein's Vienna.* New York: Simon and Schuster, 1973.

Whelpton, Eric. *Austrians: How They Live and Work.* Newton Abbot: David and Charles, 1970.

BASQUES
(basks)

People of northwest Spain and southwest France.

Population: 1,400,000.
Location: Spain, France.
Language: Basque.

Geographical Setting

The rugged Pyrenees Mountains run west to east across the narrower neck of land of southern France and northern Spain. As this mountain range approaches the Bay of Biscay in the Atlantic Ocean, it descends and breaks up into rolling hills before leveling to a short coastal plain. This is a sunny land of fertile valleys and tableland, green all year round and covered with forests of oak, birch, and ash trees and rising to valleys with running streams. Orchards, meadows, and fields fill the tablelands and slopes with fields of fruits, grapes, flax, rye, potatoes, and hemp that are watered with rainfall of 20 to 40 inches annually.

Historical Background

Origin. The exact origins of the Basque people is as mysterious as that of any people in Europe. They seem to have lived for centuries in this same region, where they call themselves Eskualdunak, a word related to their word for sun. Early Roman visitors to the west described a group of people, the *Vascone*, living in the border land between France and Spain, where the Pyrenees Mountains end in rolling hills that flatten into a plain along the coast of the Atlantic Ocean. Fiercely independent, the Vascone long resisted invasions or

Basques

San Sebastian

France

Ebro R.

Barcelona

Portugal

Spain

Atlantic Ocean

Mediterranean Sea

Distribution of Basques

Most Dense   Least Dense

government by outsiders. Roman efforts to control the land were unsuccessful. Their independence was demonstrated in their brutal opposition to Christian missionaries before the seventh century, a resistance that persisted in some form to earn them a description in the tenth century as "pillaging Basques" and condemnation by the Roman Catholic Synod of 1179. It is also seen in their leader's response to the earlier invading Romans, "We would rather die than submit."

Navarre and Castille. The Vascone drove out the Visigoths who swept into the area from across Rome in the sixth century. The Normans of the north met a similar fate, and even Charlemagne suffered a defeat when his army approached Vascone land in A.D. 778. The Vascone then separated into two governing units with loyalties to Castille and Navarre. Those who would become known as Basques were ruled by the kingdom of Navarre. In 1200 the entire land fell under the rule of Castille even though the Basques of Navarre continued to claim independence and to struggle with the imposed government. In the year 1212, the Basques joined with Castille to drive

Moors from the country. Eventually resistance dwindled and, in 1516, the Basques on the Spanish side of the Pyrenees united with Castille.

France and Spain. Basque land was then divided north and south as the French-Spanish border cut through Basque land. In 1589 the king of northern Navarre proclaimed himself king of France and became Henry IV. As they had for centuries, the Basques paid only nominal allegiance to the national rule of Henry IV, preferring their own local governments. The French Revolution swept away local government rights north of the Pyrenees, putting some Basques under French national rule while, by 1876, the Basque lands in the south had been absorbed by Spain.

Carlist Wars. Still the Basques demanded independence and that demand resulted in a Spanish defeat of Navarre in 1839 and of the other three Basque provinces in 1876. The result of these wars divided Basque land firmly between France and Spain. The arrangement with the Spanish government, however, allowed a measure of self-government to the Basques. For example, the king of Spain was not allowed to hold Basque land or to levy taxes. He could and did, however, exercise the right to receive voluntary contributions from the Basques. Basques were included in Spanish embargos on foreign trade. Local Basque leaders, *juntas*, *etats*, or *beltzars*, were freely elected either by popular vote or by groups of church delegates, or by mayors of the towns and villages.

Spanish civil war and the hope for independence. In 1936 Spain granted autonomy to the Basques of Navarre, who elected Jose Antonio de Aguise president. However, Basque independence never really materialized. With the emergence of General Francisco Franco as victor in 1936, the statute was rescinded. The Basques resisted and at Franco's request their capital city, Guernica, was bombed by German planes. Many of the Basques were forced into exile. In the 1960s the Basques renewed a demand for independence from Spain. Violent confrontations persisted through the 1970s and 1980s, even though the post-Franco governments have given a limited self-rule to the Basques. The most radical of the Basque nationalists, the ETA, were blamed for the death of an admiral in 1973 and for hundreds of deaths since then. Their activity resulted in the formation of a counter-revolutionary group, Grupo Antiterrorista de Liberacion, that was accused of the deaths of 23 Basques between 1984 and 1986.

Meanwhile, throughout the years, Basques of the northern slopes of the Pyrenees have mostly been ignored by the French government.

Culture Today

Language. The mystery of Basque origin is further clouded by the Basque language, which is not related to any language spoken nearby and was little used as a written language until the twentieth century. Basques cloud the language in legend, with the famous Abbé Diharce de Bidassouet claiming that it was the original language spoken by the Creator. Attempts to trace the language have led to the belief that the Basques have lived in their homeland perhaps longer than any other group in Europe.

A comparison of Basque with English can be made from this translation of a bit of Basque oral poetry.

Ichasos urac aundi,   The waters of the sea are vast,
Estu ondoric agueri—   And their bottom cannot be seen
Pasaco ninsaqueni andic   But over them I will pass,
Maitea icostea gatic.   That I may behold my beloved.

Encyclopedia Americana 1942, p. 314

Economy. Throughout history Basques have been independent and very much bound to the land. Farming supplemented by fishing still supports many Basques, but today an industrial movement is changing Spanish Euzkual Herria (Basque land). Coal deposits and discoveries of ore have made Basque land the center of an iron industry, and that has made it some of the most densely populated land in Europe. Still, much of the Basque economy is based on agriculture and centered at a long-held family homestead. Basque villages in the hills and valleys are loose collections of scattered family homes. The center of this "village" may be only a church and a tavern. While earlier Basques were farmers and fishers, today many Basques work as coal miners or in the iron industry. Open-air markets and traditions of giving are important parts of the rural economy. Farmers bring produce to the village market for sale or trade.

Homes and family life. Still, the *baserria*, or farm house, is the social and economic center of Basque life. A three-storied house of brick or stone, the baserria is home to the family and its livestock. Animals live at ground level, family members above. The ground level varies according to the district in which the house is built. In some places it is compartmentalized so that there is a large room for carts and carriages. In others the ground floor includes an open-air portico. In still others a large kitchen is on this floor. The earliest of these houses was built like a stone fort, with slit windows and a wooden stairway that was the only entrance to the upper floors and could be burned in time of danger.

A young working husband and wife may live in the family home with the parents and unmarried brothers and sisters on land held by the family for many years. In Basque tradition it is unforgivable to let the basseria decay or to divide the land. So baserria and land are handed intact to one son or daughter. Other children in the family may stay there as long as they are unmarried, but when married must leave the home. The members of the family decide who will best keep the basseria and others are paid for their interest in it.

In the Basque family, men and women are equal but have distinct jobs. The kitchen work belongs to the women. Stables and granaries are the responsibility of the men. Those who do not inherit the land move to the cities to work in the growing industry or to the sea where Basques have hunted whale and fished for centuries.

The family is such a strong bond among the Basques that only other neighboring Basque families are really trusted. Basque families do interact in the villages, where there is a church with a section for each family and where the only social life beyond the family is carried out.

In farming communities, the *leken cuzo*, next neighbor, is important in spiritual life as well as in the storytelling recreation. It is this neighbor who tends to the family and farm in the case of the death of a family member and who carries the cross in the funeral procession.

Religion. Basques are Roman Catholic and believe strongly in the tenets of the Church. But that faith is sometimes augmented by beliefs in witches and *lamenaks*, an imaginary race of small, cave-dwelling mischief-makers. The strongest force in Basque religion is fear, fear of the devil and its cohorts—monsters of every imaginable variety. Superstition plays an important role in Basque life. A howling dog at night might foretell misfortune, for example, or removing a tile from the roof of the home can invite evil spirits to depart.

Holidays. Throughout Spain, Roman Catholics take many occasions to celebrate major events in the history of their faith. Since most

Basques are Roman Catholic, they celebrate the same holidays as most other citizens of the country. The holidays run through the year:

January	New Year's Day
	Epiphany
March/April	Good Friday
	Easter (celebrated on a Sunday by the Basques and on Monday by their neighbors, the Catalans)
May	St. Joseph the Workman's day
June	Corpus Christi
	King Juan Carlos' Saint's Day
July	St. John of Compostela Day
August	Assumption Day
November	All Saints' Day
December	Celebration of the Immaculate Conception
	Christmas

Basques and other Spaniards also celebrate the day of the discovery of the Americas (October 12) and the anniversary of their own constitution (December 6).

Literature. Before the twentieth century Basque literature was scant. Much Basque literature was about the language rather than using it. In 1545 Bernard Dechepare wrote a volume of Basque verse, "Linguae Vascorum Primitiae." Before that century had ended, Esteban de Garibay and Andres de Poca had written the first of the histories of the Basques. A writer attempting to explain the Basque language, Abbé Dominique Lahatjuzan, completed his work in 1818. Part of the reason for the scant written Basque literature may be the difficulty of the language, which the Basques claim Satan came to learn but abandoned the project after seven years.

Arts. Basque arts include a tradition of oral storytelling as well as ritualistic plays. Before industrialization caused many Basques to gather in large communities, it was common practice to invite a neighbor family to the house for an evening of storytelling in which stories of trickery, bravery, and good and evil spirits were retold. Included in this oral tradition are short proverbs such as "A fish and a guest go bad on the third day and must be thrown out." In these stories or proverbs neighboring towns might be given special note—a town might be noted, for example, for its lack of movement except for the tongues of its inhabitants.

A well-known Basque play is the Pastorale, a very long portrayal of the conflicts between Christians and Turks in the time of Francoise I, who bought his own freedom from the Turks by giving them his two small sons. In the past, farm boys gathered on improvised stages to perform this play, with a stage manager and narrator supplying the words and a small band setting the tone for each scene. Folksongs of love, lullabies, or relations with France and Spain are popular among the Basques but, because of the lack of written records, are of uncertain origin.

Dance is popular among the Basques and includes recreational dances and ritual dances. One famous dance is the Katcha-Ranka, or Dedication of the Coffer. Dancers parade through a fishing village carrying a coffin on which sits a person representing the patron saint Peter. At the waterfront, Peter is symbolically beaten to show how the villagers will feel toward him if the fishing is unsuccessful. Even more famous are the sword dances performed by the dancers of Viscaya.

Recreation. Besides dance, Basques enjoy the game of *pelote* in many different levels of difficulty. There is often a court for playing this game associated with the village church. Pelote is a wall game like jai lai or sometimes a game played over an imaginary net. It is played at an amateur level and professionally, with professionals providing exhibitions for local inhabitants and for the tourist industry. Another wall game, played on a court 40 yards long, is *Rebot*. Equally famous is the once-a-year sport in which young Basque men risk danger by running through the village of Pamploma chased by bulls.

Planka is a popular field sport. It involves throwing a ten to 25 pound javelin in various ways. Nearly gone are the older sports in which ducks were buried up to their necks and horsemen attempted to severe the necks while riding at full speed, or a similar game in which chickens were beheaded using only blunt instruments.

For More Information

Collins, Roger. *Basques*. London: Basil Blackwell, 1990.

Gallop, Rodney. *A Book of the Basques*. Reno, Nevada: University of Nevada Press, 1970 (revised and reprinted from the original 1930 publication).

Westwood, Webster. *Basque Legend*. New York: AMS Press, 1977.

BRETONS

(bret' uns)

The French-Celtic people of Brittany.

Population: 2,800,000 (1989 estimate).
Location: Brittany, a large peninsula extending into the Atlantic Ocean from the French mainland and separating the English Channel and the Bay of Biscay.
Languages: French and Breton, a Celtic language.

Geographical Setting

The land of the Bretons is a broad, rocky plateau of gently rolling hills that slopes from the European continent to form a peninsula extending into the Atlantic Ocean. The coastline is marked by sharply rising cliffs and rugged, rocky shores broken by large bays such as that at Brest and narrow inlets that shelter small fishing villages.

Inland the region is two plateaus separated by the one river in the area that empties into the bay in which the port of Brest is located. Once cleared of rocks some of the land provides fertile soil on which Breton farmers grow grains and fruits in a climate that is mostly dry and the temperatures moderate. But some of the land was once moor-high, poorly drained swampland. Strong winds blow from the waters surrounding the peninsula, bringing moist air and fog in the winter. There is an almost uniform rainfall of from 20 to 40 inches each year.

Historical Background

Romans. When Roman legions came to the peninsula of Brittany in 57 B.C. they found a land inhabited by tribes of a Celtic people they

Basques

San Sebastian

France

Ebro R.

Portugal

Barcelona

Spain

Atlantic Ocean

Mediterranean Sea

Distribution of
Basques

Most
Dense

Least
Dense

called Amoricans, a word meaning people facing the sea. The people there called themselves Letewicians and their land Letau. The Romans also found evidence of an ancient Druid society. "Avenues" in several places on the peninsula were marked by rows of large upright stones. Later explorations uncovered graves entered through stone passages and burial sites with stone axes and objects of gold and copper buried with the ancient residents of the land. That these people were related to those who migrated from the mainland to Cornwall, Scotland, and then Ireland is suggested by evidence of similar subterranean dwellings found in Brittany and on the roughest coasts of Scotland and Wales.

The Romans were little interested in governing these people, who were organized into five tribes extending from Gerome to the Seine River. The major interest was to provide a supply line to the new conquests in the British Islands. A single Roman legion entered what was then Gaul, seized a portion of the coastline, built forts on the coastal promontories, and constructed a fleet of ships on the Loire River to continue their subjugation of the Amoricans. Under Rome, the region was divided into great estates, with the Amoricans as serfs or slaves working the land. About A.D. 277, German tribes began to penetrate Amorica.

Saxons. By the early 300s, Saxons had overrun the Roman lands and destroyed most of the villages and towns except for the strongholds at Nantes, Rennes, and Vannes. But by 345 the Romans had regrouped and the area was ruled by the Roman Count of the Saxon Shores of Britain from that year to 413. The Saxons persisted, however, encouraging the Bretons to throw off the Roman yoke, and in the early 400s the land was a loose union of *plebs*, local governing bodies who professed loyalty to the Breton King Conan Meriadoc. By the next century, the region was surrounded by the kingdoms of the Franks, kingdoms that were united under Charlemagne and Louis between 768 and 840. When these two rulers of the Holy Roman Empire had died, the area of western France fell to Charles the Bald. Under his rule, the Bretons, who had by this time grown through emigrations from Ireland and Wales (driven out by the invading Angles and Saxons of the sixth century), were never successfully brought under full unification with other French territories.

The Breton plebs were the governing units—groups of serfs, each working a piece of land, a *ran*, by the grace of a local lord or a local priest. Over the years, gifts of land by the lords to the church put much of the land into the hands of these local priests. Monasteries for the religious leaders were built and villages of serfs dependent on the church grew up around them. The rule of the people was in the hands of such collections of priests as the monastery at Redon.

Independence. Unable to control the Bretons or even to collect tributes from them consistently, the Frank leader Louis the Pious appointed a local ruler of the land in 818. Under the rule of this man, Nomenoë, Brittany became a peaceful and prosperous land. At mid-century, Nomenoë had taken advantage of the weakening Frank rule to declare independence. Although this action was recognized by the Franks, there followed a series of military encounters from invaders from the north. In the first quarter of the 900s, these actions had gained success and Brittany had been essentially reduced to the conditions of the 400s.

France and England. From that time on, Brittany was ruled periodically from outside the country or with outside support of a local ruler. For 300 years, Brittany was led by a Count based in Rennes, the first Count of Rennes having been installed with the support of Norway. During this period Brittany was closely united with its northern neighbor, Normandy. In 1169, the king of England claimed the region and made his son Duke of Brittany. Geoffrey, the Duke, soon turned against his own father and allied with the king of France. Richard the Lionhearted again claimed the land and named a successor to rule, but this successor was killed by King John of England and Brittany became a vassal state of France. Later, the Duke of Brittany was treated as a partner when France and England joined in the Hundred Years War. However, Brittany was an untrustworthy ally, joining first the French and then the English and alternating between the two throughout this long war.

Alliance with France. The Hundred Years War was followed by several minor wars over the status of Brittany in relation to France. This status began to be resolved when Anne, the Duchess of Brittany, married Charles VIII, king of France in 1491. Charles' successor, Louis XII, was so little impressed with the region that he gave it away to Claude, Countess of Angouline. It was not until 1552 that Brittany was officially incorporated into France. The land of the Bretons has remained a section of France since that time, with one bloody interlude during the French Revolution when the area sided with the royal family. After that, the Bretons enjoyed some autonomy within France and it was not until 1822 that Brittany was officially and totally reunited with France.

In the nineteenth century, the French government began to encourage development and integration with other parts of France. Railroads were built to encourage trade with other parts of the nation. Much of the swampland (moors) was cleared and canals constructed to drain the land, turning it into profitable grazing land. Brittany began to emerge from its subsistence farming and fishing to a market economy. This development was accelerated after World War II, but parts of Brittany still cling to the old costumes, customs, and Celtic language of earlier days.

Culture Today

Religion. Religion is a dominant part of the lives of the Bretons. Ancient history of a Druidic religion has left some marks on rites and ceremonies of the Roman Catholic Church, which most Bretons claim as their religion. The Breton religion is one of veneration of the dead. Blessings are said for and in the names of dead family members. At death, a Breton is placed on a *lit de mort,* a bed for the dead where it rests during a wake. Following the wake, the body is placed in a coffin for burial. Burial is in a cemetery in the middle of the town or village. The burial ceremony is followed by a celebration, a small meal attended by both family members and participants in the funeral preparation.

Various ancient stories reflect the beliefs of the Bretons in an afterlife that is closely tied to the earthly one. One story tells of fishermen who are awakened in a trance in the middle of the night and led to their ships. The ships are fully laden as can be seen by their depth in the water, but no souls are visible. Sailors are forced to sail these loaded ships to a nearby island, where the souls of the dead unload from the ships and the empty ships allowed to return home. Thus the souls of the dead reside near the living and are believed to play active roles in everyday life. Breton place names give special recognition to the dead.

Bretons believe firmly in heaven and hell and talk of the home of the devil as a cold place rather than the fiery inferno described in the literature of other lands.

Celebrations and holidays. Great days of the Breton year are *pardons*, days during which Bretons can be forgiven for their sins. Each Breton's patron saint has such a day. On this day, the Breton visits the place where the saint is believed to be buried, drinks from a nearby fountain, and then celebrates in the evening to the music of the *biniou*, a bagpipe. One of the most famous of such celebrations is at Rumengol. Here people gather in their traditional costumes at a statue of the Virgin Mary that is believed to have curing powers over all forms of ills. Another celebration is the Pardon of Fire. A bonfire is set on a hilltop, and celebrants dance and sing while trying to take a burning brand from the fire to bring joy and good health granted by St. John. Still another is the Pardon of the Sea in celebration of St. Anne built around a myth of the life and exile of the Duchess of Brittany who married a French king. Still another celebration honors St. Galonnek, an immigrant from Ireland who convinced the ancient Bretons to abandon their practice of luring ships to wrecking on the rocky coast by building fires on the nearby hills.

Farm life and farming. Cooperative farming has long been a way of life among Breton farmers. Serfs working small plots, or sometimes several widely separated small plots, often joined hands in harvesting or tilling the land. Much of the cooperation was carried out by various members of an extended family who lived together or near each other. Cooperation was a means for making the most of a sometimes difficult land using the primitive means available. Animal-drawn plows and hand harvesting of subsistence crops was a way of life on Breton farms until after World War II.

Following that war, Bretons began to turn to mechanization. Still without money to buy powered plows and harvesters, they turned to their old cooperative ways to hold joint ownership in and use of modern farming equipment. The result was more efficient farming and the need for fewer workers in agriculture. Many Bretons began to move to the larger towns, where light industry was developing or to the larger seaports such as Brest to find work in shipping. Younger Bretons moved to Paris and other large French cities in search of jobs. The result, as elsewhere in the world, has been the breakdown of the extended family and a focus on a single family unit of husband, wife, and young children. Another result for Bretons has been an aging of the population as younger family members moved away in search of a less arduous lifestyle.

Food, clothing, and shelter. Many of the small towns and villages that sprang up around churches and monasteries in the past still dot

Barns like this are seen throughout Brittany. *Courtesy of Amy A. Trenkle.*

the landscape of Brittany. The Breton farmer and villager lives in a home usually made of the most abundant building material, rock. Shaped stones frame the doors and windows of these small houses, which are roofed with thatch or shingle. In the more remote villages, people can still be seen wearing the clothing popular before the mechanical era and its Western-style clothing. Women in these outlying villages and farms dress in calf-length skirts, long-sleeved blouses, aprons, and wooden shoes, *sabots*. Breton women in many places still wear stiffly starched, lace butterfly-shaped hats. For celebrations, the dark, velvet blouses and skirts of the women are often embroidered with flower patterns. Celebrations call for some men to bring out bagpipes to supply music. These musicians identify themselves by blue trousers and gold shirts, over which an embroidered, dark, short coat is worn along with a cap or bowler type hat.

Much of the land of the Bretons has been converted to pasture. This allows Bretons to raise cattle and pigs to augment the variety of grains, fruits, and vegetables grown on the more fertile land near the seashore. In addition, fishing (particularly for lobster) adds to the available food for Bretons and for a growing market economy. Apples grow in abundance in some areas, so cider replaces the wine that in other parts of France is the most popular drink. Hams and sausages are main parts of the Breton diet.

A village scene such as this is common in the region of Brittany. *Courtesy of Amy. A. Trenkle.*

Fishing. The many small inlets that mark the coast of the peninsula are dotted with small villages and larger towns in which fishing is the major occupation. These towns have been in this century industrialized with canning factories for the fish and for the farm products that grow in greatest abundance near the coast. In addition, a few once fishing-dependent towns have developed thriving small industries in ceramics, metallurgy, and woodcarving. Central along the coast, the city of Brest provides a modern port located in a bay that is 14 miles long and seven miles wide—ample for any seagoing vessel.

The proximity to the sea, and Breton fishers' familiarity with sea travel has, in the past, made the Bretons and their land important for world exploration. One famous Breton sailor, Jacques Cartier, sailed to North America and settled what is now Canada.

Language. With railroads and highways linking Brittany with the rest of France, the French language came into greater use among the Bretons. Still, Breton, the language of the earlier Celtic inhabitants, is commonly used in the western portion of the peninsula. In the south, Brittany is marked by the Loire River with its inland port city of Nantes. From this city of a quarter million inhabitants, two newspapers are circulated in the Breton language—*L'Eclair* and *Presse Océan*. A rich literature of folk stories exists in the Breton language. Folk stories tell of magic, werewolves, and intrigue. Some seem to have been drawn from early experiences with biblical stories. For example, one story tells of a Saint Corentin who was so remorseful about breaking a fast and eating a fish that he was given power to have a single fish provide food for as many guests as came to eat with him.

For More Information

Badone, Ellen. *The Appointed Hour: Death, Worldview and Social Change in Brittany*. Berkeley: University of California Press, 1989.

Chadwick, Nora K. *Early Brittany*. Cardiff: University of Wales Press, 1969.

Davies, Wendy. *Small Worlds: The Community in Early Medieval Brittany*. Berkeley: University of California Press, 1988.

CATALANS
(cat′ l ans)

People of northeastern Spain whose capital is Barcelona.

Population: 6,440,000 (1989 estimate).
Location: Northeast Spain, mostly in the provinces of Barcelona, Gerona, Taragona, and Lérida.
Languages: Catalan, Spanish.

Geographical Setting

Along the eastern edge of the Pyrenees Mountains, the Spanish territory of Catalonia is cut by rivers flowing from the mountains and by fingers of the Pyrenees reaching southward. Forested hills and low mountains give way to a narrow coastal plain that is notched frequently by the rugged and jagged shoreline. On its southwest edge, the Ebro River, one of Spain's largest rivers, flows to the Mediterranean Sea and divides Catalonia from the province of Valencia. Twenty to 40 inches of rain fall annually, providing water for groves of oranges and olives and fields of flax, hemp, saffron, grapes, and hazelnuts. The mountains provide coal, copper, manganese, zinc, lead, cobalt, salt, and marble, while the rivers, principally the Ebro, provide hydroelectric power to make this region the center of industry and manufacturing in Spain. Barcelona, with its good deep-water port, is the center of this industrial section. The result is a population among the most dense in Europe.

Historical Background

Rome. As Rome maneuvered against its long-time enemy, Carthage, in the Second Punic War, Roman soldiers landed on the east coast

Catalans

Bay of Biscay

France

Ebro R.

Gerona

Barcelona

Portugal

Spain

Atlantic
Ocean

Mediterranean Sea

Distribution of
Catalans

Most
Dense

Least
Dense

of Spain and established a colony at Ampurious (219 B.C.) among scattered farmers and fishers who inhabited the region. By 197, the Romans had subjugated the old residents and had established the Roman province Hispania Taraconensis. Under the Romans, the people of the province lived peacefully as farmers or in small fishing villages along the Mediterranean coast. There was little need for more organization than the Romans offered, and their protection allowed the farming people to live for the next five centuries in houses and villages without walls or fences.

Visigoths. About the year A.D. 400, Visigoths who had overrun parts of the Roman Empire began to spread into Hispania Taraconensis, and by 407, the people of the province had begun to build walled villages in their defense. These were connected by a Roman highway that crossed the Pyrenees, touched Gerona, and reached Barcelona. Nevertheless, Rome lost its control of the area first to a group known as Alars and then to the Goths. But this loss was not before the Romans had developed a separate language, a sort of vulgar Latin, and had spread Christianity throughout the land, the ruler of the land having adopted that religion in 582. The Goths ruled over Catalonia for nearly 300 years until they were displaced by Moors sweeping across Spain from the south in their quest to spread the religion of Islam. Arriving in Catalonia in 711 the Moors moved northward and threatened the land of the Franks across the Pyrenees Mountains. Charles Martel led the Franks to a victory that stopped the Moorish northward movement at Tours in 732, but Moorish rulers were firmly entrenched south of the mountains. Franks and Moors struggled for the land of the Catalans, which was loosely ruled by a series of Barcelonian nobles, each given the title of count. It was not until the Moorish leader Mon al-Manour died in 1002 that the land began to revert to the older inhabitants.

Union with Aragon and Castile. As was the custom in that period, kingdoms often grew and were made stronger through marriage. In 1113, Count Ramon Berenguer III of Barcelona married the heiress of the principality of Provence. Then in 1151 Ramon Berenguer IV married Princess Petroniella of Aragon and the two regions were united, with the Count of Barcelona subject to the King of Aragon. In the thirteenth century these two forces joined with those of Castile to combat the north-moving Moors. The Catalan soldiers of Barcelona added to Aragon's strength. By the beginning of the 1300s, Aragon was expanding its sphere of influence. In 1302 the Catalan Grand Company, 6,000 soldiers, fought against the Turks in defense of the eastern Catholic church, then pillaged Sicily. The Catalans joined other people of Aragon to invade Greece and make the Duchy of Athens an appendage of Aragon. In the 1400s, Ferdinand (the Catholic) of Aragon married Isabella of Castile and Leon. This combination defeated the Moors at Granada, loosely uniting most of today's Spain.

Demand for independence. The land of the Catalans became an intellectual center and the main industrial center of Spain, while retaining its own identity and often its own government. So tenaciously did the Catalans protect their language, customs, and what they perceived as their rights that on occasion Castilian Spanish troops were needed to suppress uprisings. In 1890 labor issues resulted in a long period of unrest and by 1896 had given reason for Spanish troops to invade Barcelona. During this period, Barcelona was largely rebuilt to take its place as a major industrial port. The old wall around the city was removed and many of the streets widened to accommodate the increased industrial traffic. By the early 1900s,

Catalonia was the most powerful economic region in Spain. Forty-two percent of Spain's exports were being shipped from Barcelona.

Between 1910 and 1919, Catalans organized under one political group, the CNT, to demand Catalonian independence. In retaliation, the Spanish government at Castile banned the use of the Catalan language and flag, disbanded Catalonian cultural societies, and closed newspapers printed in Catalan. On August 14, 1931, the Catalan leader Fransesc Mació declared Catalonia a separate republic. This was short-lived, however, since all of Spain was shortly caught up in the civil war of 1936–1939. In this war, Catalonia fought on the losing "Republican" side. The end of this struggle saw the installation of a dictatorship under General Francisco Franco y Bahamonde. His decrees again eliminated the Catalan parliament and language. Streets in Barcelona were renamed to eliminate Catalan memories, and Catalan art was burned. Even under his powerful leadership, however, Basque and Catalan demands for self-government grew.

Self-government. Particularly with the Basques and to a lesser degree among the Catalans, acts of terrorism emphasized these demands. By the 1960s Basques and Catalans had been joined by Galatians and Andalucians in seeking a measure of self-government. By 1967, the Spanish government was prepared to reorganize some of these dissenters. Seventeen Autonomous Communities were established, and of these, Catalans and Basques were the first to establish their own parliaments. With the exception of 1984, when the president of Catalan was accused of fraud (a charge dropped in 1986), the parliament at Barcelona has been a strong force in Spain. In 1992, though some Catalonians remain committed to the ideal of full independence, the union with the rest of Spain now seems fairly secure.

Culture Today

People. The people of Catalonia reflect the different conquerors who dominated the land. They are a mix of the original settlers of the Iberian Peninsula (Spain and Portugal) with Romans, from whom they borrowed a language, and Goths, who ruled the region for more than 300 years. Living in an area with few natural resources, but with a fertile river basin that made it possible to be self-sufficient in food supply, the Catalans have developed into an enterprising and energetic people who early depended on industry and trade for economic growth. They have been described as frugal, industrious, and honest.

Economy. Catalans have long provided the Mediterranean with merchants and seamen. While many remained attached to agriculture in a land that was able to support itself on its production of fruits, vegetables, sheep, goats, and swine, Catalan merchants were trading goods in Sicily and along the coast of Africa. To support this trade, Catalans became manufacturers of textiles—cotton, silk, and wool—to which they added paper produced from their own forests and later weapons. In recent years, the slowly developing industrial development has encouraged immigration to such cities as Barcelona. Between 1960 and 1970, for example, nearly half a million workers moved to Catalonia from the south of Spain.

Language. In spite of this influx of people with other languages and the periodic attempts by the Spanish government to discourage the use of their own language, Catalonians have clung to the language developed during the period of Roman rule, which is described as a form of "vulgar," or common, Latin mixed with words of Arabic derivation. Throughout the dictatorship of General Franco, Catalonians struggled to preserve the language. Their success was seen in the growth of publishing. The number of books published annually in the Catalan language grew from two in 1945 to more than 500 in 1968. After the death of Franco and the installation of a republican monarchy, Prince Juan Carlos declared that all regional languages should be considered part of the Spanish cultural heritage and could be used in any medium. As much as any other factor, it is this language that separates and identifies the Catalonians. The language also gives them claim to more than the Barcelona area of Spain. Catalan is spoken in the French departments (areas) of the Pyrenees.

Literature and arts. Catalonian literature reached its greatest height about the fifteenth century with such still-famous authors as Guillaume Molinier (*Leys d'amors*) and Ausias March (*Cants d'amors*). The importance of literature in the Catalonian heritage was demonstrated early with the initiation of the Jocs Florals in 1393. In the spirit of jousts, authors gathered together in a great hall of the palace and took turns reading their works for judges who awarded prizes. These competitions flourished and then faded, to be revived in 1859. A poet who fanned the flames of independence in the nineteenth century was Carlos Bienaventura Arubau, who wrote *Oda a la Patria* in 1838.

Today more than a dozen newspapers are circulated from the Catalan capital of Barcelona, and there are more than 50 book publishers in that city.

It is in architecture perhaps that Catalonians have exhibited their greatest artistic talents. The Catalonian architecture reflects the many people who have dominated the religion. Great cathedrals sit on the sites of former Roman colosseums and Moorish mosques, while new buildings are in the sleek, rectangular styles popular in large cities today.

Recreation. Throughout Spain, *futbol* (soccer) is the most popular participant sport while bullfighting is still the country's most popular spectator sport. Catalonians are said to be more work-oriented than people of other parts of Spain, but Barcelona and other Catalan cities have many opera houses, theaters, and museums.

Holidays. The independence of the Catalonians is reflected in the holidays they celebrate. As in all of Spain, most Catalonian holidays are given some religious connotation (May 1, the traditional day to recognize workers, for example, is celebrated as St. Joseph's Day). But the people of Catalonia forsake the Spanish celebration of Maundy Thursday and instead have an Easter Monday holiday. Catalonians do not celebrate the early December holiday of Immaculate Conception, but they do celebrate Boxing Day on the day after Christmas.

For More Information

Castro, Americo. *The Spaniards, An Introduction to Their History.* Translated by Willard F. King and Selma Margaretten. Berkeley, California: University of California Press, 1971.

Read, Jan. *The Catalans.* Boston: Faber and Faber, 1978.

CYPRIOTS

(sip′ ree ots)

Greek and Turkish inhabitants of the island of Cyprus.

Population: 685,000 (1989 estimate).
Location: Cyprus, an island in the Mediterranean Sea south of Turkey.
Languages: Greek, Turkish, English.

Geographical Setting

Cyprus is a small island in the Mediterranean Sea about 60 miles south of Turkey. A roughly rectangular form extends its northeast corner in a finger pointing toward the Turkish Gulf of Alexandretta. A low mountain range rises abruptly from the northern coastline. This range, the Kyrenian Mountains, gives way inland to a flat plain which rises toward the south side of the island into the higher, more rugged Troodos Mountains. Rivers drain from the mountains into the plains area and toward the south to empty into the Mediterranean Sea, but few of the rivers carry water in the summer months. Because of the nearness of the sea to nearly all parts of Cyprus, the island has a moderate climate. The capital, Nicosia, for example, lies almost centered in the plains areas between the two mountain ranges, but still has a mild climate that ranges between 40 degrees Fahrenheit and slightly below 100 degrees Fahrenheit.

Earlier in its history, the mountains of Cyprus were covered with forests, which helped to create an even more moderate climate. But much of the mountain area has now been denuded of forests. Still with irrigation, fruits, grains, and vegetables grow easily in the fertile plains and lower mountain slopes.

Cypriots

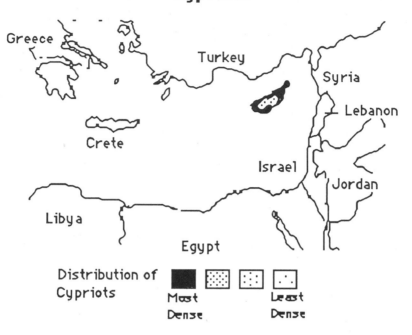

Distribution of Cypriots

Most Dense   Least Dense

Historical Background

Early settlement. The island of Cyprus was first settled before 5800 B.C. by ancestors of today's Turks and Turkmen moving westward from the Asian steppes. By 3000 B.C. these settlers had established coastal trading villages and had discovered the wealth of the forests in the mountain areas and copper in the Troodos Mountains. Between 2000 and 1500 B.C., Phoenician traders established outposts on the island, and about 1400 B.C. Mycean sailors founded settlements there. From the first settlement by these visitors from Greece until A.D. 1960, Cyprus was under the rule of foreign nations.

Kingdoms and rulers. By 708 B.C., the island was divided into seven kingdoms, all paying tribute to a Greek city-state. The inability of these seven kingdoms to unite made them easy prey for invaders, and the parade of foreign powers interested in Cyprus was unending.

Independence. Under the leadership of a Greek Cypriot president (Archbishop Makarios), Greeks and Turks lived in separate settlements or enclaves within the large towns and cities, scattered like salt and pepper throughout the island. Britain had pressed for better education and had established schools which taught the English language, but most Cypriots spoke either Greek or Turkish according to their heritage.

Chronology of Cypriot Rule

708 B.C.	Island conquered by Assyrian King Sorgen II.
690 B.C.	Egyptians drive out Assyrians and rule Cyprus.
600 B.C.	Persians control the island.
333 B.C.	Alexander the Great conquers the islanders.
294 B.C.	Ptolemy and his successors rule until 254.
45 A.D.	Claudius brings Christianity to the island.
324	Cyprus becomes part of the Byzantine Empire, which controls the island until the 1100s.
1191	Richard the Lionhearted conquers the island to rescue his bride-to-be and claims it for France.
1472	The island is ruled from Venice.
1570	Cyprus becomes part of the Ottoman Empire.
1572	The Ottoman sultan Selem II orders a forced settlement of the island by Turks. Beginning with relocation of 30,000 Turks, this settlement by exile continues unto the eighteenth century.
1878	Britain assumes control from the Ottomans and governs Cyprus as a protectorate and after 1923 as a crown colony.
1930	A Cypriot progressive party presses for independence while the majority of Cypriots join a movement for union with Greece (Enosis).
1931	The British governor of Cyprus is burned by the advocates of Enosis.
1955	A meeting of Greek Cypriots, Turkish Cypriots, and British in London fails to reach an accord on the management of the island.
1960	Cyprus becomes an independent nation under a constitution that provides that 70 percent of the legislature be composed of Greek Cypriots and 30 percent of Turkish Cypriots.

Greek-Turk separation. However, even after the independence of the country was established, many Greek Cypriots pressed the cause of union with Greece, contending that the early years of habitation on the island had left a 3,000-year legacy of Greek culture. This pressure and the election of the Greek Orthodox Bishop Makarios to lead the country soon alienated the Turks and caused them to withdraw from the government. By the 1970s, the pressure had grown and animosity between Greeks and Turks on the island had increased to the point that it attracted the attention of the Turks in Turkey. In 1974, fighting erupted between Greek Cypriots who were aligned with the Archbishop Makarios in favor of union with Greece and Greek Cypriots who opposed this leadership. The fighting among Greek Cypriots spurred the prime minister of Turkey to intervene in Cypriot affairs. Turkish mainland troops were sent into the northeastern section of the island.

Division. There followed a period of growing aggravation in which the salt-and-pepper village arrangement was no longer tolerable. A mass exodus of Turks from the south to the north and Greeks from the north to the south followed. In 1975, the Turks in the northeast claimed independence from the predominantly Greek regions and announced the formation of the "Turkish Federated State of Cyprus" separated from the Greek population by the Attila Line, an imaginary line from the north coastal town of Morphous, through Nicosia, to the eastern coastal town of Famagusta. The government of Cyprus refused to acknowledge this breakaway state and continues to claim rule over the entire island. However, the northern Turks persisted and declared the formation of a "Turkish Republic of Northern Cyprus" in 1983. Since that time, fighting between the two Cyprus governments has continued except when held in check by a United Nations peace-keeping force.

Culture Today

For hundreds of years, Greek Cypriots and Turkish Cypriots lived and worked side by side in adjacent villages or in separate enclaves within the larger towns and villages. Greek and Turkish young children played in the village streets together. Greeks and Turks dressed alike, the men in baggy pants and loose shirts held in place by a sash. A visitor to the island could distinguish Greeks and Turks only by the difference in color of these sashes—purple for Turks and blue for Greeks.

Language. Languages separated and united the Cypriots. They could attend schools in English established under British rule. But Greek Cypriots spoke Greek at home, and the Turks spoke Turkish.

The separation was aggravated by religious preferences; most Greeks were served by the Greek Orthodox Church, most Turks were Muslims. The religious differences encouraged separation of the young people at puberty—Greek boys and girls were no longer friends of their Turkish counterparts.

Greek and Turkish stereotypes. The language differences encouraged building stereotypes. Greek Cypriots felt that the Turks were too patriarchal and authoritative and more concerned with the community of their extended families than with personal gain or with national unity. The Greeks viewed Turkish reserve as untrustworthy. Turkish Cypriots viewed the Greeks as overly competitive, individualistic, and loud. These attributes tended to build distrust, also.

The result was, that even though they worked and lived near each other in similar village lives, and even though the stereotypes found representatives in both groups, the Greeks and Turks were never able to form a single Cypriot identity. Still, their lives were, in many respects, similar.

Village life. Earlier villages were collections of related extended families. In both Greek and Turkish families, the eldest male was the ruler of a group that included a wife, married sons and their families, unmarried daughters, and various other relatives such as uncles and aunts or grandparents. Although the families were patriarchal, the older women of the families had much influence in family affairs, approving marriages and deciding the quality of life of women who married into the family, for example.

As the British rule developed an industrial base on the island, more and more of both Greeks and Turks migrated to larger towns and cities in search of work. There, the village patterns of family unity continued as families settled in their own sections of the towns. Separation of Greeks and Turks continued in the large towns, as it had been in separate villages or village sections. In Nicosia, for example, as late as 1992 the Turkish section was separated from a larger Greek section by a "green line," which the two groups of Cypriots rarely cross. The villages of the end of the twentieth century have been urbanized, becoming bedroom communities for the cities in many cases. Few Cypriot villages are more than an hour's drive from a major port or manufacturing city, and many have become suburban homes for workers in the cities.

Clothing and shelter. Industrialization brought changes in clothing, also. The baggy pants and long straight dresses of the old village and farm gave way to European-style clothing of jeans and shirts, suits

Cypriot women making lace. *Courtesy of the Press and Information Department, Republic of Cyprus.*

and ties, and varied styles in the dresses of women. Still, some of the traditional dress can still be seen in the villages.

Cypriot villages were formed of single-family homes located at the bases of river valleys, where the residents could find flat land to farm and an assured water supply. Extended families lived near other members of the family in houses made of stone or wood and perched on the sides of hills. Stone and wood were abundant construction materials on the island. In today's villages hydroelectric power is not available and the country possesses no petroleum or coal resources, so many village homes rely on solar power for heating water in the house.

The invasion from Turkey and the consequent shuffling of the population resulted in serious housing changes, particularly in the larger southern Greek section. The subsequent breakdown of their society made it no longer tolerable for Greek and Turkish villages to exist side by side. Thousands of Turks left their homes in the south to migrate to the north, and thousands of Greeks moved from the Turk-controlled northeast to find homes in the south. The movement was unequal, however, with many more Greeks fleeing the north than Turks seeking sanctuary in the northeastern third of the country. The result was that Turkish migrants could find housing by occupying land and houses abandoned by the Greeks, but the Turkish houses emptied in the south would not accommodate the number of Greek

Women modeling traditional dress at Bellapais Abbey in the Turkish sector. *Courtesy of the Press and Information Department, Republic of Cyprus.*

refugees. Many Greek migrants found it necessary to make homes of garages, hastily erected government housing projects, or warehouses. Since the military intervention of Turkey resulted in the deaths of 6,000 Greeks, the taking of 5,000 prisoners, and the disappearance of another 3,000, relocation was massive and rapid. Some 200,000, or nearly one-third of the total population of Cyprus, have had to find new housing in another part of the country. This includes about 9,000 Turkish Cypriots who fled from a British-held base in southern Cyprus to Turkey and then returned to northern Cyprus.

Education. Despite the apparent fragmentation of their educational system, the people of Cyprus value education and are highly literate. Nearly all the adults of Cyprus can read and write. In both the Republic of Cyprus and the Turkish Republic of Northern Cyprus elementary and secondary education is available. School attendance is mandatory from age six to 12, and most students continue on to a six-year secondary school. Turkish Cypriots established a university in the north in 1986. Most college aspirants in the south attend universities in Greece or Great Britain, although a university was begun in Greek Cyprus in 1991.

Economy. Before the 1950s, the economy of Cyprus was agricultural, and agriculture remains a strong part of the national product. It is strongest in the Turkish northern section, which includes about 40 percent of the arable land. Citrus fruits, olives, wheat, and chickpeas are grown in this northern region and in the south. Farmers in the south also raise grapes and potatoes. In addition, in the south, cattle, sheep, goats, pigs, and chickens are raised for markets in Europe and for the Arab neighbors.

The separation of a Turkish state, even though unrecognized, created problems for the economy as well as for the people of Cyprus. The island's major seaport, Famagusta, was closed to the Greek state in which most of the industry and mining was located. Two other ports were expanded in the 1970s to attempt to compensate for this loss, at considerable expense to the new nation. The Turks who were relocated to the rich farmland of the north were, for the most part, workers of smaller farms in the south using less modern tools. The result of their replacing the Greek farmers of the north was that agricultural production lagged, and the northern Turkish state was forced to rely on Turkey for its economic well-being.

Despite the civil war, and with a great deal of help from the World Bank, industry continued to grow in the south, with products such as tiles, cigarettes, metal objects, and shoes being manufactured for export. To adjust to this increased emphasis on manufacturing, the republic of Cyprus found it necessary to expand its markets to the Arab countries. More than 40 percent of Cyprus's manufactured goods now are sold to these countries.

The relics of ancient societies that dot the landscape in Cyprus and its historical significance as a trading and sailing center and as a crossroads between Muslim and Christian culture, have made Cyprus a major tourist attraction. More than twice as many people vacation on the island each year than live there permanently.

Religion. A major divisive force in Cyprus is religion. Choosing what at the time appeared to be the lesser of the evils, the Ottoman's ousted Roman Catholicism from the island. When it returned, the Catholics found that the people were divided on ethnic lines, with nearly all Greeks following the Greek Orthodox teachings and nearly all Turks

Bellapais Abbey in North Cyprus. *Courtesy of the Public Information Office, Turkish Republic of Northern Cyprus.*

Muslims. Their religion was an important separator of villages and village people. Religious leaders discouraged intermarriages, and in fact, older children were seldom allowed to interact with people of the opposite faith. In times of war, religious symbols have become signs of the treachery of the enemy. Greeks, for example, have converted some of the former mosques in the south to other uses, often destroying the minarets that marked the sacred buildings.

Summary. This entry is markedly different from others in this book, revealing the emphatic difference in the Cypriot culture from that of other areas. It was in some ways a single Cypriot society until the Turkish separation, but it has always shown elements of two distinct cultures—Greek and Turkish—and these distinctions have now resulted in the nearly complete separation of two Cypriot societies. At this writing, feeling between the two groups remains intense, and life and economic progress is only made with the aid of a United Nations peace-keeping force.

For More Information

Markides, Kyriancos C. *The Rise and Fall of the Cyprus Republic*, New Haven: Yale University Press, 1977.

Thirgood, J. V. *Cyprus: A Chronicle of Its Forests, Land, and People.* Vancouver: University of British Columbia Press, 1987.

Volkan, Vamik D., M.D. *Cyprus—War and Adaptation: A Psychoanalytic History of Two Ethnic Groups in Conflict.* Charlottesville, Virginia: University Press of Virginia, 1979.

DANES
(danes)

People of Denmark.

Population: 5,135,400 (1990 estimate).
Location: Denmark, a peninsula protruding from Europe into the Baltic and North Seas, and its neighboring islands.
Language: Danish.

Geographical Setting

The land of the Danes is comprised of 400 islands and a peninsula, Jutland, that protrudes from the mainland of Europe and divides the Baltic and North Seas. In the entire land, no point reaches beyond 600 feet above the sea. The land is mostly flat or softly rolling hills, and is fertile farm and grazing land. The low country has pleasant summers and wet, cold winters. There is an abundance of water to make agriculture the mainstay of the economy, but Denmark's position in the North Sea, pointing to nearby Sweden and Norway has long placed the country in shipping lanes. These shipping opportunities have made Denmark a major industrial country.

Historical Background

Beginnings. The oldest inhabitants of the land of the Danes were a people called the Cimbri, who banded with Teutonic groups as they moved west. A few of the groups (Angles, Saxons, and Jutes) moved farther west and south, finally extending as far as Great Britain, and leaving the people who became ancestors of the Danes to settle the peninsula and nearly 500 islands in the Baltic Sea. In the eighth century A.D. a king from Scotland, Gorm the Old, united the area

Danes

that is Denmark with a portion of what is now Sweden, bringing the Danes under one rule. From that time until recent years, the Danes have controlled varying amounts of land in northern Europe.

Expansion. In the 900s St. Ansgar and King Harald Blastand brought Christianity to the Danes. This resulted in new acquaintances with other European groups, and the Danes embarked on conquest. King Sweyn captured England in 1013 and Canute the Great (1014–1035) added Norway to the Danish holdings, but by A.D. 1047 his successors had lost both regions. Still the royal family of Canute, beginning with his sister's son Svend Estriden, who held power from 1047 until 1076, controlled much of Denmark and expanded its international role for 400 years. Queen Margrethe reunited Norway, Denmark, and Sweden in 1387, forming the Union of Calmar. This union was broken in the reign of her son Eric and eventually Sweden declared its independence.

Independence. Freed from most international responsibilities, the Danes turned their attention to their own government, except for an involvement in the Thirty Years' War (1618–1648) between Prot-

Old stories tell of Hamlet, a tragic ruler in Denmark. The story was made famous by William Shakespeare. This castle in Denmark is reputed to be that of Hamlet. *Courtesy of Amy A. Trenkle.*

estants and Catholics. In that war the Danish leader, Christian IV, first joined forces against the Austrian-led Catholics, but then, after a defeat that forced a promise not to interfere in German affairs again, joined the Catholic forces and was soundly defeated again. Denmark has maintained a measure of neutrality in international affairs since that time. This war made it possible for Sweden under Gustavus Adolphus to invade Germany and take a powerful position in the politics of the northern regions.

Monarchy. Teutonic nobles had long been a stumbling block to strong and unified government in Denmark. Despite a series of strong kings, these nobles controlled much of the land of Denmark and held it under a noble-fief arrangement—allowing peasants to work the land for certain considerations of payment and protection by the noble. The system was an oppressive one for the vast population of landless workers. In 1660 the people of Denmark rose against their noble overlords and forced them to yield much of their power to the king. Frederick III became the first king of Denmark with absolute power, including the right of hereditary succession to the throne. The rulers of Denmark enjoyed these absolute powers until 1831, when the first attempt to create a constitutional government was made. However, the noble-serf feudalism that had existed for 600 years was difficult to abandon. The next century brought even more oppressive serfdom and wars with Sweden. Danish lands were invaded three more times, in spite of the Danish movement toward neutrality.

For the most part, Denmark held to this position of neutrality in world affairs, and when it did interfere, its own weakness resulted in tragedy for the Danes. In 1801 Denmark supported Russia in its battle with England. As a result the British bombarded Copenhagen. Then in 1807, Britain, at war with Napoleon's France, demanded that the Danes give up their navy. When they refused, Copenhagen was again bombarded, the British took command of the navy, and the Danes were forced to ally themselves with Napoleon for the next six years. The wars of the early nineteenth century resulted in the loss of the island Helgoland to England and of Norway to Sweden. Again in 1850 Austria and Prussia pressed for Denmark to join them in their battles with the Germans. In 1864 a border dispute provided the incentive for Prussians to invade Denmark and claim the islands of Schlesing and Holstein. The Danes were left with a small area of peninsular land and islands that had poorer soil and few mineral resources. The capital of the Danes remained at Copenhagen on the island of Jutland, where it had been established in the time of the Union of Calmar.

The kingdom. The succession to the throne of Denmark has been orderly since King Waldermar I in the last half of the 1100s. The monarchy has a long tradition of sharing power, which began in 1282 when nobles reached an agreement with Eric V, written as the Great Charter. This charter established a parliamentary form of government, with the parliament consisting of nobles. The charter at first gave no right to the majority of Danes, but was the basis for a constitution of 1831, which established universal suffrage and the form of government that has endured to today. This constitution was remodeled in 1848, then again in 1913 (to give women the right to vote). It survived the third great invasion of Denmark, by the Germans in World War II, and was reconfirmed by the 1953 constitution, which provided for government by a one-house parliament and also allowed women to ascend to the throne legally. Margrethe I had ruled in the 1300s but had never been crowned queen. When King Frederik died in 1972, his daughter Margrethe II became the first women to be officially recognized as Queen of the Danes.

Culture Today

Economy. In the twentieth century, the Scandinavian countries and Austria, all with relatively small populations, have found great success as welfare states. Finding little pressure to maintain powerful armed forces, and relying on citizen armies, these countries have been able to spend their resources on well-developed health services, family support services, and care for less fortunate members. Denmark was one of the first countries to introduce state social welfare programs. The state protects the Danes from unemployment, sickness, old-age problems, and disability. Danes pay high taxes for these services. In return, 34 percent of the national budget is invested in the welfare programs. One outcome of the focus on welfare is that Danes are intricately involved with their government and are very active in national elections.

The land of the Danes is small and much of it is more suitable for grazing than for growing crops. Still, 80 percent of the land has been turned to productive farming and herding. Until recent discoveries, there were few mineral resources, forcing the Danes to depend on outsiders for 70 percent of their energy needs. Denmark has continuously resisted turning to nuclear energy to resolve these needs and even discourages nuclear-powered ships from using its ports. Nevertheless, the close-knit and industrious Danes have turned their land into a successful industrial nation by combining small industry and farming.

In the 1960s and 1970s Danish industry slowed, largely due to the high cost of petroleum fuels that were provided by other countries. In 1980 the Danish government began to explore oil deposits in the Balkan Sea and off the coast of Denmark's largest landholding, the island of Greenland. Now, producing wells have been drilled, furnishing a supply of energy that has made the Danes more self-sufficient. As a result, they have begun to restore the industrial base of their economy.

City life. Today, most Danes live in towns and cities like Copenhagen and Helsingor (where Hamlet is buried) and work in small businesses and industries that usually include fewer than 100 employees. The entire country is only 16,633 square miles, making industry and farming close partners. A landowner often farms a few acres and supplements the farm's income by establishing a small business on a part of the land. Many of these small "factories" make use of the craftsmanship for which the Danes are well known. Fine wooden furniture, silverware, and porcelain are products of Danish businesses. Danes such as Kaare Klint and Hans Wegner have established reputations as major figures in furniture design. In textile design, the Danes have specialized in needlework by craftspeople such as Ida Winckler, whose embroidery pictures buildings on the Danish waterfront. Danish beer became popular with Germans during the World War II and later with Americans. It is now distributed in considerable quantities around the world.

Family life. Whether located on a farm or in a city or village, the brick and mortar home of the Dane is bordered by a garden. In the past, social activities of the Danes centered in the church and home. The garden was a place to meet family members and to continue a long-standing attachment to the soil. Today, land is scarce and private gardens are small, but Danes take pride in growing their own vegetables. The focus of social activities is shifting to public gardens and

Street musicians entertain in Denmark's capital, Copenhagen.
Courtesy of Dieter Bauer Meister.

to cafes where Danes gather to talk and to practice their favorite pastimes: eating, drinking, and listening to music. Most popular foods are the *smorrebrod*, an open-faced sandwich, and rice pudding, a dish eaten at the beginning of holiday dinners. *Frikadeller*, ground beef and pork patties served with pickled beets and potatoes, is also a popular dish. The Danish *smorgasbord* has been copied in many other countries. A smorgasbord might include herring, fish pate, fish filets, smoked halibut, shrimp, salmon, ham, salads, cheeses, and fresh fruits. The Danish diet favors fish and pork.

Still today, the family remains the basic social unit. Young people respect their parents while enjoying considerable freedom. The family members eat together, attend church together, and enjoy holidays and athletic events together. Relatives stay in contact with each other even though Danes are widespread today.

Relatives abroad. In the early part of the twentieth century, economic conditions were difficult and many Danes moved to other countries to find jobs. About one-and-a-half million Danes found new homes in the United States.

This has made for an unusual holiday celebration in Denmark. Many Danes celebrate the American Fourth of July, encouraging their American relatives to return home for the celebration. However, this celebration differs from American practices, substituting large picnics for fireworks.

Danish values. A common quality that has been attributed to the Danes is extreme politeness. Hand-shaking and hat-tipping are common practices in everyday life. The majority of Danes give this politeness and cheerfulness out of a sense of pride. Danes are proud of their accomplishments with few resources, of their buildings, which they maintain carefully and protect from destruction, and of their homes. These homes are made of stucco or brick and wood. Kitchens, bedrooms, living rooms, and dining rooms appear larger than they are as a result of the placement of light furniture and few wall hangings. Danish tables and chairs are made of beautifully finished wood, formed carefully into slender, graceful, and softly rounded shapes.

Religion. The Danes have been described as a people who aim to practice a carefree lifestyle and this is reflected in their religion. Most Danes claim membership in the Lutheran State Church but generally do not consider themselves bound by its rules. The church, officially the Evangelical Lutheran Church of Denmark, is led by ten bishops located in major urban centers. There is no single authority among the bishops, although the bishop of Copenhagen has special church duties. This church is supported by the state and 90 percent of the Danes claim it as their religion, but other churches are welcome in Denmark. There are substantial memberships in the Apostolic Church of Denmark, the Danish Baptist Church, the Methodist Church, Moravian Brethern, Norwegian Lutheran Church, Reformed Church, Seventh-Day Adventists, Society of Friends, Swedish Lutheran Church, and many others. Danish churches are not well attended by the young people, who protest that the strict Lutheranism is too old-fashioned and set in its ways to be of interest to them.

Holidays. Most Danish holidays are religious celebrations. Christmas is celebrated on two days, December 25 and 26. New Year's Day falls on January 1, and Constitution Day is June 5, but dates of the other holidays are fixed each year—Easter in March or April, Ascencion Day in May, Whit Monday in June. In addition, many Danes celebrate the American Fourth of July, as described above.

Literature and arts. Since their artistic golden age in the early nineteenth century, the Danes have also been credited with exceptional creativity. The whimsey of Danish life is reflected in the writing of

Danes preserve their heritage in this open-air museum of old buildings. *Courtesy of Dieter Bauer Meister.*

the famous Danish writer Hans Christian Andersen, whose fanciful stories for children have endured to the present day. Twentieth-century writers include the poet and novelist Johannes V. Jensen and the author Isak Dinesen, whose gothic tales have won her worldwide fame. Danish painters such as Asger Jorn and sculptors—Robert Jacobsen, for example—have achieved international recognition.

Education. As illustrated by the writing of Hans Christian Andersen, children are important in Danish life. Education of the young has been encouraged throughout most of Danish history. The system is on a European-style pattern of primary school, in which nine years of primary education are provided for everyone. Students then choose between vocational preparation and college preparation. Those who complete the secondary college preparatory course in a school called a gymnasium are honored with the privilege of wearing a special cap with a white peak. The gymnasium is roughly equivalent to the last two or three years of high school and the two years of junior college in the United States. Competition for continuation into college is strong. The Danish school system includes five universities with a total enrollment of 51,000 students.

For More Information

Larsen, Hanna Astrup, editor. *Denmark's Best Stories*. New York: American Scandinavian Foundation/W. W. Horton, 1928.

Oakley, Stewart. *A Short History of Denmark*. New York: Praeger Publications, 1972.

Rying, Best. *Denmark: Introduction, Prehistory*. Copenhagen: Royal Dutch Ministry, 1981.

DUTCH
(duch)

People of the Netherlands.

Population: 15,000,000 (1991 estimate).
Location: The Netherlands (also called Holland).
Languages: Dutch, Frisian.

Geographical Setting

About twice the size of Massachusetts, the Netherlands is bounded to the east by Germany, to the south by Belgium, and to the north and west by the North Sea. Water is as important to the country's geography as the land itself. Almost one-sixth of the Netherlands' area is water: rivers, inlets, lakes, and manmade canals. Nearly half the land lies below sea level—"Netherlands" means "lowlands"—and most of that has been recovered from the sea. Such areas, called *polders*, were once part of the seabed. Now they support the Netherlands' largest cities—Amsterdam and Rotterdam, among many others—and offer some of the country's most fertile soil. To keep the polders dry, the Dutch for centuries have built dikes, long seaside embankments that hold back the sea. The dikes have broken during North Sea storms, often with great loss of life and property to flooding.

Also on the coast runs a series of sand dunes, culminating in the north with the Frisian Islands, which are actually low-lying dunes. The coastline itself is jagged, broken by a number of inlets. The largest inlet was the Zuider Zee, which Dutch engineers blocked off from the sea by a huge dam (nearly 19 miles long) in 1932. The resulting lake, called the IJsselmeer, has since been shrunk by the recovery of several polders, the largest of which is called Flevoland. Similar proj-

The Dutch

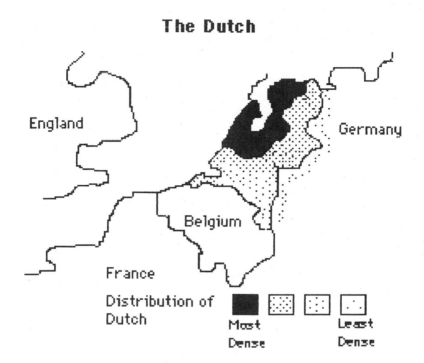

England

Germany

Belgium

France

Distribution of Dutch

Most Dense — Least Dense

ects have recently blocked off several smaller inlets in the southern area called Zeeland (zay land). East of the polders, a wide strip of higher ground borders Germany. The Rhine, one of Europe's great rivers, runs through this area into the polders, splitting into smaller rivers: the Lek, the Waal, and the IJssel. The Maas, rising in France (where it is called the Meuse), flows north through Belgium and into the Netherlands before turning west to the sea.

The Dutch climate is rainy but temperate. The flat land allows strong winds to blow almost constantly. The practical Dutch have harnessed the wind by building windmills, used to pump water from one place to another. Moisture from the sea creates puffy, windswept clouds, often featured by the famous Dutch landscape painters of the past.

Historical Background

Romans and Franks. While roving groups of Stone Age peoples hunted and fished in the Netherlands as long ago as 16,000 B.C., the area was not settled until about 4000 B.C. Those who lived in eastern Netherlands around 2000 B.C. left piles of huge boulders—known as

"Giants' Graves" today—as memorials to their dead. In historical times, the Frisians (whose Dutch descendants still occupy Friesland, northwest of the IJsselmeer) fired the opening shots in the endless battle against the sea. They built massive mounds of earth and clay called *terps*, on which their villages might remain dry during storms during which water would rage through the lowlands. Around 60 B.C., Roman armies under Julius Caesar conquered the Saxon, Celtic, and Frisian groups that had occupied the Netherlands. Roman occupation, punctuated by unsuccessful Frisian uprisings, brought roads and improved dikes to these early Dutch peoples. In the A.D. 400s, as Rome weakened, the Germanic Franks brought the Dutch (except for the stubborn Frisians) into their kingdom, which was centered in France. The Franks adopted Christianity in 496; by the late 700s, under threat from the Frankish emperor Charlemagne, the last Frisian and Saxon pagans had converted as well.

Middle Ages. After Charlemagne's death in 814, the Dutch fell under the rule of his three grandsons, among whom the empire was divided. From the 700s to the 1100s, Dutch (and other peoples of northern Europe) were subjected to violent and sudden raids by Viking sailors from Scandinavia. During this unstable time, power passed to local nobles, whose arms and castles offered protection in return for rent, labor and taxes. The system, called *feudalism*, lasted in Holland (as in the rest of Europe) until the 1400s–1500s. In the 1100s and 1200s, the Dutch began creating polders, by building dikes and dams to block off expanses of sea, then draining the resulting lakes and swamps. They built the cities of Amsterdam, Rotterdam, and the Hague on new polders during this period.

William of Orange. From the 1300s to 1500s, much of the Netherlands fell under the dukes of Burgundy, a powerful French feudal dynasty. In the early 1500s, Charles V, Duke of Burgundy, inherited the thrones of both Spain and the Holy Roman Empire. Thus, much of Europe became united under one ruler. At the same time, the Protestant Reformation divided the continent on religious lines. Like other northern peoples, many Dutch accepted Protestantism, while southern lands such as Spain supported the Catholic side. While the tolerant Charles, a Catholic, was liked by his Dutch subjects, his more rigid successor, Philip, was not. In 1568, the Dutch prince William of Orange mustered an army to drive the Spanish from the Netherlands. Though William was assassinated in 1584, his efforts eventually resulted in freedom from the Spanish, and he has been known since then as the Father of the Netherlands.

Golden Dutch century. Resistance to the Spanish united the low-landers, who previously had local (rather than national) loyalties. In 1579, the Union of Utrecht unified the seven northern lowland provinces; two years later, those provinces declared the Netherlands an independent country. The new national spirit energized the people, as did the continuing opposition of the Spanish, who did not recognize the Netherlands until 1648. Well before that, however, Dutch traders, excluded from Spanish-controlled ports around the world, established their own trade networks. Their profits soon surpassed those of the Spanish, and by the 1620s the Dutch shipping fleet was the world's largest. Dutch explorers and colonists claimed territory from South Africa to South America, from Tasmania and New Zealand to parts of Canada and the future United States, from the Caribbean to Indonesia. Riches flowed to the tiny northern country, which dominated the world economically for over 100 years.

Spurred by this phenomenal economic growth, Dutch culture also flourished during the "Golden Age" of the 1600s. Porcelain, silver work, sculpture, architecture and especially painting found new and vigorous expression in the hands of Dutch artists and craftsmen. Dutch arts of the Golden Age were supported by a prosperous middle class, rather than by religious or aristocratic patrons, as had been the case with previous European artistic movements. Rembrandt's paintings (like his most famous one, *The Night Watch*) were often group portraits commissioned by local officials, members of trading families whose public service reflected a sense of civic responsibility. Other artists such as Jan Steen or Jan Vermeer portrayed the daily life of working people, landscape painters like Jacob van Ruisdael captured the Netherlands' natural beauty.

Graceful decline. Many opportunities had come to the Dutch because of squabbling between the great powers of Spain, France and England. However, wars with these states eventually led to the decline of Dutch power in the 1700s. Gradually, the balance of colonial power shifted in favor of England. The beginning of this change can be marked by the sale in 1664 of the Dutch colony of New Amsterdam, which the English renamed New York.

Modern Netherlands. Over the next 200 years, decline as a colonial power was matched by changes at home. Territory was lost and gained as the Low Countries (the Netherlands, Belgium and Luxembourg) decided their borders. During the 1800s, Dutch monarchs (descended from William of Orange) democratized the government, establishing the constitutional monarchy that exists today. In the 1900s, industry—chemicals, textiles, and electrical manufacturing—rather than mercantilism became the focus of trade, with the Dutch importing raw materials and exporting finished products. World War II remains the darkest period in recent memory. During the five-year German occupation, cities and towns were ruined and tens of thousands of civilians were starved, bombed, or shot to death. The Germans were especially hard on the Dutch, who resisted them by hiding Jews (whom the Germans wished to kill) and by sabotaging the German war effort in the Netherlands. One Dutch Jewish girl, Anne Frank, recorded two years of hiding with her family. The Franks were aided by Dutch non-Jews who brought them food. Though the family was discovered and Anne died in a concentration camp, her courageous and moving diary has provided generations of young readers with a vivid picture of life in the nightmare world of Nazi occupation.

Culture Today

Dutch character. The Dutch are known for being a simple and tolerant people with a passion for order and neatness. These characteristics can be traced back to the Golden Age and further. Their desire for religious tolerance helped inspire their revolt from Spanish rule; their organizational ability allowed the growth of a complex trade empire, while colonial efforts fizzled because the Dutch possessed no real desire to rule over foreign lands. Even in Dutch eyes, tolerance has sometimes been carried to extremes. During wars with England and France in the 1600s and 1700s, Dutch merchants were criticized by their countrymen for carrying on trade with the enemy— to the extent of insuring their ships! Today, Amsterdam has drawn criticism for its liberal attitude towards prostitution, pornography and drug use. Yet both tolerance and order are necessary in a land that fits 15,000,000 people into just over 16,000 square miles, a population density that is Europe's highest. Furthermore, nearly half the population lives in an area called the *Randstad* ("Rim City"), which takes in the urban areas of Rotterdam, Utrecht, and Amsterdam, and amounts to only 16 percent of the land. Since the 1950s, the Randstad has been the subject of intense planning and management.

At one time windmills were used to drain water off of low-lying land.
Courtesy of the Netherlands Board of Tourism.

Shaping the land. The people's constant battle against the sea has been credited with instilling the Dutch love of neatness and order. Dikes are now strengthened with steel and concrete as well as stone and dirt, and canals in both city and country help to adjust water levels today as in the past. The Zuider Zee Dam (mentioned above), built in 1932, allowed the creation of large polders, some of which were finished only in the 1980s. The latest weapon in the Dutch armory is the tidal barrier, huge, connected dams meant to restrain tidal surges during North Sea storms. The worst disaster in modern Dutch history came in 1953, when a terrible storm broke dikes in the southern Netherlands. Sea water flooded 460,000 acres, killing 180,000 people. Shortly afterward, the government undertook the Delta Plan, a huge barrier 32 years in the making that now protects over 400 miles of inlets and tidal flats in the south. Further plans are continually discussed in the Dutch media; one would connect the Frisian Islands by a series of dikes.

Food, clothing, and shelter. Dutch food is characteristically plain, no-frills fare, with the emphasis on nourishment rather than fancy presentation. Fishing is part of the Dutch heritage, and seafood remains a favorite, particularly herring, oysters, and eels. Herring come in many guises—raw, pickled, or salted—and are traditionally picked up by the tail and dropped lengthwise into the upturned mouth. Red meats include veal and pork; poultry is also eaten. Dairy products are a traditional staple. Dutch *gouda* and *edam* have become popular cheeses worldwide. The Dutch also have a special fondness for whipped cream, which accompanies many of their sweet desserts. A wide variety of fruits and vegetables, some native to former colonies, graces many a Dutch table. Tea, coffee, and beer are popular, though the national drink is Dutch gin (*jenever*), an alcoholic drink flavored with juniper berries.

Traditional costumes vary regionally, showing the local loyalties, once paramount, that still flavor Dutch life. Most include baggy black pants and colorful, wide-brimmed hats for the men, with voluminous black dresses, colorfully embroidered bodices and lace bonnets for the women. Though still worn by some older people, such costumes have mostly been replaced by modern clothes. Two well-known exceptions are the towns of Volendam and Marken, just north of Amsterdam, where the costumes have become a tourist attraction. Throughout the Netherlands, those who work outdoors still wear *klompen*, the aptly named famous Dutch wooden shoes.

A typical outdoor cafe in the Netherlands. *Courtesy of the Netherlands Board of Tourism.*

The Dutch are a home-loving people, preferring small, comfortable dwellings to large, impersonal ones. Experiments with modern block apartments have proved unpopular, despite the high population density. When possible, homes almost always boast neat, colorful flower gardens in front, often complemented by hanging plants near the door and windows. Tulips, originally brought from colonies near the equator, have become the favorite flower (as well as providing a major industry, the international sale of tulip bulbs). Houses give cities like Amsterdam a distinctive look: tall, narrow, gabled structures, set up against each other, built by rich merchants of the past. Often today they have been divided into apartments. Throughout the Netherlands, living in a converted barge on a canal offers an exotic alternative. Whether in such a houseboat, or on dry land, the Dutch strive to make their home *gezellig*, an important Dutch word roughly translated as "cosy" or "homey." Knick-knacks abound: colorful Dutch tiles, for example, or the painted blue-and-white porcelain called Delftware (made in the Dutch city of Delft). The Dutch homemaker's passion for cleanliness is legendary, with spotlessness being an ever-present yet ever-receding goal.

Family life. Dutch parents tend to be affectionate, relaxed and naturally tolerant with their children. Along with gezellig, which might include a quiet evening of family conversation, the quality of *deftig*—a modestly dignified respectability—is important in home life. Most Dutch homes have a large front window, in which the curtains are customarily kept open, leaving the living room in full view of passersby. It has been suggested that this accessibility is to assure the neighbors that all is deftig within. Yet, while partly open to view, the Dutch home is a very private place. Only close friends and family will be invited in. If the Dutch are to meet someone they don't know well, the appointment will inevitably be made for a public spot.

Language. Dutch is closely related to German and sounds (to an English-speaker's ears) even more guttural and hard. The language evolved out of the spoken dialects of the early Germanic tribes. Today some 25 dialects still exist, though most people can also slip into "standard Dutch." About 400,000 Frisians speak the Frisian language, which is also closely related to German. In Friesland, road signs are bilingual in Dutch and Frisian. The independent Frisians keep their own traditions intact, referring to the rest of the Dutch as "Hollanders."

Holland, used by the English as interchangeable with *Netherlands,* actually denotes the two Dutch provinces of North and South Holland. The Dutch call the language they speak "Nederlands." The English term *Dutch* stems from the same word that gave rise to *Deutsch* (German for "German"). From this confusing situation arose the misnomer "Pennsylvania Dutch," who were actually German settlers. Dutch settlers themselves brought many words into American English: place names, such as *Catskill, Gramercy* (originally *De Kromme Zee*), *Harlem* (named for the Dutch town of Haarlem), and *Brooklyn* and food names, like *coleslaw, waffles* and *cookies.* English is now spoken by many Dutch and is especially popular with the urban young.

Religion. Although religion was a powerful influence in the past, nearly half of the Dutch today classify themselves as non-religious. Roman Catholics, about 36 percent of the population, predominate in the south; Dutch Reformed Protestants, at about 20 percent, live mostly in the north. One more example of the people's liking for order is the way that religion has held over in the organization of social institutions. From schools and hospitals to newspapers, television stations and even stores, society is organized into religious and secular *zuilen*, or "pillars." Yet far from being divisive, the zuilen act to help society work together. In the 1960s, the Catholic and Protestant political parties merged to form the dominant Christian Democratic Appeal party.

Literature and the arts. The best-known contributions of Dutch writers have been in the field of philosophy. Desiderius Erasmus (1467–1636), called the Sage of Rotterdam, was one of Europe's foremost humanist scholars. His ideas stressed the individual's understanding of the Bible and contributed to the Reformation. Baruch Spinoza (1632–1677), son of Portuguese Jewish refugees, was rejected by the Jewish community for questioning Jewish beliefs. Spinoza also related the individual to God and laid important groundwork for future philosophers.

No entry of this length can do justice to Dutch painting. Before the Golden Age, Hieronymus Bosch (c. 1450–1516) painted surreal pictures that resonate with modern viewers, and Peter Brueghel the Elder (1529–69) created powerful and realistic representations of Dutch life. Frans Hals (1580–1666), a prolific artist sometimes called the first modern painter, captured fleeting emotions in a way that prefigured Impressionist art of the 1800s. Rembrandt van Rijn (1606–69), recognized as the greatest Dutch painter, deftly used light and shadow to help emphasize the emotional tone of his portraits, still-lifes, Biblical scenes and landscapes. Perhaps the greatest of many well-known landscape painters was Jacob van Ruisdael, whose rich, dark greens and browns impart a sense of tension to his cloud-ridden, often stormy scenes. Among Impressionist painters, Vincent Van Gogh (1853–90) sold only one painting in his short and tragic life, but today is one of the most popular artists of all time. His unique, swirling brushstrokes and startlingly vivid colors evoke moods from despair and unease to unbridled joy. Among the many modern Dutch artists, Piet Mondrian and Willem de Kooning are two of the best-known.

While painting reigns supreme, as shown by their many excellent museums and galleries, the Dutch also enjoy music, dance, theatre, cinema, and sculpture. A rich tradition of crafts also exists, most notably pottery, tile work, glassware, and silver.

For More Information

Beresky, Andrew, editor. *Fodor's '92 Holland.* New York: Fodor's Travel Publications, 1992.

Catling, Christopher, editor. *Insight Guides: The Netherlands.* Singapore: APA Publications, 1991.

Colijn, Helen. *Of Dutch Ways.* Minneapolis: Dillon Press, Inc., 1980.

Ozer, Steve. *The Netherlands.* New York: Chelsea House Publishers, 1990.

Schama, Simon. *The Embarrassment of Riches: An Interpretation of Dutch Culture in the Golden Age.* New York: Alfred A. Knopf, 1987.

ENGLISH

(ing′ lish)

The people of England, a mix of populations including Anglo-Saxon and immigrant ethnic groups.

Population: 48,780,000 (1992 estimate).
Location: England, the southern portion of a large island off the coast of mainland Europe.
Language: English, a Germanic language.

Geographical Setting

England lies off the coast of mainland Europe on an island shared with Scotland to the north and Wales to the southwest. The island is Great Britain, officially part of the United Kingdom of Great Britain and Northern Ireland. Separating the island from mainland Europe are the English Channel and the North Sea. At its closest point, England is about 20 miles from France.

The English land mass is roughly triangular. Its eastern border measures about 350 miles in a straight line; the western border would measure about 425 miles, and the southern border, 325 miles. The total boundary would fit a blunt triangle with sides of about 1,100 miles. However, the terrain is cut by numerous streams and rivers, waterways that create jagged indentations in the coastline, making it over 2,700 miles long. The many estuaries and coves in the coast have figured prominently in history, providing ports for trade and entry routes for raiders. Also attracting raiders were England's resources: its game-rich forests, fertile soil, and pastureland. The resources would prove even greater than expected, compounded by its less visible minerals, such as coal and natural gas.

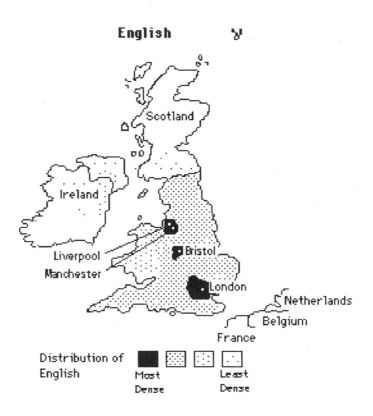

English

Scotland

Ireland

Liverpool
Manchester

Bristol

London

Netherlands

Belgium

France

Distribution of
English

Most
Dense

Least
Dense

Historical Background

Celts and Romans. Speaking a language that predates modern Welsh, the first known inhabitants of the English countryside were Celts around 500 B.C. They lived in hilltop communities, practicing agriculture and occupying round wooden houses. The women spun and wove woolen cloth while the men ploughed and herded, yet women were apparently treated as equals. When the Romans conquered the country in A.D. 43, two of the largest Celtic tribes (there were 15 principal tribes, denser in the south than the north) were ruled by queens who fought from their chariots. One of them, Queen Boudicca, a huge leader with a harsh voice and flowing red hair, staged an uprising against the Romans in A.D. 60, after the Celts had been defeated. She lost.

The Romans ruled the countryside for some 400 years, their greatest influences lying in their building of towns and roads, new phenomena in the region. They built about 50 towns in southern England, four of them for retired soldiers: Colchester, Lincoln, Gloucester, and York. These towns were the size of villages, but had shops, city halls, and forums.

Anglo-Saxons and Danes. Christianity penetrated the country in the 300s, taking hold slowly. In this same century, Roman rule began to disintegrate as outsiders like the Saxons, a Germanic people, plundered the countryside. They were later joined by the Angles, the Jutes, and the Frisians, who invaded and colonized the country in small groups, then flooded it in search of fertile land. The Britons, or defenders of the country Julius Caesar had dubbed Britannia, offered staunch resistance to the collection of invaders known as the Anglo-Saxons for much of the fifth century. Ultimately, they were defeated. Those Britons who survived and stayed probably became slaves of the conquerors. The Romans' towns were razed, and their villas disappeared.

Preferring the valleys to the hillsides, the Anglo-Saxons constructed villages. An excavation of one such village has uncovered over 100 small wooden huts. Led by kings, their society consisted of nobles, or thanes, who served the kings in war. The masses were farmer tenants who rented land from the nobles, paying them in kind (lambs, crops) or service, working their lands two days a week. Called a *hide*, a farmer's holding consisted of from 40 to 120 acres spread out in one-acre strips. The strips did not lie next to one another but were scattered over two or three common fields. After harvest time, these fields would become grazing ground for all the villagers' livestock.

From the sixth through the seventh centuries, the Anglo Saxons were converted to Roman Catholicism, but they remained illiterate until the reign of Alfred the Great (871–899). Alfred, constantly in poor health and never long at peace, taught himself to read and write in Latin and English. He had just begun fashioning a more spiritual, educated society, when England was beset once again by invaders—this time, the Vikings. Coming from Denmark, Norway, and Sweden, they defeated the Anglo-Saxons, then turned to settlement. Ultimately the country was split in half, the Vikings setting up the *Danelaw*, or Viking territory, in a treaty (886) between Alfred the Great and the Danish king, Guthrum. The Danelaw occupied the north and east while Saxon England continued to exist in the south and west. Alfred set about building a navy superior to the Vikings' and conquered the Vikings, but they remained in the Danelaw for nearly 200 years, influencing Anglo-Saxon language and other customs. Preoccupied with law, the Vikings introduced the jury system.

Alfred's conquest of the Vikings was followed by a long period of peace. The tenth century saw England consolidating into a single kingdom, its territory organized into shires, headed by local officials and the shire reeve, or sheriff. Crops failed at times or livestock were afflicted by disease, so small farmers became more and more indebted to large landowners. Society continued to consist of a king and nobles, but grades of farmers developed. Freemen held land on condition of payment in military service or money rent to an Anglo-Saxon noble. Serfs held land on condition of performing labor for him. At the bottom were the landless.

Normans. Duke William of Normandy in France claimed the English throne and in 1066 assembled an army to enforce his claim. Crossing the channel to England, he combined heavy-armored cavalry and crossbowmen in his army to disrupt the enemy from a distance before pushing home his final charge. His victory at Hastings ensured Norman rule over England.

Under the Normans, the concept of landholding changed. They assumed the king was sole owner of all land, which he would grant to tenants-in-chief (called barons) in exchange for military and other services furnished to him by them. The Church held land, too. Overall, about one fifth of the territory went to the king, one fourth to the Church, and one half to the tenants-in-chief. These barons occupied manors, or landed estates, which spanned one or more villages. Over time about 900 manors spread through England, each populated by 60 to 100 occupants. A baron, the lord of a manor, would lease most of his land to small tenants, who paid him for its use in money, kind, or services.

French became the spoken language of the ruling classes in this period, many words penetrating into the common Anglo-Saxon tongue. Also introduced by the Normans were castles and tournaments. By 1100, thousands of castles had appeared in the country, intended as barons' strongholds. The barons were obligated to maintain forts for the king and they meanwhile developed their own regional spheres of power. Tension developed between the barons and King John, climaxing in 1215 with the signing of the Magna Carta.

This document had little effect on the bulk of the population. Rather it limited the power of the king, freeing the few nobles and merchants from the arbitrary taxes of the monarch. "No freeman," said the charter, referring only to the minority that owned land, shall be "imprisoned, deprived of his lands, outlawed or exiled . . . save by the lawful judgment of his peers" (Cowie 1973, p. 179). More important, the document set up a committee of 24 barons to make sure John kept his word to the nobles. The first meeting of such a committee occurred a few decades later, in 1265, attended by knights (soldiers) and burgesses (town merchants) as well as barons. It became a firmly established body when King Edward III sought money to fight the Hundred Years' War (1337–1453) against France. This committee was the origin of the English Parliament.

Middle Ages. Norman society introduced heraldry (coats of arms) and tournaments. Imported from France, the tournament was a rough training ground for young knights, in which a mock battle was fought in an open field, knights on each side lashing out at one another to unhorse the "enemy." Later the combat narrowed to a contest between two horsemen riding at full tilt against each other in boarded enclosures. There developed a tournament called the Round Table, in which all manner of sports were practiced, from wrestling to high jumping to jousts, the knights eating at a round table to set aside rank, their shields placed behind them. King Edward III sponsored such a Round Table tournament in 1344.

Such jousts were attended by the nobles, but the Hundred Years' War meanwhile elevated the status of common folk. With the advent of the longbow as a weapon in this conflict, the prestige of the armored knight fell. Longbows placed the trained peasant archer on equal footing with the noble in war, beginning to rob him of his distinction as a fighter.

Back home, the English population grew and some prospered. Towns were rebuilt on the old Roman sites, the church becoming the hub of social life, its bells ringing even to signify the right time to plant peas and beans. Each week there were markets, stalls where fishermen sold their herring; butchers, their meat; and country-women, their eggs. Sheep-raising grew, especially in the north and among the clergy. Flocks of 20,000 to 30,000 were not uncommon, giving rise to a profitable trade in wool and then cloth.

At least 109 new towns appeared in the 1100s and 1200s, but in the 1300s wages dropped as the number of workers rose. The standard of living declined sharply until the Black Death struck in 1348. Spread by rats and transmitted by fleas, "It passed most rapidly from place to place . . . swiftly killing ere mid-day many who in the morning had been well, and . . . not permitting those destined to die to live more than three, or at most four, days. On the same day twenty, forty, sixty, and very often more corpses were committed to the same grave" (Hibbert 1987, p. 32). In the end, the Black Death appears to have decimated more than a third of the population. The 4,250,000 population of 1300 plummeted to under 2,500,000 by 1380.

Fortunes brightened for the survivors. With such a drastic drop in population, wages rose and the price of land fell. The end of the fourteenth century proved rosy for the masses who had managed to stay alive. A new class appeared, the yeoman farmer, who owned 60 to 100 acres of his own. Meanwhile, war with France continued and the king imposed new taxes, backed by nobles who were threatened by the prosperity of the serfs. The masses rebelled in the Peasants' Revolt of 1381. Demanding an end to poll taxes and serfdom, the peasants dragged the nobles who devised the tax from chapel, executed them, and carried their heads on pikes around London. They broke into monasteries and churches in protest against the tithes, or the tenth of a peasant's earning collected by the priests. Led by Wat Tyler, the rebels finally agreed to a meeting with King Richard III, then 14 years old. He conceded to some demands—confiscating Church estates, for example. Unexpectedly, a supporter of the king knocked Tyler off his horse and another rushed to kill him during the meeting. The rebels brandished their weapons, but Richard quieted them with, "Sirs, will you kill your king? I am your captain. Follow me" (Hibbert 1987, p. 37). Later, over 100 more rebels were killed, but conditions did change. The right to fix wages passed from the nobles to justices of the peace.

In the next century, the nobles lost more power, fighting a civil war (War of the Roses, 1455–1485) among themselves that hastened their destruction as a ruling class.

Church and town. In general, the people had faith in their religion but not in its representatives. The church may have sat in the center of town, but it was rarely packed with citizens. The monasteries of the early Middle Ages were seats of learning, art, and health, but already in Geoffrey Chaucer's *Canterbury Tales*, published at the end of the fourteenth century, monks and friars were attacked as knaves. Typical of a type of religious leader in his day, a priest in these tales "ran to London to earn easy bread/By singing masses for the wealthy dead" (Hibbert 1987, p. 42).

Meanwhile, industry grew in towns, giving rise to a new institution—the guild. Guilds were societies of merchants or craftworkers who fixed prices, wages, and standards of quality. There were merchant guilds, saddlers guilds, weavers guilds, and more. The cloth industry dominated, employing some 20,000 men and women by 1475. It was a fragmented business (and remained so for centuries) with workers dyeing, spinning, or weaving piecemeal in their homes.

Some merchants grew rich, monopolizing power in the towns and living in mansions. First timber, then stone, was used to build the average town homes. They stood in rows and were multistoried, each story projecting over the one below. House dwellers dumped kitchen refuse and the like into their small yards or into the narrow streets in front of the gable ends of their houses. Periodically, rakers would cart the garbage off, but the cleanliness never lasted long.

Both Church and town underwent drastic change in the 1500s. King Henry VIII's conflicts with the church grew as he sought annulments and divorces for his marriages, which had failed to provide an heir. In 1536, King Henry dissolved the monasteries, selling their lands to nobles rather than the peasantry. The next monarch officially reorganized the Church. Queen Elizabeth I assumed the title of Supreme Governor of the Church of England, placing it under royal English control and removing it from the authority of Rome.

Elizabeth's reign (1558–1603) also saw an upheaval in agriculture due to enclosures. Landowners enclosed common fields—that is, they fenced in a piece of land that had until then lain open for common use. At first, the purpose was to increase their pasturage, and later, their farmland. In either case, the average peasant lost acreage. There were violent riots to protest enclosures, the most serious erupting in 1549, when Robert Ket led a large-scale revolt against the landlords of Norfolk. The government sent in an army of 12,000 that defeated the rebels. Ket was hanged, and the nobles clamored for more hangings until the Earl of Warwick chided them with "Will ye be ploughmen and harrow your own land?" (Morton 1965, p. 174). Ultimately the enclosures drove the peasants into towns, where at first all manner of work could be found, from domestic service to chimney sweep.

Civil war. The power of town merchants continued to grow, especially after 1588 when their ships were used to drive the Spanish Armada from English waters. During this period, the merchants formed

An old painting illustrates the art of canvassing electors in England in the 1800s. *From the Library of Congress.*

charted companies, which were given exclusive privileges to trade in parts of the world: the Virginia Company in North America, the Royal African Company in South Africa, the East India company in East India. A British Empire blossomed and was later secured in the war against Napoleon. It provided ready markets for English goods, stimulating industry back home.

An upper-class power struggle broke out. Backed by merchants and yeoman, Parliament wanted to control the army and approve the king's appointment of ministers. He refused, supported by the nobles. Meanwhile, the populace was preoccupied with its own problems. Famine set in and there were cases of starvation. Most of the English had little interest in issues of the civil war, but it ravaged the land: crops were destroyed, livestock seized, and houses destroyed. In the end, 100,000 men were killed and the king lost. Parliament's troops, led by Oliver Cromwell, closed in on the enemy at top speed. They were taught to halt on command and to wheel and fight in unison or separately. The army would remain loyal to Cromwell while the Commonwealth lasted (1649–1660). He lost the support of others though, feeling forced to resort to military rule. Famine set in again, and the monarchy was restored, with a major change in power. Before 1649 King Charles I was thought to rule by Divine Right; after 1660 King Charles II ruled by consent of Parliament.

While the upper classes struggled for power, the populace became preoccupied with witch hunts. Proclaiming himself a witch-finder, Matthew Hopkins toured the country and charged a fee to identify witches. The last execution took place in 1706. Charged with causing their neighbors to spit pins, a woman and her 11-year-old daughter were hanged. The law against witchcraft was finally repealed in 1736, but accusations continued for decades.

Industrial revolution. Conditions would improve for a time, then deteriorate. Food riots broke out when the price of corn went up or wages dropped. Peasants burned down mills and attacked corn dealers. In 1756–57 alone, there were 100 disturbances. With changes in industry came more rioting, as machines replaced workers and as factories replaced jobs that had been performed with the aid of an apprentice at home.

The Industrial Revolution began in England 50 years ahead of other countries. Great strides were taken in the clothing business due to many inventions. John Kay doubled the weaver's output with the flying shuttle, and James Hargreave doubled the spinner's output by inventing the spinning jenny. James Watt invented the steam engine in 1775, a discovery that hastened many an industry, especially coal mining. A fever of canal building from 1790–1794 produced a network of waterways that transported goods.

Meanwhile, workers flocked to towns as four million more acres were enclosed from the mid-1700s to the mid-1800s. They found jobs mostly as domestic servants—more people worked in this capacity in the eighteenth century than any other except agriculture. Industry attracted many workers too. "People left other occupations and came to spinning for the sake of high wages. I recollect shoemakers leaving their employ and learning to spin; I recollect tailors; I recollect colliers; but a great many more husbandmen left their employ to learn to spin . . ." (Morton 1965, p. 339). Wages dropped, and workers complained.

In protest against unemployment caused by the new machines, craftspeople called Luddites smashed equipment. They took their name, it seems, from Ned Ludd, a boy who entered a cottage one day and vented his anger on two knitting frames. Thereafter Ned was blamed whenever frames were smashed, and machine breakers carried straw effigies of him in their raids. The movement faltered in 1812, and some Luddites were hanged, but their spirit lingered on in tales and song.

Slums. War against Napoleon Bonaparte ended in victory in 1815; afterwards poverty increased at home. In desperation, armed poachers snared game on the estates of nobles in the countryside. A type of guerrilla warfare broke out, with rival gangs of nobles and poachers trying to outwit each other.

Conditions in towns were dismal too, though some factory owners were forward-thinking. The potter Josiah Wedgwood constructed a village for his workers near his mansion. Other workers were housed in cellars or had to fend for themselves. In London there were both splendid neighborhoods and slums. The word *slums*, first used in the 1820s, was coined from *slump,* meaning "marshy place" and referring to the early industries and dwelling structures built on low ground near canals. In between the wealthy residences and the slums were respectable neighborhoods of two-story houses occupied by some factory workers with dependable incomes. Those employed as servants generally fared well too (a typical middle-class family commonly employed six servants in the 1800s).

The poor who took irregular jobs in the mines and sweatshops suffered most, working 12 or more hours at a stretch. Coal miners worked 24-hour shifts underground, men's bodies growing overdeveloped in some areas, stunted in others. Notorious for its filthy, stifling, poorly lit rooms was the clothing sweatshop. Housing for the poor was abysmal, too. A family cooked, washed, and slept in the same small, insect-ridden room, with only a dark cellar for coal and food. In the words of Charles Dickens, the town structures were generally "red brick, or brick that would have been red if the smoke and ashes had allowed it" (Ashley 1982, p. 135).

Suffering worsened under the Poor Law of 1834, which forced every able bodied person in need of relief to enter a workhouse. Conditions, reasoned the legislators, would be so miserable inside the workhouse that the poor would be inspired to find outside work. Families were split up, and inmates given lowly tasks, such as stone breaking.

Victorian Age. Along with slums, the profession of the peddler grew during the age of Queen Victoria (1837–1901). London street names revealed where the wares were peddled: Wood Street, Milk Street, Bread Street, and Ironmonger Lane. Street cries resounded through the different markets: "Will you buy my sweet bloomin' lavender, three bunches a penny?" or "White sand and gray sand! Who'll buy my gray sand?" (used to dry ink). A social ranking developed among the peddlers. At the top were the patterers, who sold cheap literature, then the costermongers with their carts of produce, next the street entertainers, and lastly the chimney sweeps. Men sold the heavier, more profitable items, such as books and stationery, while women hawked flowers, fruit, and the like.

Also in Victorian times social reforms began to attack abuses of the age. The Act of 1833 prohibited textile factories from employing children aged 9 to 13 for over 48 hours a week, and provision was made to enforce the act. Corn Laws, passed to keep prices up, were repealed in 1846. The Act of 1891 limited the workday of women dressmakers to 12 hours. Other needs were addressed too. In 1891 elementary education became mandatory and free. The fervor for social welfare would continue into the twentieth century.

World Wars. Guided by leaders such as Emmeline Pankhurst (1858–1928), women agitated for the vote, breaking windows, serving jail sentences, fasting, and suffering forced feedings. World War I interrupted the fight, as women took jobs in the army, navy, munition works, and public transport. Proving their worth, they earned voting rights in two stages: in 1918 (women over age 30) and in 1928 (women over age 21, like men). That same decade saw the birth of new industries: motor vehicles and talking pictures. Yet unemployment rose (22 percent in 1932) and lasted until World War II. Some 750,000 English soldiers had been killed in World War I. Less than half as many were killed in World War II, but its air attacks claimed the lives of 60,000 civilians, injuring 240,000 more and destroying English factories and houses.

More social welfare followed the war. Aiding parents with children, the government instituted family allowances. The Education Act of 1944 made secondary schooling mandatory and free. State medical service was established in 1946, with the nation taking over hospitals and providing free medical care.

Britain's empire dissolved in the 1950s and 1960s, its colonies declaring independence. Their heads of state formed a commonwealth that would meet periodically. In 1973, the English entered into another new alliance when the United Kingdom joined the European Economic Community. Meanwhile, emigration from former colonies to London and other cities had soared, changing the complexion of English society.

Culture Today

Ethnic England. Major ethnic populations in London reflect a new mix of English. In the 1980s the city claimed about 450,000 Asians, 350,000 Afro-Caribbeans, 240,000 Jews, 236,000 Irish, 58,000 Cypriots, 26,000 Poles, and 31,000 Italians. There is a sizeable Chinese community (50,000), but most Asians come from India, Pakistan or Bangladesh. India's emigrants have a long history in England; coming from northwest India, gypsies had settled in the country by 1579; about 500 of these gypsies now live outside London.

Many Bengalis live in the East End, where the major source of employment is the textile workshops reminiscent of the past. Despite social reform, "the sweating of sewing-women," asserts one author, "has persisted in one form or another until the present day" (Ashley 1982, p. 143). Children, too, spend long hours laboring in the workshops. The community saw severe racial violence between whites and Bengalis in the 1980s—windows were smashed and cars damaged.

Violence also struck in the Afro-Caribbean community, with citizens rioting against the police. Slavery of blacks stopped earlier in England than other areas, when the courts ruled (1772) in favor of James Somersett, an escaped slave. Over 15,000 blacks lived in London at the time, dressed in showy liveries (once including a silver dog-collar around the neck) and given haughty names. By the 1790s most had freed themselves of slavery simply by leaving their owners.

Racial conflict with the Jews dates back to the Middle Ages, when they had to wear two stone tablets on their clothes and suffered massacres in London, Norwich, and York. But mostly the Jews lived in peace. King Edward I expelled the group in 1290, when, legend has it, some wealthy Jews hired a ship for France but were robbed and left to drown at the mouth of the Thames, making the water turbulent there. The culprits were later hanged, but Jews were not welcomed back to England until 1656 and did not win complete equality until the Jewish Relief Act of 1858. In London, the East End became home to poor members of the group, and some of its businesses still appear in the Old Jewish Quarter there.

Religion. A mix of churches, temples, and mosques reflects the ethnic makeup of England today. Muslims are estimated at over 1.5 million. Among the Christian denominations, the Church of England claims most members (roughly 27 million), and the reigning monarch continues to serve as its supreme governor. There are two Church provinces in England, Canterbury and York, and each has its own houses of Parliament to initiate legislation concerning the Church. Moreover, the archbishops and bishops of these provinces have seats in the nation's House of Lords.

Government and nobility. The sovereign is the titular head of state in England, but executive power is placed in the cabinet headed by the prime minister. Parliament, the House of Commons and the House of Lords, makes or revokes all laws. Elected for five years by direct vote, members of the House of Commons initiate most laws and have the real power. The House of Lords consists of "Hereditary Peers" and "Life Peers." While it can suggest amendments of laws, the House of Lords cannot prevent laws from passing once approved by the House of Commons.

Monarchs directly affect membership in the House of Lords by awarding peerages to distinguished commoners. (A peer is someone with a right to a seat in the House of Lords.) Peerages are granted to noteworthy individuals for their service to the nation. In contrast to those peers who inherit their titles, these noteworthy individuals (called Life Peers) hold their titles only during their own lifetime. Altogether the United Kingdom recognizes five degrees of peers—in descending order, they are dukes, marquesses, earls, viscounts, and barons. All the Life Peers are barons.

Other honors bestowed on commoners today are the baronetcy and knighthood, which is still conferred by the touch of a sword. These honors do not entitle recipients to seats in the House of Lords. In recent times, knighthood has been awarded to scientist and Nobel Prize winner Dorothy Hodgkin and sculptor Henry Moore for the advancement of art, literature, and science. Most honorable of all military awards in the United Kingdom is the Victoria Cross, instituted in 1856 to recognize bravery in the presence of an enemy.

Law. The United Kingdom has no written constitution. Rather the country relies on precedents and procedures of government. There are several sources of law: Acts of Parliament, called Statute Law; Common Law, or unwritten, age-old practice; and Equity, which softens some of the harsh common-law rules. In criminal and civil cases tried in England, the House of Lords is the highest court of appeal.

Courts and jury trials were not always mandatory in England. Once, the accused was subject to trial by ordeal. A freeman had to plunge his hand into boiling water. If the scars healed in three days, he was proclaimed innocent. Serfs were bound and thrown into cold water. If they sank, they had proved their innocence. Trial by ordeal was outlawed in 1215 but other unsavory methods were used in the name of justice. For minor offenses, an accused would serve time in stocks or a pillory until the date of the trial. Stocks were wooden frames with holes for the ankles, a pillory had holes for the neck and wrists. To publicly disgrace the accused, the frames sat on the village green. Those in the pillory sometimes died from the confinement.

The last stocks were removed from London in 1826, ending that tradition. Other traditions, such as public dissent, have continued to the present. The late twentieth century has seen wage strikes and a rise in unemployment. Continuing a twentieth century tradition, the government passed new welfare legislation in 1990: The Housing Benefit Scheme, to aid the needy in paying rent. Among the continuing welfare policies is the National Health Service, now providing free medical care to all, except for prescriptions and dental treatment, which is free only to the poor.

Some major industries have been nationalized in England, the first one being the coal industry in 1946. Currently there is more support in the country for increased private enterprise and less government involvement in daily affairs. Many industries are now being denationalized.

Economy. In the past, farmers pulled down fences to protest enclosures of common fields and the Luddites smashed machines to protest their use in industry. In the twentieth century, workers in print and newspaper businesses have displayed similar resistance to the advanced methods of photographic and computerized typesetting. Far fewer English earn their livelihoods in agriculture or industry (mines, manufacturing, construction) than in the past. Whereas in the mid-eighteenth century, 75 percent of the population farmed or raised livestock, in 1990 only about two percent worked in agriculture (raising wheat, barley, potatoes, sheep, and cattle). About 30 percent labored in industry in 1990, mostly in manufacturing.

Since World War I, women's role in the workforce has continued to rise. The Equal Opportunities Act of 1975 requires that a vacant post be open to members of either sex.

Food, clothing, and shelter. Diet has depended through the years on the era and family income. In Celtic times, mead, an alcoholic beverage of fermented honey and water, was popular. The Anglo-

Saxons used barley to produce ale; beer, made from malt and flavored with hops, grew popular in the 1500s, brewed in the home. Taverns were frequented in the early 1700s. In the 1800s, they became known as pubs, or public houses, and by 1830 there were 400 in London alone. Tea shops, the first public places in which women could have a meal on their own, appeared in the late nineteenth century.

Meals in early times consisted of vegetables and oatmeal for the poor and little better for those with more means. Chaucer describes a widow's meals in the "Nun's Priest Tale (Hibbert 1987, p.21):

> Her board was mostly served with white and black,
> Milk and brown bread, in which she found no lack;
> Broiled bacon or an egg or two were common,
> She was in fact, a sort of dairy woman.

By the mid-1700s, the poor still relied on bread and cheese, but the rest of the people were becoming meat and potato eaters. Ever since, meat, especially beef and mutton, has dominated the English diet, but in reduced amounts since World War II. Shops emerged in the 1800s that indicated tastes of the time: hot pie shops, selling warm

A typical English country cottage. *Courtesy of Monica Gyulai.*

beefsteak pies, puddings, kidney meat pies, and fruit pies; and fish and chips shops, serving food that was standard fare in working-class families before 1914. Particular foods are credited to the English: ice cream, probably invented when the King Charles I's cook added cream to sherbert and stirred it an ice-encased tub; and the sandwich, perhaps, by John Montagu, Earl of Sandwich, who had sliced beef placed between toast so he could continue playing cards. In fact, toast is touted as an English invention. England typically had high-quality meat and vegetables, so the cooking here remained plainer than in most of continental Europe. Indeed the English developed a reputation for poor cooking, which they are only now shaking off.

Clothing, like food, depended on the era and income, and also came to be used by women in their struggle for equality. In Anglo-Saxon and Norman times, men wore tunics and breeches, and women wore long dresses. Both costumes were covered by cloaks tied with a cord at the neck. Common women still wrapped themselves in hooded red cloaks at the turn of the 1800s. Farm laborers had adopted smock-frocks by then, while some of their wives continued to wear bedgowns in the fields, along with linen caps under straw hats. For swimming, women of the time wore a long flannel cloak, tied at the neck but loose at the bottom so it would spread out on the water to conceal her body. Late-1800 feminists adopted the bloomer, a short skirt with trousers gathered at the ankle, suggested by Amelia Jenks Bloomer. Women bobbed their hair and raised their hemlines from the ground after World War I; after 50 more years they, like women elsewhere, wore male-style trousers.

While the Normans built castles, surrounded by walls, moats, and drawbridges, villagers lived in cottages with thatched roofs. The 1530s saw a number of the castles, ruined by then, converted into Great Houses. These were houses with dining chambers that doubled as game rooms, ballrooms, and theaters. Other rooms in the Great House were parlors (private sitting rooms), bedchambers, and withdrawing chambers, where servants slept within call. (This last chamber changed to a drawing room, used to receive visitors.) There were also galleries (for walking, fencing, or dancing), and much money was spent on gardens. In the 1700s, the irregular garden came into vogue, including rolling expanses of grass, walkways, streams, and genuine ruins (such as Gothic temples and dead trees). Many of these Great Houses were converted into museums during the depression of 1929. By then, English towns included mansion-style flats and small row houses with brick walled gardens in front and back. Flats, or apartments, became popular after World War II due to the shortage of building space; many of the large older houses have been divided into flats. Also, houses built since this war are in Georgian (1714–1830) architecture. An Englishwoman, Octavia Hill, founded a trust to recondition slums in the 1860s. Her example is still being followed by government spending to rebuild worn-out inner-city housing.

Education. Not only women but children also were put to work for centuries. As early as age 7, poor children would often be placed in training as servants for the wealthier households. Being beaten at home was common and those who escaped it could expect whippings at school. Not only beating but other bodily punishments were rife (Hibbert 1987, p. 455): "I have been woken many times by the hot points of cigars burning holes in my face."

Early curriculum was simple: the alphabet, prayers, and mostly Latin grammar (hence, the name "grammar school"). Students were usually forbidden to speak English, even penalized for it. They learned from the hornbook, a sheet with letters of the alphabet mounted on a wooden frame shaped like a table-tennis bat and covered by some transparent horn. Boys might progress to "public" schools, where they learned arithmetic, merchants' accounts, and more, preparing for the university. (The first British public schools were actually highly respected private schools; such public schools

Magdalene College is one of the colleges that make up Oxford. *From the Library of Congress.*

now attract only about ten percent of the student population.) By 1200, Oxford was already a celebrated place of learning for the clergy. Cambridge gained its reputation in the 1400s. Scholars who could not afford the expenses paid their way by acting as battlers—servants of richer scholars—or by reciting poems for the wealthy. Other schools (charity schools, dame schools, ragged schools, boarding schools) appeared before the advent of a free state education system. Now most students enroll in free "comprehensive schools," so called because they provide general education and offer vocational training or college preparation. Needy students who attend a privately run "independent school" may receive monetary aid from the government to pay the school's fees.

Language. The English used today descends from Old English, the language of the Anglo-Saxons, and Middle English, which took precedence in Chaucer's time, during the 1300s. In the twentieth century, different dialects of English are used by different strata of society. Non-regional standard English is most popular among the upper middle classes. The lower middle and working classes often still use a regional dialect. There are different dialect areas in the country, as shown in a map of different terms used by children of the late twentieth century to mean "truce."

Cockney is the dialect used in London. Some of its features are neglecting to pronounce the initial "h" (*'ard* instead of *hard*) and using a short "i" instead of a short "e" sound (*git* or *kitch*). It has been suggested that the varieties of pronunciation in different dialects may explain some of the irregular speech patterns in current standard English (such as *blood* and *food*). Certainly, foreign influences on the language brought by different invaders of England are still present. From the Vikings came words such as *husband, outlaw*, and *wrong*. From the French come *pantry* and *chamber*.

Leisure. Hunting, pigeon fighting, bear baiting, bowling, puppet shows—all have been popular English pastimes. Hunting was long a favorite sport, deer being the principal quarry. Hare hunting became popular in the 1800s, on foot with the help of beagles. Another early favorite was football (soccer). Played by commoners, it began as a brutal game that led to broken necks and even death. The sport was outlawed for a time, then revived and a Football Association formed in 1863. With a season that lasts from late August to early May, football has long been the national sport. Rugby, derived from foot-

Each word on this map has meant "time out" in its particular region of use. *Adapted from Wakelin 1977, p. 81.*

ball, was invented in 1871 at Rugby School. Cricket, another early game, was standardized through the nineteenth century, and is today the major summer sport. In the 1870s, the English invented lawn tennis, which grew popular as a game for men and women to play together.

Fairs were annual events for selling wares, and they attracted a host of entertainers. There were acrobats, fortune-tellers, and keepers of bears that danced. The English circus started when trick horseback riders exhibited their feats on fields rented for the purpose. The most celebrated rider was Philip Astley; accompanying his act, Madame Margeretta balanced herself on a wire on one leg while carrying 13

English people gather in pubs to drink and play. This is reputed to be the oldest pub in England. *Courtesy of Monica Gyulai.*

glasses balanced on a tobacco pipe. Another familiar sight was the minstrel player, who set verse to song, often accompanied by harp music; minstrels appeared everywhere in England, even in the households of the nobles.

English theater has a long-standing history. From the 1300s to the 1500s, there were miracle plays, dramatizing stories from the Bible. They had a lively, comic spirit—the story of Noah, for example, portrayed his wife as maddeningly resistant to getting into the ark. Besides humor, audiences demanded horror and surprise: severed heads, bladders of blood, trap doors, and the like. Much credit for advances in theater goes to David Garrick, who made his debut in 1741 as King Richard III. Instead of a forced-style, Garrick adopted a familiar one, prompting a fellow actor to observe, "If the young fellow is right, I and the rest of the players have been all wrong" (Hibbert 1987, p. 418). Called the greatest actor of his time, he managed the Drury Lane theater for 30 years and instituted major reforms: separating the audience from the stage, hiding the stage lights, using cut-out scenery, and insisting that the actors keep their eyes on each other rather than nodding to friends in the audience.

Classic English plays have been performed up to the present. Leading actors, such as John Gielgud and Laurence Olivier, have dominated the stage. Supported by government, two new groups were formed in the 1960s and 1970s—the Royal Shakespeare Company and the National Theater. Though theater remains vital, cinema has outpaced it as the more popular public entertainment for most of the twentieth century.

Holidays. Acknowledging the importance of servants in English society, December 26 is Boxing Day, the occasion on which boxes of gifts are given to providers of services. Guy Fawkes Day (November 5) commemorates an attempt in 1605 to blow up Parliament for repressing Roman Catholics in England. Children create stuffed dummies of the rebel leader Guy Fawkes and walk the streets in quest of money, chanting the standard, "A penny for the Guy." In the evening, fireworks are set off and the dummies burned on bonfires. The English also have Bank Holidays, so called because banks as well as other businesses and schools are closed. Falling on a Monday, one Bank Holiday occurs in each of the four seasons.

Arts and sciences. The rich and steady stream of English authors includes giants who have excelled in every genre from poetry (Elizabeth Barrett Browning) to drama (William Shakespeare) to the novel (Charles Dickens) to the short story (D.H. Lawrence). Elizabeth Browning's "The Cry of the Children" laments nineteenth-century child labor. William Shakespeare's history plays concern the courtly intrigues of several eras. Charles Dickens' *Oliver Twist* travels from the workhouse to comfortable English family life, and D.H. Lawrence's "The Rocking-Horse Winner" exposes working-class thoughts and feelings. In children's literature, the Robin Hood and King Arthur legends are set in Norman times. Though Irish, Jonathan Swift (*Gulliver's Travels*), Oscar Wilde (*Importance of Being Earnest*), and George Bernard Shaw (*Pygmalion*) have written incisive masterpieces on English society. The English themselves created the comic magazine *Punch*, exposing the shams of English society in witty comment and illustration. Standing in a poor, run-down cottage, for example, Mr. Punch makes an acid suggestion to his landlord: "Your stable arrangements are excellent! Suppose you try something of the sort here?" (Gaskell 1990, p. 115).

The prime minister Benjamin Disraeli, by birth a Jew, wrote *Sybil*, calling England's rich and poor "two nations" as ignorant of each other as if they lived on different planets. An Englishman of Afro-Caribbean origin, Samuel Coleridge-Taylor, incorporated ele-

Beatrix Potter, creator of Peter Cottontail, is one of England's most revered authors. *Courtesy of Alisa Rabin.*

ments of black music into Europe's concert tradition in *Hiawatha's Wedding Feast.*

Twentieth-century rock music has had a leveling effect on English society. In the 1960s, the Beatles openly presented themselves as working-class teenagers rather than disowning their origins, as others, aspiring to nobility, had done before them. This democratizing effect of popular music on English society would survive the transition to punk rock during the 1970s and then to music videos in the 1980s.

Thomas Gainsborough painted works such as "Blue Boy," for the wealthy industrialists of the late 1700s. Joseph Turner painted scenes of English life and history, studies of changing colors and light as the weather changes. In woodcraft, Thomas Chippindale created fine furniture for the rich industrialists in a style that has remained popular. The most famous architects of the Industrial Revolution were the Adams brothers, who designed brick country homes for the wealthy, which are still used today.

In the sciences, Sir Isaac Newton first defined the laws of gravity, Sir Alexander Fleming discovered penicillin, and Charles Darwin described a theory of evolution that has served as a base for scientific investigations since the 1800s. Most of these discoveries were reported through England's Royal Academy of Science, which helped set the standards for quality investigation and reporting so that scientific studies today are considered unacceptable unless they are reported in such a way that the experiments can be repeated and checked. Memorable in medicine is Mary Seacole, an Afro-Caribbean. Her efforts on behalf of sick and wounded British soldiers earned her the title "black Florence Nightingale."

For More Information

Ashley, Maurice. *The People of England: A Short Social and Economic History.* Baton Rouge: Louisiana State University Press, 1982.

Gaskell, Martin. *Slums.* Leicester, London: Leicester University Press, 1990.

Hibbert, Christopher. *The English: A Social History 1066–1945.* New York: W.W. Norton, 1987.

McAuley, Ian. *Passport's Guide to Ethnic London.* Lincolnwood, Illinois: Passport Books, 1987.

Morton, A.L. *A People's History of England.* 3rd ed. Berlin: Seven Seas Books, 1965.

FAROE ISLANDERS

(fair' oh eye' lan derz)

People of Norse origin who settled in the Faroe Islands.

Population: 50,000 (1991 estimate).
Location: North Atlantic Ocean.
Languages: Faroese, Danish, English.

Geographical Setting

The Faroe Islands lie midway between Scotland and Norway in the stormy North Atlantic, about 400 miles below the Arctic Circle. To the southeast are Scotland's Shetland and Orkney Islands; to the northeast is Iceland. The Faroes consist of 17 inhabited islands, along with numerous smaller, uninhabited ones. The islands are generally aligned in a northwest-southeast direction—the result of erosion by strong currents from the northwest. These currents are actually part of the warm-water Gulf Stream, which drives northeast from the Caribbean. A small branch shoots north below the Faroes, then hooks south through the islands to rejoin the body of the current. To visitors flying in, the barren, treeless Faroes look like a fleet of battleships steaming north: the current leaves a wake which makes it appear that the long, narrow islands are moving.

The Faroes can be thought of as falling into three groups, arranged roughly in the shape of a thick T. On the west arm of the T are the largest two islands, Streymoy and Eysturoy, with the smaller islands of Vagar and Mykines to the west of them. A group of small islands makes up the Nordoyar or "north islands," on the T's east arm. Several islands lie on the stem of the T, the largest of which are Sandoy and Suduroy. The Faroes' interiors are rugged and rocky; one island alone, Vagar, has enough flat area for an airport. Only coastal

Faroe Islanders

Faroe Islanders

parts are settled. The capital and largest town is Torshavn, near the southern tip of Streymoy.

The Gulf Stream's interaction with cold Arctic currents brings foggy, wet, windy weather to the Faroes. Temperatures (because of the Stream) rarely fall below freezing, though winter storms are frequent and violent. Rainfall is heavy, about 50 inches annually, with nearly two-thirds of the days overcast. The high latitude means that winter days are as short as five hours, though correspondingly longer in summer.

Historical Background

Norse settlers. Though some Irish hermits probably reached the Faroes in the 700s, they either fled or were absorbed by Viking settlers in the 800s. From the 800s to the 1100s, Viking (or Norse) sailors enjoyed an era of great exploration and discovery. Sailing from Norway, they carried out raids on the shores of northern Europe, opened trade routes along Russian rivers to the Mediterranean, and reached the shores of North America. They also colonized Greenland, Iceland, and other North Atlantic islands, such as the Faroes, the Shetlands, and the Orkneys. It was a violent time, and though the first Norse to reach the Faroes were probably warrior-sailors, later settlers were mostly farmers and fishermen escaping with their families from upheavals at home. Many probably came from settlements on the Shetland and Orkney islands. With other Norse peoples, the islanders became Christian around the year 1000.

Norwegian rule. From the 1100s to the late 1300s, the Faroes were part of a trading network linking Norway's Atlantic colonies with the Norwegian port of Bergen. Though to some extent the islanders were allowed to keep their own laws, they paid taxes to the Norwegian crown and were essentially under Norway's control. The islanders relied on imports such as grain and timber (for building boats), exporting woolen cloth, feathers, and dried fish. The land is poor for farming, being more suitable for raising sheep, which rapidly became (with fishing) a main source of livelihood.

Rise of Danish power. Gradually, Norway's trade became directed eastward, to the Baltic. At the same time, Danish influence grew, until Norway and Denmark united under the Danish crown in 1380. Copenhagen, the Danish capital, came to replace Bergen as the Faroes' connection with Europe. In the 1400s, the Greenland colonies petered out, and the Shetlands and Orkneys came under Scottish rule. Only Iceland and the Faroes remained as Denmark's island possessions.

Protestant Reformation. As throughout Europe, the religious upheavals of the mid-1500s profoundly affected life in the Faroes. Denmark became a Protestant country, which meant tearing down and replacing the structure of the Catholic Church. In the Faroes, the new religious institutions were put in place by Danish authorities, strengthening Danish political and economic control. The last trade contacts with Bergen were broken in 1619, when Denmark brought the Faroes under a royal monopoly that lasted until 1856. Danish became the language of religion, government, and trade. Yet Faroese, based on old Norse, survived as a spoken language, and the islanders retained their own distinctive culture.

Modern revival. In the early 1800s, liberal Danish political leaders attempted to redress the poverty caused by isolation and economic stagnation. The new Danish policy aimed at making the islands an integral part of Denmark. Thus, from 1816 they constituted a Danish county (*amt*) and were administered by Danish governors. The Danish also undertook efforts to bolster the islanders' economy, particularly by improving their fishing fleet. Banks and new villages were established, as well as a local governing council. However, rather than making the Faroese more Danish in outlook, increasing prosperity brought instead a greater sense of Faroese identity.

Emergence of a middle class. The crucial factor in the Faroes' economic and cultural revival has been the growth of commercial fishing. For centuries, Faroese men had fished in small open boats, providing food for the table and trading any surplus for goods. By the 1880s, however, fishing was growing into a major export industry, slowly replacing woolens as the chief source of revenue. With the fishing-based economy came a relatively prosperous middle class: civil servants, merchants and fishermen who made Torshavn into a modern city and sent their children to be educated in Denmark. In the late 1940s, the islanders began to acquire modern, long-ranged vessels, and today fishing supplies fully 98% of Faroese exports.

Culture Today

Far Islands, Islands of Sheep. Two rival stories compete to explain the islands' name. According to one version, the Irish monks who lived there in the 700s called the islands something like *fear an*, Gaelic for "far islands." Even before the Vikings' arrival, sheep were kept on the islands in large numbers, probably brought by the monks— hence the other claimant to the origin of the islands' name, *faar oy*, or "islands of sheep" in old Norse. Most Faroese believe that this is the basis for the islands' modern name, *Foroyar* in Faroese.

Population growth. The relative prosperity of the last 150 years has led to dramatic population growth and increased urbanization. From about 5,000 in 1800, the population grew to 15,000 in 1900, 38,000 in 1970, and 50,000 in 1990. Most live on the six largest islands of Streymoy, Eysturoy, Vagar, Suduroy, Sandoy, and Bordoy. About one-third live in Torshavn, with more in the capital's suburbs and outlying communities. Smaller towns and villages throughout the islands continue to flourish, however, especially since the fishing limit was extended from 12 to 200 miles in 1977. (The fishing limit prevents non-Faroese ships from fishing within 200 miles of the islands.)

As in the past, the rugged interiors of the islands have kept settlement to coastal areas.

Government. In 1948, the Faroes' status as a Danish county was abolished, and the islands became a self-governing community within the Danish state. Denmark controls foreign affairs, while the islands look after taxation, currency, customs, and cultural matters. Other areas are decided jointly by Denmark and the Faroese legislature, the *Logting*. From the Logting's members are elected the *Landsstyri*, an executive committee whose foreman or *logmadur* is the equivalent of a president. Both the logting and the logmadur are ancient Faroese democratic institutions revived in modern times.

Food, clothing, and shelter. The Faroes' environment has decided the people's traditional foods. Only the most robust vegetables can be grown in the poor soil: onions, potatoes, rhubarb, for example. Mutton and fish have been staples, with birds and whales being delicacies. Though much is imported today, the islanders retain a fondness for such dishes as *skerpitjot*—raw, wind-dried mutton that has been hung in a shed for at least a year. The sharp, cheesy meat (akin to beef jerky) is offered to guests soon after they enter the house. Not only the meat, but virtually all parts of the sheep are used, either for food or for material goods such as wool. Cod, haddock, herring and halibut are among the many fish taken from Faroese waters and are prepared in a number of ways, most often boiled, ground, dried, salted, or pickled. The islanders also eat whale meat and blubber.

Birds living on seaside cliffs provide feathers as well as tasty nourishment. To catch the birds, a group of men lowers one man over the cliffs at the end of a rope. The man on the rope carries a *fleyg*, which resembles a large lacrosse racquet, with which he picks the wheeling birds out of the air. He gets one bird every 10 or 15 minutes, wrings its neck, and attaches it to his belt. On his signal, the others haul him up, and the catch is shared out among them. The birds' eggs are also collected and eaten.

The Faroese retain their distinctive national dress, though it is nowadays worn mostly on special occasions. Men wear a brightly embroidered woolen vest, red for the young men, dark blue for the old, with a row of silver buttons. They also wear knickers (knee-pants) of dark blue, with light blue stockings for the younger and, again, dark blue for the older men. Black leather shoes with a silver buckle, a dark woolen jacket, again with silver buttons, and a hat like a ski-cap complete the ensemble. Young men's hats are red with a narrow black stripe, old men's, dark blue. Women wear a long, heavy skirt, perhaps dark blue with red stripes, black stockings, a dark, laced bodice, topped by a lighter colored apron and shawl. All of the woolen material is homespun.

Because the islands are treeless, most homes were traditionally built of stones and sod. Only wealthier islanders could afford timber for houses. Today, however, most live in comfortable wood homes, complete with electricity and central heating. Often the houses are set right on naked rock, and are painted in bright reds, greens and blues.

Family life. The islanders' harsh, demanding life has made Faroese society quite conservative, despite the great socio-economic changes of the last 150 years. Traditional divisions between the sexes have largely been maintained in the culture today. Men and older boys work outside the home, often together (as in catching birds), women and girls carry out domestic tasks. Men don't help with dishes or cleaning, and women don't expect or desire them to. Any man who did so would be met with puzzlement and mild derision. Gender divisions have survived in the Faroese society.

Until a few generations ago, the family (along with hired help and other household members) would gather in the kitchen during the evening. Men might card wool or repair tools; women would knit or perform other chores. A roaring fire warmed the small, snug room, which was the home's center. At these evening gatherings, called *kvoldsetur*, adults and children would sing the old ballads, and older men and women would tell ancient stories of trolls, giants, and ghosts.

Literature and the arts. As these oral traditions became less important in daily life, however, scholars such as Jakob Jakobson (1864–1918) recorded them in written form for future generations. During the 1900s, a number of Faroese poets, playwrights, and novelists have gained followings both in the islands and, to some extent, abroad. Dictionaries, journals, and newspapers have also been produced. Faroese painters have won recognition in recent years, but folk music and dance remain the most important art forms. The Faroese *dansiringur*, or ring of dancers, is the sole survivor of a popular dance form once found throughout Scandinavia. The participants link hands, repeating the simple steps at different tempos, depending on whether the words of the song are sad or happy. The dance may go on all night, depending on the occasion, accompanied by singing, drinking, and merrymaking.

Language. Faroese is a Germanic language descended from old Norse and influenced by Gaelic. Its closest cousins are Icelandic and Norwegian. Since Danish was for centuries the language of business and government, Faroese survived only in spoken form, not being written until the 1800s. Only in the 1890s was the spelling regularized. Danish is still used widely, and some Faroese writers use both. English became familiar during World War II, when Britain occupied the islands to prevent their falling into German hands (Germany had occupied Denmark). Many older people still speak English, and television, movies, and music are making it more popular among the young as well.

Grindadrap. The Faroese institution best known to the outside world is also the most controversial: the *Grindadrap*, or slaughter of a group of whales. The *grind* are pilot whales, which swim in groups called pods. When a pod is sighted near the island, the word goes out, and the men drop everything and race for their boats. They herd the whales into shallows by throwing rocks into the water, then beach them and kill them. It is a busy, hurried operation, and a messy one, as the men must carve up the animals immediately, before they spoil. Environmental groups such as Greenpeace have objected to the Grindadrap; others say that the hunt is an ancient part of Faroese culture, and that the species is not under threat of extinction. While the procedure often disgusts visitors (and even guidebook writers), it has for centuries provided the people with food and with a vibrant, elaborate and ceremonial occasion. The meat and blubber of the whales is divided and distributed according to who sighted the whales and to the contributions of the men. While a local official decides the divisions, the people dance all night, and the men drink and sing. Whatever else it may be, the Grindadrap remains perhaps the most characteristic Faroese occasion.

For More Information

Swaney, Deanna. *Iceland, Greenland, and the Faroe Islands: A Travel Survival Kit*. Hawthorne, Australia: Lonely Planet Publications, 1991.

Williamson, Kenneth. *The Atlantic Islands*. London: Collins, 1948.

Wylie, Jonathan. *The Faroe Islands.* Lexington: University Press of Kentucky, 1987.

Wylie, Jonathan and Margolin, David. *The Ring of Dancers: Images of Faroese Culture.* Philadelphia: University Press of Pennsylvania, 1981.

FINNS
(fins)

People of southern Finland.

Population: 4,953,000 (1989 estimate).
Location: Finland, mostly in the southern and western regions.
Languages: Finnish, Swedish.

Geographical Setting

Finland is the northernmost country on the mainland of Europe, lying between Russia on the east, Estonia on the south, Norway on the north, and Sweden on the west. Much of the land is surrounded by water: the Gulf of Bothnia on the west and the Gulf of Finland on the south. Most Finns live in the coastal lowlands of the south and southwest, or in the central lake district. With the country's mildest weather and most fertile soil, the lowlands have been a magnet for most of the country's farmers, but the milder weather has also attracted urban populations. Helsinki, Finland's capital, is in this lowland country. Offshore from the lowlands, Finns live on islands, of which there are about 30,000. Thousands of lakes fill the center of Finland, and north of them lies the sparsely settled, harshly cold region.

Finland's coast receives warm air from the Gulf Stream, so its climate is mild for a north country. Winter temperatures along the coast average between 25 and 30 degrees Fahrenheit; summer days have highs of 55 to 65 degrees.

Historical Background

Origin. The earliest known people of Finland are the Lapps, who still make up much of the population north of the lakes. As early as 7500

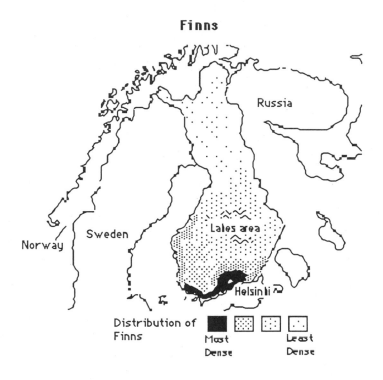

Finns

Distribution of Finns — Most Dense / Least Dense

B.C., the Lapps lived as nomadic hunters in the area now known as Finland. About the first century A.D., ancestors of the Finns moved into the country, probably migrating from the region in present-day Russia between the Volga River and the Ural Mountains. Gradually the Finns forced the Lapps farther north. Farming, hunting, and fishing for their food, the Finns divided themselves into three separate tribes and eventually settled in communities in the south by A.D. 1000.

Swedish Rule. In the twelfth and thirteenth centuries, Sweden conquered all of Finland and introduced Christianity to the inhabitants. In 1323, the Pahkinansaari Peace Treaty established the boundary between the Swedish land and the Russian country based at Novgorod. Originally, the Swedes and the conquered Finns were Catholics, but after the Reformation, the Swedish king converted to Lutheranism and this religion became the official religion of Sweden and Finland. For nearly 600 years, Finns were part of Sweden, governed in Swedish style and using the Swedish language. Finns found themselves in turmoil from the 1500s to the 1700s as Sweden and Russia fought for control of the territory. In the Great Northern War (1700–1721), Russia temporarily won all of Finland and by the end of the war still controlled the province of Vyborg. After another war in 1788–1790, a group of Finns tried to create an independent Finland under Russian protection, but that effort failed.

Russian domination. In 1808, Russia invaded Finland again, winning control of it in 1809. Finland technically was an independent duchy, forming its own parliament (the Diet) and making its own laws. However, the Russian tsar was the grand duke of Finland and held real political power. Still, Finns moved toward more independence. In 1821, Helsinki became the capital of the duchy, and in 1861, Finns established their own monetary system. This was a period marked by increased attention to the Finnish culture and language. Many advocated replacing Swedish with Finnish as the official language—an act that finally took place in 1902.

While Finns wanted to express their own culture, Russia was in the throes of a pan-Slavic movement toward a single law, religion, and language for all Slavs and their possessions. In 1899, Czar Nicholas II established a program which encouraged the use of the Russian language. Elements of self-rule gained by the Finns—parliament, money, and postal service—were abolished, and the Finnish army was incorporated into the Russian military. A six-day strike in 1905 helped lead the restoration of self-government, and in 1906, the Finns held national elections in which women as well as men were allowed to vote. Again in 1909, Russia began to suppress the Finnish culture. But troubles within Russia made Russification difficult.

Independence. Finland remained neutral during World War I, but commerce stalled because Finnish ships were blockaded in the Gulf of Bothnia. When the October (1917) Revolution in Russia overthrew the tsar, the Finns declared independence, and a new Communist government in Russia accepted the new nation. However, division within Finland between the Red Guard (sympathetic to the new Russian socialists) and the non-socialist White Guard erupted into civil war when the White Guard attempted to expel Soviet soldiers from

Finland. The White Guard supported by Germany was victorious over the Red Guard supported by the Russians in May, 1918. A republican constitution was adopted in 1919 and Kaarlo Juho Stahlberg became Finland's first president. The new country remained unstable as both Sweden and Russia disputed its boundaries.

World War II. Although it was officially neutral in the 1939–1945 war, Finland was twice invaded by the Soviet Union. The Winter War of 1939–1940 ended with a peace treaty that forced Finland to surrender a border region, Karelia, including one-tenth of the population of Finland and a tenth of the land, to the Soviets. In 1941, Finland could remain neutral no longer and reached an agreement with Germany that allowed German troops to use Finnish soil as a base for attacks on the Soviet Union. This pact angered the Soviets, who then bombed Finland. Communist troops moved deeper into Finland and on September 19, 1944, Finland signed a treaty favorable to the Soviet Union.

Neutrality. Carl Gustav Mannerheim, a war hero from the civil war and a leader in Finland's efforts against the Soviets in World War II, became president of Finland in 1944. Two years later, poor health demanded his resignation and Juho K. Paasikivi took his place. Immediately, Paasikivi placed Finland on a path of strict neutrality. Relations improved with both the Soviet Union and the Scandinavian countries. Then in 1955, the economies of Norway, Sweden, Iceland, Denmark, and Finland were tied together with the formation of the Nordic Council. Under this agreement, a resident of one member was entitled to receive social benefits and accept work in any other council member country. As a result, many Finns moved to Sweden, where more jobs were available.

Urho Kekkonen was elected president in 1956, and by stressing Finland's neutrality in international politics continued to be reelected until 1981. In the 1970s, the Finnish government passed a special measure extending Kekkonen's term of office to assure the Soviet Union that Finland intended to retain its policy of neutrality.

Finland benefited from trade with the Soviet Union. With the breakup of that country, Finland can only hope that its proximity to Russia and the other former Soviet republics will enable it to take advantage of the changing economic situations of its neighbors.

Culture Today

Economy. Finland's national government provides the Finns with a wide range of social services. Social security includes national pensions and sickness and disability insurances. The government provides for care of children of working parents, and provides financial aid and housing assistance to aged, disabled, and maladjusted citizens. A National Health Act of 1972 established health centers in each town and abolished doctors' fees. Much of the cost of health service, including hospital costs, are paid by a national government that apportions nearly 30 percent of its budget for social welfare.

Finland is an agricultural nation, but it has growing industries based on its most abundant natural resources—forests, granite, and materials for making cement. Lumber, plywood, pulp, and paper are manufactured for export through seaport cities such as Helsinki and Turku. The Finnish people struggle to balance these exports with the necessary imports of energy materials. Finland has no coal or oil deposits of its own. However, the fast-flowing Finnish rivers provide abundant hydroelectric power.

City life. Because of their nation's industrialization, Finns moved to the cities between 1950 and 1970 at the rate of 16,000 a year. More than two-thirds of Finland's inhabitants now live in urban areas, mostly in the south. The new city dwellers, born and raised in the country, still relish the outdoors. During the winter, city residents can be seen spending their weekends "on the ice"—skiing, skating, ice fishing, or strolling. During the summers, urban residents abandon Helsinki and other cities for vacation cottages in the country.

Food, clothing, and shelter. Fish of all kinds are important staples in the Finnish diet. The greatest delicacy is crayfish, which the Finns call *rapuja*. Salmon, herring, sardines, and reindeer meat are also eaten in several forms—smoked, broiled, or sauteed. This meat is often eaten with a side dish of boiled potatoes covered with butter and dill sprigs. Rye bread and coffee complete most meals. In the farm homes, rye bread is sometimes made in large batches and hung on rafters to dry so that one cooking lasts the family for some time.

Finnish country women still dress in a long skirt, with a bodice and an apron. A scarf is a common headdress. The Finns often decorated their dress with touches of their favorite color, red. However,

A Finnish farm family in everyday dress. *From the Library of Congress.*

most urban Finns dress in Western-style clothing—dresses for women, suits for men, and jeans for both men and women.

In the country, the farmers live in separate houses on small farm sites or in the villages. The homes are wood structures with shingle roofs. A dominant feature of many homes is a large kitchen, which may have been expanded to accommodate the family crafts industry. Those who migrate to the cities find the most available housing to be in large, multistoried apartment buildings. Only eight percent of the city dwellers own a single-family home.

Recreation. Sports of all kinds are popular in Finland, especially the winter sports of skiing, ice hockey, ice skating, ski jumping, and cross-

Water sports are popular in Finland as evident from this photograph of a Finnish Polar Bear Club swimming in winter. *From the Library of Congress.*

country skiing. Finns often compete well internationally in these sports. The interest in all sports is seen in Helsinki, where a great stadium—built for the 1938 Olympic games (which was abandoned because of the coming World War) and finally used for the 1952 Olympics—is still maintained.

Finns are proud that many foreigners immediately think of a sauna, the Finnish bath, as characteristic of their culture. They believe that the sauna is an important part of relaxing and remaining healthy. Almost every home has one. Most Finns take a sauna at least once a week. In the sauna, stones are heated over a stove or furnace and the temperature reaches 175 to 212 degrees Fahrenheit. People sit or lie on wooden benches until they are perspiring heavily, and some throw water on the stones to create steam, which makes the room seem even hotter. Occasionally, some Finns whip themselves with light birch sticks to stimulate circulation. Following a stay in the sauna, they take a cold shower or jump into an icy lake. After repeating the process, they lie down to recover, allowing their body temperature to return to normal.

Friendships are bound and business transacted in the sauna. An invitation to visit a Finn and take a sauna together is a sign of friendship. The saunas have caused some business turmoil as women in business feel left out of the decision-making because they are excluded from the male saunas.

Holidays. Finnish people celebrate the holidays that are universal throughout Christianity—Christmas, Epiphany, Good Friday, Easter, Ascension Day, and All Saints' Day. In May or June, Christian Finns also celebrate the fiftieth day after Easter, Whitsunday. June 24 is Midsummer Day in Finland and also the day of celebration of the flag. Along with their neighbors of the former Soviet Union, Finns celebrate Labor Day on May 1 with parades and dances.

Women. In 1906, Finland became the first country in the world to grant women equal national voting rights. (New Zealand had granted local voting rights to women in 1893.) Today, more than a quarter of the Finnish parliament members are women. More than 60 percent of the students taking university examinations are women. Still, though women are employed in almost every industry, including business, forestry, and engineering, as a whole they are paid only 75 percent as much as men.

Education. Finns are highly educated—almost all adults can read and write. Public elementary schools are mandatory for nine years beginning at age seven. After finishing the basic schools, students have a choice of a secondary school leading to the university or one directed toward vocational training. The secondary schools offer three years of academic work leading to one of Finland's 13 universities or 26 technical institutes.

Literature. The first known Finnish literature was a book by Michael Agricola, Bishop of Turku, in 1544. Since then, Finns have had a rich literary history. The national epic, called the *Kalevala*, is a collection of poetry, legends, stories, and proverbs. A country doctor, Elias Lonnrot, collected the folk legends for the Kalavela during the early nineteenth century, in a period when Finns were beginning to discuss political independence and developing a national conscience. This work contains nearly 600 poems and 50 ballads in a book called *Kanteletar*, 7,000 proverbs in *Suomen Kansan Sanalaskuja*, and 2,000 riddles in *Suomen Kansan Arvoltuksia*. More recent authors include Aleksis Kivi, Frans Eemil Sillanpaa, and Mika Waltari. Sillanpaa won the Nobel Prize for Literature in 1939 for his account of the struggles of rural people in the days when Finland was controlled by Russians. Waltari became an international best-selling author in 1945 with his *Sinhue the Egyptian*, a novel about ancient Egypt.

Arts. The Finns have had a deep impact on some modern arts and crafts. Eero Saarinen is an architect of the modern movement who experimented with great concrete structures that attempted to remain scaled to human needs. His influence is seen in bright, modern structures in Finnish cities and in such structures as the TWA terminal building in New York. This building, with its wing-shaped roof, is his best-known work. Alvar Aalto had a deep impact on architecture and design in his own country and spent much of his time after 1940 in the United States and Europe.

Finnish architecture blends modern styles with natural shapes. After World War II, the garden city of Tapiola was created ten miles west of Helsinki to showcase the modern designs and to incorporate working-class and middle-class housing. This model city is now an integrated suburb of Helsinki.

Other Finnish artists are also internationally known. Painters such as Albert Edelfelt and Akseli-Gallen-Kallela have created church murals using the Kalevela for their themes. Composer Jean Sibelius based most of his symphonic poems on the Kalevala. He later turned to more sophisticated music and gained an international reputation. The importance of music to Finns is evident in the hundreds of musical festivals produced every year.

Government. Finland is a republic with a government structured similarly to the British government. Citizens over the age of 18 vote for members of a college of 301 electors, who then select a president to govern for six years. He selects a prime minister and together they choose a cabinet. The legislature, the Eduskunta, consists of 200 members elected for four-year terms. The president may dissolve this parliament at any time and call for new elections. Also, at any time, the parliament can force a cabinet to resign by withholding support for its programs.

The country is divided into 500 communes in 12 provinces. Council members who direct each commune are selected in local elections, but the president appoints governors of each province. Local communes are responsible for operating hospitals, schools, police and fire departments and other local services.

For More Information

Engleman, Max and David Kirby. *Finland: People-Nation-State.* Bloomington, Indiana: Indiana University Press, 1989.

Singleton, Fred. *A Short History of Finland.* Cambridge: Cambridge University Press, 1989.

Vesilind, Priit J. "Helsinki: Finland's Capital Has Its Heart in the Country," *National Geographic*, August 1981, p. 237–255.

FLEMINGS
(flem' ings)

Roman Catholic people of Flanders.

Population: 4,500,000.
Location: Northern Belgium, the Netherlands.
Language: Flemish (Vlämsch), a west Germanic language.

Geographical Setting

The land of the Flemings is dominated by the Schelde River, which flows through Antwerp in Belgium and then separates into several broad estuaries as it flows into the North Sea. Most of the land is low, some of it below sea level, and flat—the western edge of a great plain that extends from Belgium into Russia. In some places, sand dunes more than 100-feet high separate the ocean from the fertile soil deposited. In other places, dikes, sometimes equally high, have been constructed to separate sea from soil and fresh water from salt water. There are no mountains in the region and few wild trees. However, the silt deposited by the sluggish rivers and mixed with sand churned up by the ocean have made Flemish land excellent for growing such crops as flax and wheat and for raising cattle and poultry.

The climate of the region is very damp. Winters bring severe storms, and the whole year may see as few as 40 days of sunlight.

Historical Background

Beginnings. Before A.D. 400 the land of the Flemings was inhabited by Celts, but in the 400s a wave of Franks moved across Europe and gradually pushed out or merged with the earlier inhabitants. A predominantly Celtic group remained in the south of Belgium and be-

Flemings

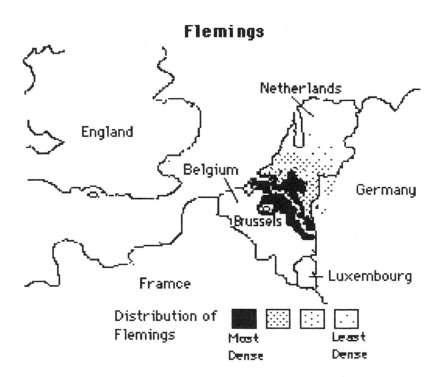

Distribution of Flemings
Most Dense — Least Dense

came known as the Walloons. The Franks and Celts of northern Belgium and the Netherlands formed a new group, the Flemings. They lived independently until Charlemagne united them with the Franks into one empire in the 760s.

Franks. By 900 the empire expanded by Charlemagne had begun to disintegrate and the Flemish land was broken into feudal states. Left more to themselves, the Celts founded cities and became traders while the Flemings kept to the old ways of farming and herding. Still, the entire lowland remained a feudal region until the Burgundians of France claimed and held power there in the fourteenth and fifteenth centuries. However, by this time the Flemings had begun to separate themselves from other Germanic peoples by developing their own language. Various dialects arose between the seventh and twelfth centuries from an ancient language known as Old Low Franconian. By the twelfth century a written language had evolved, and by the thirteenth century a Fleming body of literature had begun.

Austria and Spain. In 1477 Belgium and the Netherlands were claimed by Austria. Then in 1616, Spain claimed the territory. After a change in Spanish rulers, northern Flemish land was returned to Austria in 1713 while the south remained with Spain. One result was that the south held to the Roman Catholic Church while the north followed Protestant leaders. In 1792, an Academy of Brussels acknowledged the differences by recognizing the Flemish language along with French. Then in 1794, France claimed the southern lowlands. This area remained under French rule until 1815, becoming further entrenched under Catholicism. Despite the religious difference between peoples of the north and south, the entire lowland was united into the Netherlands at the Congress of Vienna following Napoleon's defeat in 1815.

The issue of language remained difficult. Beginning in 1818 and continuing through the first half of the nineteenth century, champions of Flemish such as Jan Franz Willams argued for the use of Flemish in literature. In 1846, Karl Lodewijk, recognized as the greatest Flemish poet, stirred interest in Fleming nationality by writing about the greatest Flemish cities—Ghent, Bruges, and Antwerp.

The growth of cities. These cities grew over the centuries as the Flemings became major suppliers to the world of lace and fine cloths produced from the flax that grew well in the country (*cambric* takes its name from the city of Cambria; *lisle* from Lille). The cities of Flanders became major trading centers and grew in size and beauty so that they rivaled the cities of Italy. Bruges in the west, Ghent in the east, and the great seaport of Antwerp in the north were the principal trade centers in Europe for cloth. The city of Ghent took on the appearance of Venice when canals were built as highways throughout the city.

Catholics and Protestants. By the early 1800s the Walloons and some of the Flemings in the south were firmly Catholic but the northern Flemings were firmly Protestant. The situation proved untenable for the Catholics, and both Walloons and Flemish Catholics seceded to form Belgium in 1830. Much earlier, the Walloons of southern Belgium had adopted the French language and the Flemings had made Flemish (akin to Dutch) the most common language. So from the first, today's Flemings have been divided among themselves by religion and government, and from other Belgians by language. The result has been that the Flemings in Belgium have long sought a form of self-government. As early as 1477 they had secured a special privilege from Austria to preserve their way of life and their language.

The city of Ghent serves as the capital of East Flanders. *Courtesy of the Belgian Institute for Information and Documentation.*

Their efforts in recent times have resulted in a limited form of self-government in the Flemish area of Belgium (Flanders) and in the Walloonian lands. Today, the Flemings of Belgium are Roman Catholics who speak Flemish. Many Flemings still seek their own state in an eventual break of Belgium into two states, and some Belgians argue for the inclusion of French speakers in an expanded France.

Culture Today

Farm economy. While their Celtic partners in south Belgium were developing a great trading and industrial center on the coast of Europe, the Flemings held to their farming heritage from feudal times. The land is rich and three-fifths of it is suitable for planting. Fleming farmers, raising wheat, barley, rye, oats, sugar beets, potatoes, hogs, and cattle, occupy holdings of 50 or less acres—small enough to discourage rapid movement toward mechanization.

Industry. Belgium has, however, become one of the most industrialized nations of the world. Manufacturing and trade development began in the south and was slow to spread to the Dutch-speaking northerners. The most recent industrial growth, however, has occurred in the Flemish areas—the Flanders province in Belgium and the Netherlands. A wide range of products are manufactured and are oftentimes transported over water. The canal and river systems of transportation are more developed in Belgium than in any other region of its size. Brussels, Belgium's largest city, has become the headquarters of the European Common Market and NATO, leading some to describe it as the "capital of Europe."

Language. Meanwhile the overwhelming issue for the Flemish has been language. Flemish speak and write Dutch although there has been a considerable movement toward Flemish as a literary language, preserving the spellings and punctuation that existed in the sixteenth century. Walloons of the south of Belgium speak French. Participation in the most important city, Brussels, is hindered by the language barrier. There French-speaking people live in the city, Dutch-speakers in the suburbs. Both languages are recognized. Belgian schools, in which attendance is required until age 18, are taught in whichever language is dominant in the school district.

The Flemish language arose from more ancient dialects around the seventh century. It appeared in several tribal dialects with such names as Frisian and Franconian. Gradually the Franconian dialect began to dominate the region and became the language of writing. During the French rule beginning with Charlemagne, many French words were added to the language, further separating it from its close neighbor, Dutch. Today, Flemish is the language of some people in southern Holland as well as of the provinces of Antwerp, Lemburg, Brabent, East Flanders, and West Flanders in Belgium. It is so closely related to Dutch that some believe it to have been the original language and Dutch a more recent dialect.

Literature. As early as 1150, Henrik von Veldeke was leading a plea to develop literature in the local dialects of the Low Lands—dialects that included Flemish and other languages similar to Dutch. However, these advocates gained little success. In the fifteenth century, the ruling Dukes of Burgundy encouraged the use of French and brought French words into the Flemish language. Before the nineteenth century, works of Flemish literature were in a language indistinguishable from the Dutch.

There was no formal literary language until 1818, when Jan Frans Willems began the literary tradition with his writing *Sur la Langue et la Littérature Neerlandaise, par Rapport aux Provinces Méridi-oneles des Pays-Bas.* Willems championed Flemish as a literary language and gathered a number of authors to support this movement. Still it was not until Holland and Belgium separated in 1830 that there was a strong movement toward preserving the old Flemish language. In the nineteenth century, early Flemish literature was revived as examples of the language—including *Spiegel Historical*, written by Jacob van Maerlant in the thirteenth century. By 1886, the success of the group started by Willems had resulted in the formation of the Royal Flemish Academy (Koninklije Vlaamsche Akademie) and the adoption of Flemish along with French as official languages of Belgium. The Academy supported a number of novelists and poets in producing works in the Flemish language, and the volume of literature grew. Madam Courtmans wrote 58 stories in the late 1800s. Rosalie and Virginia Loveling became successful novelists. Finally, Abbé Guido Gezello published popular poetry.

Government. Quarrels over which language to use or where to draw boundaries have affected the government of the Flemish. Belgium is a constitutional monarchy. During the twentieth century, the royal office has passed from father to son. With headquarters at Brussels, the king, his ministers, and two houses of parliament loosely govern both the Fleming Belgians and the Walloons, each with their own territorial governments. Today, the language barrier has forced decentralization so that Flanders and Walloonia are more directly governed by regional cabinets. Even this arrangement does not satisfy the need for Catholic Flemish independence, however. The country is further divided into 590 village areas, each presided over by a burgomaster. These local rulers are the effective governors of the Fleming people in Belgium. Since Flemish is closely related to the Dutch language, Flemings in Holland are less isolated from their countrymen than those in Belgium.

Religion. The common bond between the Flemish of Belgium and the Walloons is religion. Fewer than 100,000 of the nine million Belgians belong to faiths other than Roman Catholic. This religion and the possibility that they could be absorbed into France or the Netherlands are ties that hold the Flemings together in government with the Walloons, even though they are of different heritage and appearance. The Flemings are descendants of Frankish people and have the lighter complexion of Nordic people. The Walloons are shorter, darker descendants of the early Celts.

Holidays. Most of the holidays of the Flemings are religious celebrations. Christmas is a two-day celebration in which children court favors by setting out bundles of straw for Santa's reindeer and wooden shoes to be filled with gifts. National holidays in the Netherlands are Queen's Day (April 30) and National Liberation Day (May 5). This last holiday celebrates the liberation of the Netherlands from German occupation in 1945.

Food, clothing, and shelter. In dress, the Flemings and Walloons appear similar, both having abandoned traditional costumes for the dresses and business suits of a modern European nation. Farm families can still be seen in traditional dark-colored clothing, with men wearing caps and women wearing aprons.

Heavy fog blows in from the ocean, damaging crops and making living conditions unattractive. In this atmosphere, good nutrition, warm clothing, and habits of cleanliness are essential, and these are carefully attended to by the Flemings. The country produces abundant quantities of dairy products and eggs, which make up a major part of the diet along with wheat and rye breads.

Arts. Particular to the Flemish heritage has been a tradition of success in painting. It has been dominated by the works of Peter Paul Rubens, which reflected a Flemish interest in detailed landscapes, vivid colors, and rich textures. A first wave of old masters included Jan Van Eyck, who some claim to have invented the art of painting in oil in the fifteenth century, Hubert Van Eyck, Margarete Van Eyck, Hans Memling, Rogier van der Weyden, and Moro. Hubert and Jan Van Eyck established an art center at Bruges. A second wave of Flemish masters included the more famous Peter Paul Rubens, Anthony Vandyck, Jakob Jordaens, and Frans Snyders.

For More Information

Delepiere, Octave. *A Sketch of the History of Flemish Literature from the Twelfth Century Down to the Present Time.* Studies in European Literature #50. London: Haskel, 1972.

Hermans, T. J., editor. *The Flemish Movement: A Documentary History 1780–1980.* London: Athions Press, 1991.

FRENCH
(french)

The collection of Teutonic peoples who live in France.

Population: 51,968,000 (1990 esimate).
Location: France.
Language: French, a language derived from old Latin.

Geographical Setting

The land of France rises gently from the Atlantic Ocean to high mountains on the south (Pyrenees) and north (Alps, Jura, and Vosges). Four great river systems (Loire, Seine, Garonne, and Rhone) rise from the mountains and flow across the broad, rolling plains to the sea. Except for a volcanic mass that rises to 600 feet in the central southeast, France is marked by the basins carved by the four rivers and their tributaries. The result is well-watered, fertile farmland on which abundant crops of grapes, wheat, and other grains flourish. The four rivers also provide the most favorable harbors for the country. Most of the coast is rocky or low and sandy, with few large coves adequate for seaports. Two large peninsulas protrude westward into the Atlantic—Normandy and Brittany. These two regions differ from the rest of France in their rugged coasts and in the rise to higher plateaus at altitudes of about 1,000 feet. Most of France is, therefore, farmland. But in the northeast, deep valleys in the mountains separating France and Germany provide rich deposits of coal and iron. This region, whose government has passed between France and Germany through the years, is one of the most highly industrialized areas of Europe.

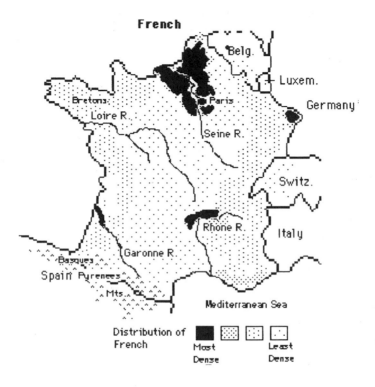

French

Distribution of French — Most Dense ▓ ▒ ░ Least Dense

Historical Background

Origins. The French today represent a blending of people from different regions who moved to the rich farmland bounded by the Atlantic Ocean and the Rhone River. Originally, the people called French were a collection of independent Gallic tribal clans with such names as Parisie and Senones—names that are place names in France today.

Rome. By 300 B.C., migrants near the Mediterranean Sea had moved westward to settle in small groups along the Rhone River. In 125 B.C., the townspeople of Marseilles invited Romans to move into the area to prevent invasion by the Celts. The Celts turned toward the sea, moving to the British Islands. But as the power of Rome weak-

Relics of Rome are found throughout France. This amphitheater is located near Neims. *Courtesy of Amy A. Trenkle.*

ened greatly in the fifth century A.D., a Germanic people known as the Franks arrived and occupied much of what is now France. The Franks drove out invading armies from Africa to secure France and united the peoples of the region. Its rulers espoused Christianity and Catholicism, forming the Holy Roman Empire. The dominance of religion in French life was to continue through World War II. Under Charlemagne this empire controlled most of Europe by the eighth century. However, the Empire was short-lived. By the tenth century the Holy Roman Empire had disintegrated into many feudal fiefdoms.

Beginning of unity. It remained for Hugh, who came to power in 996, to separate the fiefdoms of France from those of the rest of Europe and establish a kingdom whose ruling house would reign for 800 years. Weaker kings of this house were unable to stop raids by the Danes in the tenth and eleventh centuries. The Norsemen left their name to one feudal kingdom, Normandy. During the period of the Crusades, the French king Louis IX traveled with the Crusaders and began to bring world recognition to France. However, the claim to the French throne by an English king, Edward III, triggered á 100-year-long war (1337–1453). The conflicting claims by England and France slowed France's unification process. It was during this period that Joan of Arc led French forces in an attack to regain the city of Orleans from the English and helped prevent England's controlling all of France. For her efforts, she was later taken captive by the English, who burned her at the stake.

Monarchy. It was not until the sixteenth century that the country was again unified under a single monarch, Francois I (1415–1547). France then entered an age of great intellectual and artistic achievement. Francois I commissioned 600 paintings that formed the nucleus of the now-famous art museum, the Louvre. Toward the end of the 1500s an Edict of Nantes proclaimed religious freedom for the French citizens, but this was renounced a century later. The playwright Molière wrote and staged comedies that made the customs of the French famous. In time France became powerful enough to expand. Under Louis XIV (1638–1715), the armies crushed the Germans. Also, under Louis XIV, the Roman Catholic religion became firmly entrenched when the king purged many Protestant believers. Secure in power and wealth, Louis XIV began spending French money for luxury, building show places like the Palace of Versaille. The contrast between peasant farmers and nobles grew, and even the nobles came into disagreement with the king.

Revolution. In 1789, the kingdom was overthrown in a revolution led by small business people and intellectuals and backed by peasants. The rule of the French fell to a radical Committee of Public Safety. The Committee promoted national identification in France but failed in promises to the peasants. Meanwhile, other nations, particularly Austria, threatened the French unity.

Napoleon. In 1796, a young General Napoleon Bonapart was sent to the plains of Lombardy (Italy) to fight the threatening Austrians. His victory and the resulting tributes he demanded then and in following adventures resolved the financial difficulty of the government and catapulted Napoleon to fame. In 1799, Napoleon took office as head of the French government. Soon after he named himself Emperor of France. Napoleon took charge of the Revolutionary legacy

Fortress towns were common throughout France in the fourteenth century. This is Fort at St. André in Villereuve-les-Avignon. *Courtesy of Amy A. Trenkle.*

of spreading a sense of French identity among the different peoples of France. He established uniform laws throughout the country, the Code Napoleon. He also developed a highway system for his troop movements, which was the beginning of the highway system that unites France today. The Napoleonic army was finally defeated at Waterloo in 1815.

A new monarchy. The nation again became a monarchy, but now with an assembly representing the wealthy French and advising the king. Three decades of governmental strife followed, including the reign of Charles X, who attempted once more to establish a dictatorship, dissolving the government of the Chamber of Deputies and suspending freedom of the press. After his reign, Napoleon III (Napoleon's grandson) came into power (1848). He shortly persuaded the French people to name him Emperor of France and abandon the four-year election cycle that was the law. Napoleon III ruled until 1870. Under his leadership France began to expand its industry and to claim territory worldwide.

Republic. Once more the government failed and France weakened. In 1871 Prussians invaded France and succeeded in obtaining the provinces of Alsace and Lorraine in the industrial regions and in gaining millions of dollars as settlement. Napoleon III's government fell and, after a brief military rule, France established the two-house parliament and presidential rule that has continued to today. Thereafter, France began a period of decline. The country was further split by a military incident known as the Dreyfus Affair, in which a Jewish army officer was brought to trial on a charge of treason but was later acquitted. The charges appear to have been raised by anti-Semitic Frenchmen.

The World Wars. It was not until World War I that France again found itself embroiled with Germany, and the French appeared to be firmly united. French governments from 1905 to 1914 bent extensively to the will of the Germans for the sake of peace, but war between the two countries began in 1914. From 1914 to 1918 this war was fought mostly on French soil. Eight million Frenchmen served in the army, and 1,300,000 were killed in the battles. France joined other Western countries in industrial development after World War I, but no longer with the spirit of a leading nation. Development was interrupted once more when Germans occupied France in 1940 at the onset of World War II, adding to the embarrassment of the French people.

Fourth Republic. With this war over, France again formed a republic. From 1946 to 1958 the country was led by 26 different governments. Finally, in 1958, the French leaders asked General Charles De Gaulle, who had led the battle against German occupation, to head the government and gave him dictatorial powers for six months. The government stabilized, General De Gaulle continued to lead the country until 1969 as a reorganized "Fifth Republic." Since that time, France has steadily regained its pride and has become one of the leading industrial nations of the world, while the central government has alternated between conservatism to democratic socialism.

Culture Today

Variety. The French are a diverse people. Briefly describing their culture necessitates focusing on similarities of language, values, and customs. To that end, since Paris is the heart of France, or the soul of the French people, most emphasis must be placed on the French capital and cities. Neglected is the variety of the French, which spans cosmopolitan city dwellers; Bretons (see BRETONS), who have a legacy of Celtic customs; a few Basques and Catalans (see BASQUES, CATALANS), with their own languages, along the Spanish border; and Cevinols, east of the Rhone valley, who cling to their peasant village lives, which are radically different from the lives of French people in the city.

Language. More than any other factor, it is the unique French language that identifies the French. It is a Latin language adopted in the days when the French ruler was the Holy Roman Emperor, and ruled with the blessings of the pope. Before that, the various French groups spoke Germanic languages, mostly Celtic, the language of the common people as recently as the sixth century. Celtic, German, and Greek words have been added to the Latin-based language, reminders of the various peoples who have influenced France from its beginning.

City dwellers. One-fifth of all French people live in Paris and its suburbs. Paris is the heart of the country, with roads and highways radiating from Paris much like a spider's web. Many more of the French work and live in smaller industrial cities such as Grenoble and Toulouse. Although their history is one of small villages and rich farmlands, France today is more aptly represented by industrialization. A small percentage of farmers continue to grow potatoes, wheat, sugar beets, and oats in quantity, particularly in central France. But mechanization and the unyielding nature of land in a few areas such as Britanny have resulted in many young French people leaving the farm to find work in the industry and businesses of the city. The industrial areas are located in regions with rich natural coal and iron

An open-air market is a common sight in French villages. This one is at L'ile Sur Sorque. *Courtesy of Amy A. Trenkle.*

resources—the energy and raw materials used to produce items such as textiles, chemicals, and weapons.

French values. Until World War II, France was a nation of small industries. The people prided themselves on individuality and independence. They thought of their country as "France, mother of arts, arms, and laws," and clung to the revolutionary values of liberty, equality, and fraternity. During World War II, General Petain, who led the German-supported government of France, added that the French believed in "work, family, and fatherland."

The French people hold to the Catholic Church, and are said to respect the state but scorn government, respect law but tend toward anarchy, and honor individualism.

French marry young and consider marriage with a sense of purpose. The church binds them together along with the language, in spite of their multi-headed origins—Belgic (Teutonic), Celtic, and Aquitanian (people who early spoke the Basque language). Their religion remains one of the binding forces of the French, enabling a French priestly caste to have special respect and great political influence. The French are said to be bound together by national unity, a priestly caste, the affirmed dogma of the Church, and the many special shrines dear to French believers.

Family life. Despite the shift in the ways people earn their livelihood, many of the traditional ways have been retained. These traditions center around family members who work and play with equal vigor and who have a deep interest in food. On the farms south of Paris as well as in the industries and offices of the cities, people still follow the custom of eating an early and small breakfast (a roll and coffee), then taking a two-hour break for a family lunch. After lunch, the French person works until seven or eight o'clock in the evening, then has a light supper.

Food, clothing, and shelter. Every region has its own special dishes; the variety of French dishes is great, as illustrated by the number of cheese dishes in the French diet. The different regions have developed at least 245 kinds of cheeses.

Housing also changes according to the region in which the people live. Home to the French family varies from the white-walled, red-tiled farmsteads of Brittany to the high-rise flats of the Paris suburbs. Most of the farmhouses are long and narrow, and the French often prefer to live close together in small homes or apartments. Even in the cities, however, French prefer older houses, which they furnish simply. In Paris, old and new housing accommodates 100 people or more for every acre of land. Yet even in this city, the family remains the focus of social life. The French seem to prefer meeting and dining with family members. Everyone shares in family chores and activities. Husbands often help in the kitchen.

Arts. Both women and men pursue the arts, building on a heritage that features authors such as Victor Hugo (*The Hunchback of Notre*

A typical town shop with residences above in a town in France. *From the Library of Congress.*

Dame), Madame George Sand (*The Country Waif*) and Alexandre Dumas. Singers build on a tradition set by the troubadours of medieval France, who created such forms as the ballad. Painters follow the lead of artists such as Edgar Degas. Ballet dancers served as subjects for many of his paintings, the ballet being another form of art with origins in France. From World War I to World War II, the French people excelled in many art forms. Paris was the world capital of fashion design. Painters and writers from all over the globe migrated to Paris to study their craft. But since World War II, the French appear to be mostly interested in work, money, and advancement. While designers and artists in Paris are still important, their writers and artists are fewer and have more competition than before from cities like New York and London.

France has a long tradition of excellence in architecture. Remnants of early Greek architecture remain from the period of the Roman Empire and its successors, and these serve to inspire current architects. The French are most noted for their use of public squares, which are the hubs of French cities and places for great buildings and sculpture. The French willingness to experiment in design of buildings is very visibly demonstrated in the Eiffel Tower, a framework of iron and steel girders that rises above Paris.

Literature. French-language writing and poetry spoken by bards begin with the *Prose of St. Eulalia* and the *Life of Saint Léger*, the latter being a 250-verse poem written in the tenth century. More famous was the early epic poetry, the *chancons de geste* (songs of romance and galantry) that included the *Chanson de Roland*. This epic was part of a great folklore of sagas about Roland, his English counterpart, Arthur, and an array of Greek and Roman adventurers.

From those beginnings, the great names of French literature are many. Corneille wrote *Le Cid* in the 1636. Racine wrote about Alexander the Great at the end of that century. Molière, a great dramatist who once completed a play in six days, and Voltaire were followed in the nineteenth century by Victor Hugo and Alexandre Dumas (father and son), Guy de Maupassant, and Emile Zola. France continues to be a center for literary and artistic studies. Of all the French authors, some feel that Molière, whose real name was Jean Baptiste Poquelin, was the most versatile. Writing in the seventeenth century, he produced drama about real people in the real situations of the day, and like Shakespeare, with whom he is sometimes compared, Molière produced works of comedy, tragedy, and satire on subjects that proved timeless.

In the eighteenth century, Voltaire (pen name for Jean François Marie Arouet) followed the strong French literary tradition with his examinations of the problems of society. He condemned what he saw as the French's blind adherence to church doctrine, claiming that the average follower's belief in what was told them was only faith in the priests.

Since World War II, French authors and playwrights have spent much effort in the same vein as that of Voltaire. French modern writing examines current issues of society such as feminism, financial scandals, the role of physicians in perpetuating or discontinuing life,

The Eiffel Tower overlooks Paris, France. *Courtesy of Leah Cadavona.*

the absurdity of the legal system, or the obligations of intelligent people toward those not so intelligent.

Religion and tradition. An early religion of the area of France was the Druidism of the Celts. But early in the development of the nation, Roman Catholicism was espoused by the French rulers. In France today, it is the middle class and the old people who cling to traditional ways. Roman Catholicism has dominated French religious life since the time of Charlemagne, but today only 12 percent of the French regularly attend church. It is the middle class who insist on weddings and funerals in the church. These people also entertain in the old style, mostly with family members. They prepare formal dinners served at elegant tables where wine is the most common beverage. The bonds of the average French person to the church are strong. The French remember their heritage in such slogans as "France, eldest daughter of the Church."

Education. Children are important among the French. School begins at six years of age. After primary school (at age 11), French students

The famous Notre Dame Cathedral lies on an island in the Seine River at Paris. *Courtesy of Amy A. Trenkle.*

attend secondary schools until age 15 and then may enter a lycée or college to prepare for the university or may attend a business training institute. Other students prefer vocational training. Except in remote farmlands, the French are mostly class conscious. Because of this, few working-class young people attempt the lycée. Instead, they enter a trade school or become apprentices under a labor union constitution that has governed most French workers since 1946.

Government. Unrest is almost a way of life among the French. Many years of struggle against Germans, followed by sometimes violent attempts at independence by such colonies as Algiers, have been in recent years replaced by labor unrest and by dissension among the youth and the political parties of France. The president of France is directly elected by the people and has the primary task of appointing a Council of Ministers and a Prime Minister who is responsible for the functioning of the government. French law is made by elected representatives in the two houses of Parliament (the Senate and National Assembly). In France, members of the larger National Assembly are elected by the voters in a general election, but the members of the Senate are elected by the National Assembly. Members of the National Assembly serve for five years, while one-third of the Senators are elected every third year to serve for nine years.

Recreation. Present-day conditions are affecting the traditional ways of the French. The two-hour lunch is being abandoned by some as they commute farther and farther to work, from village to farm or from suburb to inner city. Still, life is better for French people than for citizens in many places in Europe and leads to a unique summer for French city workers. These workers enjoy long vacations, five weeks in the first year of work. And most French workers in business and industry insist on this time during the summer months. In these months, some French industries seem almost vacated, as workers migrate to the countryside or the Mediterranean seaside for the annual retreat. The French also enjoy theater, television, and reading. There are 50 million radios and 22 million television sets in the country; 43 million books are printed in the French language yearly.

Holidays. Two holidays stand out as distinctly French: Bastille Day and Liberation Day. Both mark turning points in French history. July 14, Bastille Day, marks the anniversary of an important event in the French Revolution. For 400 years, the Bastille, a prison, had stood in Paris as a symbol of tyranny. People disliked by the current ruler were often imprisoned there under secret warrants and then forgotten. At the beginning of the French Revolution in 1789, a citizen mob surrounded the prison and demanded that it be opened. Supported by an armed guard, the mob forced entry to the prison and found seven forgotten prisoners there, some having been imprisoned, for little cause, for 30 years. The next day, workers began to tear down the old jail as a visible symbol of the new freedom of the French people. Bastille Day is celebrated each year much like the Fourth of July in America. Liberation Day, May 8, marks the end of German domination following that country's defeat in World War II.

For More Information

Jackson, Hampden. *A Short History of France from Early Times to 1972.* London, Cambridge University Press, 1974.

Nourissier, François. Translated from French by Adrienne Foulke. *The French.* New York: Alfred A. Knopf. 1968.

Willings, Heather. *A Village of the Cevennes.* Southampton: The Camelot Press Ltd., 1979.

GERMANS
(jur′ mens)

People of Germany who are widely represented in most Central European states.

Population: 77,000,000 (1991 estimate).
Location: Germany, other Central European states.
Language: German.

Geographical Setting

The land of the Germans can be divided into three geographically varied regions. The north German lowlands are flat plains along the Baltic and North seas. Inland these plains rise to rolling hills south of Berlin and to a series of intermediate mountains. In the southeast, the lands rise into the forested foothills of the Alps and to the mountains themselves. Great rivers—the Rhine, Oder, and Danube—begin in the mountains and wind their way through the country. Rich ore deposits of coal and iron border the Rhone Valley in the southwest. The climate is moderate and even throughout the country; the higher elevations in the south provide the same cool conditions as the lowlands farther north. Much of Germany is rich farmland and farming is still an important factor of the economy.

Historical Background

Germans and Romans. The early history of Northern Europe is one of small bands of Germanic and Celtic peoples living along the swampy coastline and isolated in the forests. They first came to the attention of Roman visitors to the area about 101 B.C. The Roman forces were able to defeat some of the larger tribes, such as the Teu-

Germans

Distribution of Germans — Most Dense / Least Dense

tons, and Romans dominated the area, but with little interest, until A.D. 9. At that time, one tribe was able to defeat the Roman army of General Varnius, and from then on, the Germanic tribes were outside the influence of Rome. The tribes evolved into small feudal kingdoms but were again disbanded by the invasion of eastern Huns about 375.

The Germanic duchies. Teutonic princedoms were again loosely united as part of Charlemagne's Holy Roman Empire, but after the death of Charlemagne, German states again began to be established. By A.D. 900, the Germans were organized into five duchies: Bavaria, Franconia, Saxony, Scandia, and Lorraine. Each was ruled by a duke, who reigned supreme even though a king supposedly was the ruler of the entire old empire. In 911 the last of Charlemagne's successors died and eight years later the federation of German duchies chose Henry I, Duke of Saxony, to be king. Henry's army beat back a Danish invasion, then succeeded in stopping frequent Magyar raids from the southeast. From that time until 1024 Germany was governed by Saxon kings. The kingdom extended through what is now Czechoslovakia.

Wars with Italy and the Church. When Henry was succeeded by his son Otto, Germany began a 100-year policy of expansion. Otto sought to gain land from the small kingdom of Italy. Continuous wars with Italy and with the Catholic church rulers consumed successive German rulers at the expense of holding their own government. Over the next centuries, the leadership of Germany reverted to an array of small states. These were ruled by nobles and clergy, and, in addition, a number of free towns were established and formed a Hanseatic League of traders. The nobles chose a king to lead them and the seat of government followed that king wherever he traveled. The German Empire and the old French kingdom met at the Rhine River, with Franks and Celts claiming the west and Germans claiming land east of the Rhine through Poland and Austria. By the time of Frederick II (died 1250) the German section was again an assortment of small independent states.

Catholics and Protestants. In 1437, Frederick III was chosen king and began a long reign of the house of Habsburg (Hapsburg). At some times, the rule of the nobles and the Habsburgs became oppressive to the large number of peasants and, while reforms in the Catholic Church were being demanded by Martin Luther, the peasant unrest grew to rebellion (1524). Martin Luther sided with the nobles in this rebellion of 300,000 peasants—a dispute resolved with victory for the nobles. Soon many of these rulers joined with Martin Luther in a Protestant movement against the church. By 1555, the western prince-states had adopted Protestant Christianity and had declared for freedom of religious choice. However, in the east, the Habsburgs of Austria had held to Catholicism and were determined to restore this religion throughout Germany. By the first decade of the 1600s the states had divided into a Protestant League and a Catholic League. The issue evolved into the Thirty Years' War. An early defeat of the Protestant League weakened German states and resulted in invasion by the Danes and the entry of Sweden into the battles. Although Sweden's King Gustavus Adolphus was defeated in this war, Cardinal

Richelieu, leader of France, supported the Protestants and extended the war for 13 years until the Peace of Westphalia in 1638 ended the struggle. The German states restored Protestantism. The French managed to win over the regions Alsace and Lorraine to Catholicism, and many princedoms claimed by the Habsburgs of Austria and Spain were given independence. By 1785, in order to protect themselves from possible problems with Russia, the princes of Prussia, Saxony, and Hanover formed a League of German Princes.

France and Austria. The united German states were no match for the forces from France, however, and were a target in the expansion of France under Napoleon. France controlled many German states until 1806, when Napoleon relinquished claim to them and the Old German Empire disintegrated. Germans found themselves ostensibly ruled by Austria, with a capital at Frankfurt but without a defending army or treasury. However, the northeast princedom of Germany, Prussia, grew in strength and the ruler of Prussia came to rule all of the German people except those in Austria between 1828 and 1842.

Bismarck. A union of German states was to serve the people for 50 years, with the semi-autonomous states providing support for the central government. Before the middle of the nineteenth century, the leader who was destined to strengthen this central government and make it self-supporting and internationally significant, Otto von Bismarck, had served in two state parliaments (diets)—those of Saxony and Prussia. In 1851 Bismarck became a member of the central German Diet and began a German leadership career that was to transform the union of states into an empire. Bismarck became chancellor of Germany after a war with France in 1871—the day-to-day director of affairs in the reign of William of Prussia who had become Emperor of Germany. Under him, Germans regained Alsace and Lorraine from France, and their country was transformed into an industrialized nation. By 1878 Bismarck's Germany had become a sufficiently powerful nation that it could intervene in the Russian-Turkish War and influence the settlement between the two countries. Bismarck established an Imperial Court, which acted as a supreme court of the land, and developed an Imperial Civil Code. In the 1870s he led a program known as Kulturcampf directed toward reducing the political influence of the pope in Germany. However, in 1888, Emperor William died and Bismarck's influence in German affairs began to wane.

Wilhelm. By 1890, the emperor of Germany was Wilhelm, an erratic ruler who refused to have government decisions made by others. Bismarck resigned in 1890, and Wilhelm became the Kaiser Wilhelm, King of Prussia. He was in command at the time of World War I. In the early 1900s, Wilhelm built his own large army and allied himself with Austro-Hungary and Italy—nations that shared German concerns about the apparent alliance of France, England, and Russia. Wilhelm continued to develop a national unity among the Germans largely through the army, which he exhorted to "shoot down, if need be, your own mothers and fathers, brothers and sisters in order to fulfil your flag oath." Even though Germany had prescribed a constitutional government directed by two houses of parliament, the Reichstag and the Bundesrat, Wilhelm ruled with an iron will. He was described by his own chancellor, Bernhardt von Bulow, as a warlord in peace, an indecisive leader in war, and in defeat, an evader. According to von Bulow, William II (Kaiser Wilhelm) was an open-minded man but one who never would concentrate, with no tact and at times a lack of dignity.

World Wars. Continuous disputes with the French over territories around the Rhine continued through two World Wars. Defeated in

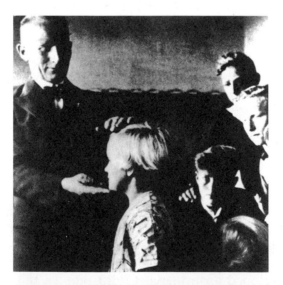

As early as 1934, Nazi instructors were demonstrating the ideal head shape and measurement to assure pure Aryanism. *Courtesy of the Simon Wiesenthal Center.*

1918 after the four-year World War I, Kaiser Wilhelm resigned and retired to isolation in Denmark. The German people immediately began to rebuild their devastated land. By the 1930s, they were on the way to recovery. However, a small group of dissidents, known as the Nazis and led by Adolph Hitler, had come into power. Its goals were to purify Germany by removing people with all but the purest Teutonic blood and to expand German territory throughout Europe. In 1940 Germans under the leadership of Adolph Hitler occupied France, Czechoslovakia, Poland, Austria, and Hungary and acted on the policy of extermination of unwanted peoples that nearly resulted in destroying the Jews and Gypsies of Europe.

Hitler's troops rounded up Jews in Germany and in other countries they occupied. The Jews were forced to wear identifying insignia, to pay exhorbitant taxes, and to give up their lands and property. Systematically, Jews and political prisoners in Western Europe were shipped from Belgium, France, Germany, Greece, Italy, and Holland to forced-labor camps and to prisons. Concentration camps, which held Jews captive without regard for the accepted norms of arrest, appeared in France, Germany, and Austria, as well as in Poland and Czechoslovakia. There were camps built to exterminate the Jews, and

Students were drafted into the Nazi movement. Here young Nazis participate in burning books considered to be undesirable. *Courtesy of the Simon Wiesenthal Center.*

some were shot, drowned, or starved to death. Altogether nearly six million were killed by Nazi command. There was some national resistance. When 11 Jewish refugees who had been deported from Finland were murdered, that country refused to allow any more deportations. Most of Denmark's 7,200 Jews escaped to Sweden in 1943, with the help of Danish sea captains. The refugees joined some 3,000 other European Jews who had fled to Sweden.

When Germany was defeated in World War II, the country was divided into several parts governed by the various countries of the opposing armies. Eventually the Western countries that had opposed the Germans combined their sections into a European-influenced West Germany. This part of Germany was established as a democratic republic in 1949. The territory of Germans in the east was formed into a Russian satellite, and East Germany became a Communist people's republic. For nearly 40 years, distrust among Germans was encouraged by the Soviet Union, on the one hand, and by the West, on the other hand. Both feared a united Germany. Finally, in 1990 a revolution in East Germany deposed the Communist regime there and the leaders sought reunification with West Germany. The two German states agreed to reunite under a two-house parliament and the pattern of free elections that had been developed by

A derisive depiction of Jews in a German periodical before World War II.
Courtesy of the Simon Wiesenthal Center.

BORNESTRASSE SYNAGOGUE, FRANKFURT (BEFORE AND AFTER)

In their zeal to purge all non-Aryans, Nazis systematically destroyed Jewish buildings. *Courtesy of the Simon Wiesenthal Center.*

West Germany. Since then, Germany has worked to balance the economies of an east with a developing industrial sector but firmly entrenched in agriculture and a west with a long-standing industrial sector. The differences between the two partners is reflected in their per-person share of the gross national products—$12,000 in eastern Germany and $20,000 in western Germany.

Culture Today

The German image. The German people have an almost universal reputation for diligent work habits, intelligence, and stubbornness. In reality they are as varied as the land on which they live. They are bound together by a common origin in the early Teutonic tribes and by a language that is part of the same family of languages as English and has been used by the Germans since the earliest Teutonic settlements.

Economy. Today 61 million Germans live in the western former Federal Republic of Germany while 17 million form the former eastern German Democratic Republic. The countries were economically very different, with individuals owning much of the resources of the west, but with 99 percent of the industry and 90 percent of the land

The Berlin Wall, once a barrier between East and West, is now broken. Remnants provide sites for murals and graffiti. *Courtesy of Monica Gyulai.*

Away from Berlin, the separation between East and West Germany was, for more than 40 years, held by guards and fences. *Courtesy of Amy A. Trenkle.*

of East Germany held by the state. West Germany enjoyed greater natural resources and greater industrialization. About 50 percent of German land is useful farmland, but today mechanization has reduced the number of workers in agriculture to 10 percent of the work force. Since 1990, the two Germanies have reunited and are struggling to integrate these two very different economies.

Throughout Germany, workers are known for their industry and precision. This industry and quality has led Germany in its recovery from two disastrous wars, albeit with considerable help from the European Economic Plan (Marshall Plan) instituted by the allied forces after World War II. More than 50,000 precision parts and tools are manufactured in the country.

Today the German economy is the most powerful in Europe. That the currency of the European Community (Common Market) is based on the value of the Deutschmark is an indication of this strength. Germany is also beginning to dominate the economy of an Eastern Europe beginning to be freed from Soviet rule. The position that Germany twice tried to achieve through military action is now being secured by peaceful economic means.

Education. Germans have traditionally given education high respect. Universities such as those at Berlin and Heidelberg were established in the days of small princely states and have been centers of science, philosophy, and literature. At these universities, musical masterpieces were produced for the German cathedrals.

Scientists such as Robert Koch and Nicolaus Copernicus and philosophers such as Immanuel Kant peopled the German universities of the past. Today, education in Germany is compulsory beginning at age six. At the age of 14 students complete an elementary education and have begun secondary school. They then elect or are directed toward either a *volkschule,* to prepare for skilled jobs or a gymnasium, the secondary preparation for the university. Education is compulsory until age 18. There are 19 universities, eight technical schools and 48 music or theology colleges. Competition in the schools is rigorous. Tests for entry into the gymnasium or the university are difficult.

The quality of education in Germany is witnessed by the long period in which Berlin was the intellectual capital of the world, and by the 44 Nobel prize winners who worked in Germany between 1901 and 1944 (11 of these winners were German Jews).

Early German Universities			
Vienna	1365	Leipzig	1409
Heidelberg	1386	Rostock	1419
Cologne	1388	Berlin	1809

Language and literature. The German language of today evolved from an earlier version that was heavily influenced by Latin. The first writings in the language, which, until about 1150, was a form known as Old German, were developed in the eighth century after some German contact with the Roman Empire. Between 1150 and 1500, old German evolved into a blend that was influenced by the French and known as Middle German. But from 1500, a German blend of Moravian and Saxon languages replaced the earlier version. This latest blend has become the common literary language. Its development was encouraged in the early stages by Martin Luther.

Perhaps the most well-known work in the old German was the story of a struggle between father and son, *Heldebrandslied,* written in the ninth century. An earlier work, *Beowulf,* is Germanic, but ascribed to an earlier Anglo-Saxon language. During the early history of the language, a great number of poets arose who created poetry passed from generation to generation orally. Much of this folk literature was lost when Christianity arrived among the Germanic tribes and discouraged the old poems.

Much of the early German writing was religious. When Germany was absorbed into the French Holy Roman Empire, great court epics were added to the literature. However, folk stories, often in poetic form, continued and again became dominant in the fifteenth and sixteenth century. In the 1700s, J. G. Herder set the path for German literature and intellectual development. His work led to a break with the past and to writings that were inseparable from philosophy and science. Such writers as Johann Wolfgang Goethe, Johann Gottlieb Fichte, Heinrich Heine, Thomas Mann, Frederick Nietzsche, and Immanuel Kant wrote of daily life, philosophy, and religion in works that endure today.

During the reign of Adolph Hitler, much new exploration was discouraged in both literature and art. Hitler sponsored events that displayed the types of literature and art his new regime considered degenerate. The suppression of great writing was much the same as that experienced in the Soviet-dominated countries, including East Germany, under Josef Stalin. Stalin prescribed what would be acceptable to the Communist management and called it "social realism." The writing under Hitler and Stalin became limited only to those works that were politically correct.

Music. Beginning with Heinrich Schütz (b. 1585), who is described as the father of German music, German composers have a long history of creating music of worldwide and long-lasting interest. The list of German composers reads almost like a *Who's Who* of classical music: Johann Sebastian Bach, Ludwig van Beethoven, Frans Schumann, Richard Wagner, Franz Schubert, Felix Mendelssohn (a German Jew), and, more recently, Richard Strauss and Arnold Schönberg. These composers created musical dramas, massive religious works, and lyrical works that set the standards for classical music today.

Science. Adopting the spirit of investigation of France and England, the German Gottfried Wilhelm von Leibnitz founded the Berlin Academy in 1700. By the end of the eighteenth century, Germany had become an important contributor to philosophy and science. Justus Liebig established a chemical laboratory in the 1800s from which grew a great array of famous chemists and German interest in chemisty that has helped to make Germany a great industrial power.

A. G. Werner, working at Freiberg, developed the idea of continental creation that led to the present concepts of continental drift and plate tectonics. Rudolph Virchow established a base for the science of bacteriology and was followed by Robert Koch's discovery of the bacillus causing tuberculosis. During World War II, Werner von Braun and his colleagues developed rocketry, making Germany the first nation to have rocket weapons.

Clothing, food, and shelter. After World War II, West Germany became a very industrial nation. More and more people moved from farm to cities in search of jobs in the factories. These people have adopted Western dress and music. Only at festivals and as an occasional symbol of a trade or craft are the traditional costumes seen today. For example, a journeyman carpenter might still be seen wearing a felt hat, corduroy suit with pearl buttons, bell-bottom trousers and a red kerchief. The older costumes of the Germans reflect their varied beginnings and are regional. In the Bavarian section, near the Alps, men still wear the traditional plumed hat and vest. In Triberg, both men and women once wore stovepipe hats. In another region, old costumes might feature flower-laden hats and ornate coats. Today

Germany is a country of large industrial cities and old, well-kept smaller towns and villages such as this one in the Black Forest. *Courtesy of W. Paul Fischer.*

these costumes are seen mostly during celebrations. Old festivals are important in Germany. One festival, Rosemontag, is celebrated in August with fireworks. On such occasions the men might also be seen in the traditional lederhosen, short leather pants held up by suspenders with a decorated band across the chest.

The farmers of Germany grow in greatest quantity potatoes, wheat, oats, and sugar beets, along with other vegetables. From the farm produce, Germans bake coarse bread and create such dishes as sauerkraut. Bread, potatoes, and sauerkraut are staple foods in Germany. The main meal is eaten at noon and often features veal or pork. A light supper might consist of bread, cheese, and sausage.

Throughout Europe, the old castles still stand. This is Neuschwanstein Castle in Germany. *Courtesy of Amy A. Trenkle.*

Recreation. Germans favor traditional forms of entertainment—listening to the classical music of masters such as Richard Wagner or sitting in small ale houses to share drinks of strong beer and stories of the past. As in other Western countries, music has formed one cultural division between young and old. German youth, even those raised in the more guarded East Germany, often establish their own cultural identities through the rock music disdained by their elders.

Many German folk stories are ancient tales of adventure, such as "die Lorelei," the story of the singer who tempted travelers along the Rhine, drawing them into the rocks. Much of German folklore and other literature has spread throughout the world. Examples are the poems by Johann Wolfgang Goethe, plays by Bertolt Brecht, novels by Hermann Hesse, and classic folk stories such as the "Bremen Town Musicians."

Religion. Religious differences have characterized the German people and have resulted in complete religious freedom in west Germany today. Fifty-one percent of the people are Protestant. Most practice a form of Lutheranism—the Protestant Reformation church created by the German religious leader Martin Luther. Forty-five percent are Catholic. The religious inclination of the people persisted in East Germany despite Communist attempts to discourage it. Still, fewer

German people work and play hard. Many enjoy intellectual challenges. These men are playing chess with large pieces on a checkerboard set in a town park. *Courtesy of W. Paul Fischer.*

than half the people of the former East Germany espouse any religion. Of those who do claim a religious affiliation, about seven percent are Catholic and 35 percent are Protestant. Most Protestants in Germany belong to the *Evangelishce Kirche in Deutchland.*

Holidays. Most of the holidays celebrated in Germany are related to the Christian religion that is dominant in the country. However, these holidays are not universally celebrated. Christmas, a November 18 Day of Prayer and Repentance, Good Friday, and Easter are recognized throughout the country, but other religious holidays—Epiphany, Assumption Day, Corpus Christi, and All Saints' Day—are celebrated in some *länder* (states or provinces) and not in others. A new national holiday, Day of Unity, is celebrated throughout Germany on October 3.

Government. Until 1990, Germans were divided politically under two different government structures with different philosophies. West Germany was governed by a president elected for five years by a Federal Assembly. Members of the assembly represent the Bundestag, the lower of the two houses of the legislature. The upper house of the bicameral legislature was the Bundesrat. The Bundestag had 499 members while the Bundesrat had 49. Several political parties vie for seats in parliament; the dominant parties are the Christian Democrats and the Social Democrats.

East Germany, on the other hand, had one party and a single legislative group, the Volkskammer. As a result, an election in East Germany might show that 99 percent of the people supported representatives of the Communist party. The symbol of political division in the country was the Berlin Wall, which had been erected to prevent Eastern and Western Germans from visiting or moving to the other side.

In 1990, the two Germanies united and adopted the West German pattern of government, with the upper house of parliament, the Bundesrat, made up of 68 members who are chosen according to the populations of 16 länder (states). Each state determines the terms of office and times of election of new representatives to the Bundesrat. The lower house of parliament, the Bundestag, now consists of 662 members elected by the people of Germany for four-year terms. This lower house chooses a Federal Chancellor to lead the government. In the new Germany, each state has considerable freedom to rule and is totally responsible for education, policing, and environmental protection.

German qualities, real and imagined. The Germans have been described as stubborn, dogmatic, tenacious, proud, given to precision in work and speech, avidly religious, and totally practical. Some of these qualities, if they can be said to be true of many or most Germans, place them in direct contrast with even their near relatives, the Austrians. Instead of precision, for example, one author describes what might be a national slogan for the Austrians, "Punctuality is a waste of time" (Bailey, p. 373).

The zeal for precision in work among Germans is suggested by the recoveries made in technical industries after the two disastrous wars. And their practicality can be illustrated by an interview with Albert Speer, Hitler's minister of armaments, following his 20 years of imprisonment for war crimes. Asked why a man of his cultural background and good taste could have fallen in with Hitler, Speer responded, "I was bribed." Asked again how a man of his upbringing and wealth could have been bribed, Speer's answer was "I was 28 years old, a struggling young architect; my father had money, I hadn't. I was given the biggest architectural commissions in recorded history. That is how I was bribed."

How could a nation just recovering from one great defeat convince itself that it was the greatest people on earth and rally to the call *Deutchland uber alles*, or "Germany above all"? The answer may lie in the amazing successes in all aspects of industry and scholarliness. Or the Germans may have been forced to this reaction by comments such as that of Georges Clemenceau after World War I, a comment known to all German school people: "There are 20 million too many Germans."

For More Information

Gerber, Margy, editor. *Studies in GDR Culture and Society.* Lanham, Maryland: University Press of America, 1988.

Kohn, Hans. *The Mind of Germany: The Education of a Nation.* New York: Charles Scribner's Sons, 1960.

Johann, Ernest, Berthold Spangenberg, and Hans Dollinger. *German Cultural History from 1860 to the Present Day.* Munich: Nymphenburger Verlagsbuchhandlung, 1983.

GREEKS
(greeks)

Long-time residents of the country of Greece and their descendants.

Population: 10,200,000 (1989 estimate).
Location: Greece.
Language: Greek.

Geographical Setting

Greece is composed of a peninsula and many islands with few rivers and little rainfall. More than half the region is mountainous, with Mt. Olympus in the southeast being the highest point. The many islands are mountaintops protruding from a land sunken under the sea millions of years ago. Most of Greece is, therefore, so rocky that an old legend ascribes its creation to a god throwing away rocks after having created the rest of the world. The randomly tossed rocks, according to Greek legend, resulted in a rocky mainland surrounded by more than 600 islands.

Surrounded by the Aegean Sea, the Mediterranean Sea, the Ionian Sea, and the Adriatic Sea, no part of Greece is far from water. There are no large flowing rivers in this rugged land, but the Greek way of life has long been tied to sailing. Greek cities began as shipbuilding and trading centers growing up around the many natural harbors. Shipping, along with fishing and farming, is still a major occupation.

Historical Background

Origins. In the centuries before 2000 B.C. Greece was inhabited by small bands of peoples isolated from each other by the rugged, rocky

Greeks

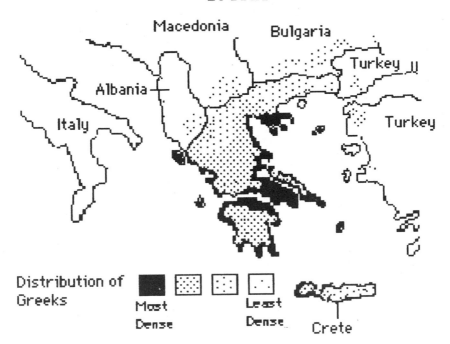

Distribution of Greeks

Most Dense — Least Dense — Crete

terrain and by the ocean, which separated the islands on which the people lived. By 2000 B.C., however, the Greeks had organized into a number of city-states, mostly serving as centers for trade with eastern monarchs. The achievements of the city-state societies can still be seen in the magnificence of ancient structures in Athens and on the island of Crete. It was on this island that Greek society began, first as the Minoan civilization.

Minoan civilization. The Minoan Empire was a hub of trading and shipbuilding for the Mediterranean area. Before 1400 B.C., the Minoans had developed skills in shipbuilding, construction of great stone buildings, and pottery, and they had developed a written language. They followed a well-organized religion under which they worshiped a Mother Goddess. About 1400 B.C. this culture disappeared, but the Minoan influence continued on the mainland of Greece until 1100 B.C.

Northern invaders. About 1100 B.C. invaders from the north swept across the Greek peninsula and Crete. The old centers of society, Tuyus and Mycenae, were destroyed and, for a time, the Greek writ-

A wall carving from the Temple of Apollo in Greece. *From the Library of Congress.*

ten language disappeared. Eventually the western mainland cities of Athens and Sparta became leaders in Greek society and learning. By the eighth century B.C. the cities had developed strong governments and had organized armies. Each city-state was separated into a military section (the acropolis) and a civilian section (the polis). Although large for their time, the city-states were small enough to allow for popular participation in government. In the early days of these city-states, women enjoyed equality with men in government, sports, art, and literature. The practice of democracy had been developed, a form of government these early Greeks would bequeath to peoples of the future.

About 600 B.C. Greek thought was reflected in the works of a large number of philosophers. Thales, Anaxagoras, Pythagoras, Solon, and many other learned Greeks taught and wrote about ideas that were to dominate world of thought for more than 2,000 years.

Greeks and Persians. By the sixth century B.C., Persians had conquered much of the east and had begun to move south along the Danube. Their domination extended to major Greek cities and helped to spread the Greek arts and ideas. In 499 B.C., the Persians attempted to control Greece, but people from Athens, Eretria, and Miletus defeated the invaders and succeeded in burning the Persian capital. Six years later, Persians attempted to punish the Greeks, but a great storm

The Temple of Diana is part of the Acropolis near Athens, Greece.
Courtesy of Alisa Rabin.

destroyed much of their fleet and left the Greek culture intact. Again the Persians grouped for attack and destroyed many Greek states. But Athenians under General Militiades gathered at the Battle of Marathon and forced the Persians to withdraw. Again, in 480 B.C., the Persians invaded. This time resistance came from Sparta until a traitor led the Persians to surround the Greeks and destroy the whole Spartan army. Finally, Persian persistence resulted in unification of the Greek states. Led by Athens, Greek armies and navies destroyed the Persians in 454 B.C. and Persia withdrew from Europe.

Philosophers. Beginning with the birth of Pericles in 429 B.C., Athens led Greeks into a golden age of architecture, philosophy, art, literature, and drama. Vast theaters were built, the largest of them in Athens. Audiences crowded into the theaters to watch tragedies or comedies by writers such as Sophocles and Aristophanes. Athens became the "school of Greece" and of the Western world. The philosophers Socrates, Plato, and Aristotle put forth ideas that would revolutionize the world of thought: Plato gave ideas a place among real things, and Aristotle presented a view of nature that was to dominate the Western world for nearly 2,000 years. Pottery, often painted in orange and black, was beautifully decorated with scenes from everyday life.

The period from 350–333 B.C. saw Alexander the Great extend Greek culture and Greek influence around the Mediterranean. To be an orator was regarded as a high accomplishment among the Greeks of this time. One of their greatest orators, Demosthenes, gave speeches urging the Greeks to unite against their common enemies— this at a time when the city-states were weakening and subdividing into districts.

Romans. In the second century B.C., Romans conquered the Greek states, passing heavy taxes even on the cities that were not completely occupied. The defiant Greeks were totally controlled from Rome by 127 B.C. In the first century, Saul of Tarsus brought Christianity to Greece and the ancient religion of Zeus and Olympus began to disappear.

Byzantine. About A.D. 330 the government in Rome faded, and a new capital of part of the Roman Empire was founded in Constantinople under Emperor Constantine. Religious differences between peoples of the empire resulted in disputes throughout the Mediterranean area. In 394, Emperor Theodorius abolished the Olympic Games (originally dedicated to the Greek god Zeus) as a move to destroy the old religion. In his name, Christian fanatics burned many old records and killed Hypatia, one of the leading Greek philosophers.

Huns and Goths. In the next century, Greece was to be split by Huns and Goths who overran the western part of the country. In 476, Germans invaded Italy and the Roman Empire fell. Now the Byzantine government from Constantinople took the opportunity to gain control of all the Mediterranean shoreline from Italy to Egypt and of the land around the Black Sea.

Crusades. The great empire of Constantinople began to crumble when Frankish and Venetian crusaders from Central Europe united in a war on the capital city. While not totally successful, the two allies did succeed in dominating Greece and operating it as a feudal state under a number of dukes and counts. By the sixteenth century, Greece was divided among Venetians, Franks, Catalans, and Germans.

The Ottomans. In the 1400s Turks began to advance into the area to spread the Islamic religion. By the end of the fifteenth century most of Greece had fallen to the Turks. As the Turks began trade with Europe, they found some of the Greeks to be able ambassadors. These aristocratic couriers spread a revival of the Greek culture throughout Greece and Europe.

Although most Greeks resented Turkish rule and rebellions were frequent, Turkey remained in control until 1821. Egyptian forces took some of the Greek land in 1825. Then in 1827 Turks and Egyptians joined forces to battle Russia, England, and France. In the Battle of Navarius Bay the Turk-Egyptian fleet was destroyed. In 1830, the three powers agreed to establish a Greek monarchy under their protection. King Otho, a prince of Bavaria, became the first king of Greece in 1833. Otho was deposed in 1862, and in 1863 power was given to the son of King Christian of Denmark, who became King George I.

England acquired the island of Cyprus in 1878. At the same time, the island of Crete became the focus of Turkish-Greek disputes. Despite these interventions, Greek economy developed steadily until World War I. The Balkan wars against Turkey in 1912 and 1913 resulted in almost all of the ancient Greek land being reunited under Greek rule.

World War I. In World War I Greece remained neutral until 1917 when the Greeks joined Allied forces. Following the war new territorial demands were made by Turkey. Some of these Turkish demands were honored at the Lausanne Conference of 1923. The regions of Thrace and Eolerne were ceded to Turkey. Turks and Greeks traded great populations to adjust to the new boundaries. In 1935, by a 97 percent vote, the Greek people agreed to reinstall the monarchy. King George II returned to Greece, but real power was wielded by General John Mataxes. Mataxes' rule was fascistic but dedicated to Greek independence. Under his guidance, the Greeks refused to be intimidated into joining Germany and Italy in World War II. In 1940 Italy invaded Greece but was driven back into Albania. The actions of Italy and Germany and the Greek resistance resulted in severe damage to Greece and disruption of the Greek economy. Damage was increased when British forces occupied the land. In the process of occupation, an edict by British General Scobio resulted in a battle for Athens in which 11,000 people were killed.

Civil war. After conflict with foreign nations had subsided, Greece found itself on the edge of civil war. This war erupted in 1947 and lasted through much of 1949. In this struggle, the Communist forces were defeated and the monarchy restored under King Konstantinos. Once again Greece was divided as Communist forces set up government in northern Greece while the south remained under the rule of the monarchy. By 1967, Greek unity had been restored by the army colonel Georgios Papadopoulos, who became prime minister in that year, then regent in 1972. Finally, in 1973, King Paul abdicated and Papadopoulos became the first president of a new republic.

The republic has been plagued with difficulties inside the country and from without. Disagreements with Turkey over petroleum prospecting in the Aegean Sea and the status of the island republic of Cyprus have periodically reoccurred. Not until 1985 did Greece and Albania reopen the borders that had been closed since 1940, and not until 1988 did the two countries agree to promote trade across the border. More recently (1989), Greeks and Albanians disagreed over repatriation of Albanians who had sought sanctuary in Greece and over treatment of the 300,000 Greeks in Albania. Until 1975, Greece was governed by an oppressive military force. A 1975 constitution restored parliamentary government under a president and single-house parliament, but a 1986 legislation relieved the president of most of his executive responsibilities. Greece is directed by a 300-person parliament and a prime minister. In 1981, Greece joined the European Community.

Mix of peoples. Throughout all this turbulent history, Greeks have affected and been affected by the people who have made demands on their land. The first inhabitants, Vlacks, fled north and west into Romania; the small number remaining in their homeland represent the original Greeks. Throughout the years they were joined by other peoples—Romans, Huns, Goths, Franks, Turks—and merged with them to form a new people. Today's Greek society results from the mixing of the various cultures throughout the country's history.

Culture Today

Economy. Greek people are predominantly farmers, herders, and sailors. They grow wheat, corn, potatoes, sugar beets, and maize and raise a variety of livestock. About one-fifth of the population works in agriculture. In recent years, industrialization has placed nearly half the work force into offices and factories. However, many of the industries are based on agriculture. The Greeks manufacture margarine, olive oil, yarns, linen, and other fabrics. The growth of their industries

An underground site of an ancient city near Athens attracts tourists in the twentieth century. *Courtesy of Alisa Rabin.*

has caused many Greeks to move to the cities. One-fifth of all Greeks live in the major city of Athens. Today Greece has more than 600 trading ships with 20,000 seamen.

Village life. Nearly one-half of the Greek people live in villages of fewer than 1,000 citizens. Most earn their living by farming or fishing. Farmers on the islands raise olives and press them for oil or preserve them in vinegar or brine. Mainland farmers, too, raise olives, but also wheat, rice, fruits, vegetables, and, in the north, tobacco, a major Greek cash crop. Much of the farming is done without mechanization. Greek farms are often smaller than 10 acres and are tilled by horse- or donkey-drawn plows, and the harvest gathered by hand and wagon.

Few villages in Greece are more than 60 miles from the sea. Many seacoast villages have harbors filled with small boats that are used for fishing or for traveling among the many islands.

Men mostly farm and fish. Women of the village take care of the house, which is built of stone or brick and flat-roofed. The houses often lack running water or central heating. Heat is provided by a wood stove that is also used for cooking. In many villages, water is available from a village spring or well, and women carry water from this source in large earthenware pots.

Men and young people of many villages also tend sheep and goats, moving them higher or lower in the rocky hills around the village with the seasons. The wool from the sheep is transformed by some village women into colorful cloth and bright carpets and wall-hangings.

Villages are built around a square surrounded by shops. There is almost always one or more coffee shops on the square in which the village men gather after work to drink strong, Turkish coffee, smoke cigarettes or hookahs (water pipes), and discuss the events of the day.

Food, clothing, and shelter. Greek ships travel throughout the world, bringing ideas from other countries to Greece, so it is not surprising that Western-style clothing has replaced the traditional peasant clothing. The old costumes of tight white pants bound at the knee and worn under a tunic and perhaps a vest can be seen only in remote villages or in the colorful shows and festivals that attract tourists to Greece. In the mountains, this costume is still worn by sheepherders, and in the city, elite military guards still dress in this fashion.

Foods have been less subject to change. Traditional foods are still the most popular in Greece. The most common meat is lamb, often ground and wrapped in vine leaves (*dolmathes*) or prepared in layers with eggplant (*moussaka*). The fishing industry provides a variety of

A marketplace in Athens. *Courtesy of Alisa Rabin.*

seafood. The main dishes are commonly cooked in olive oil. Popular Greek cheese (feta) is made from goat's or sheep's milk.

As among peoples in most parts of the world, Greeks have migrated to the cities in recent years. Here they live in government—supported apartments or in small homes built in the suburbs of the great old cities. Still, about half the population live in outlying areas in villages of a few thousand people.

Art. Greek interest in art is illustrated by the early innovations in architecture. They built large buildings of marble with characteristic columns supporting the roofs. Among the most reknowned examples is the Parthenon of Athens, which was dedicated to Athena, the goddess of wisdom. Little remains of Greek painting of the past. However, the beautiful figures and colors of ancient Greek pottery attest to great skill in the graphic arts. Statues of the gods and ancient Greek heroes, reliefs carved on temples, tombs and sacred walls also illustrate the great artistic skill of Greek craftspeople. A great theater stood in ancient Athens, capable of seating 17,000 people to watch dramatic productions that sometimes lasted for as long as three days. While Greeks pride themselves on preserving the ancient arts, Greek accomplishments in the arts have continued to the present. On stage and screen, Greeks such as opera singer Maria Callas and movie director Elia Kazan carry on their heritage in theater and live performance.

Religion. Ancient religious beliefs have given way to Christianity. Almost 97 percent of today's Greeks are participants in the Holy Eastern Orthodox Church. The pre-Christian religion is kept alive in literature through a rich legacy of mythology, featuring heroes such as Apollo, god of the sun. However, the deep roots of Christianity seen in the gospel of St. Luke, which was originally written in the Greek language, is manifested in an array of Greek celebrations.

Holidays. Greeks usually do not celebrate their own birthdays. Rather each Greek person celebrates the birthday of his or her patron saint. A man named John, for example, would celebrate St. John's day. The Greek New Year is dedicated to St. Basil and is celebrated with gifts and parties as well as symbols of the ship that brought St. Basil to Greece, red and blue paper ships carried by the children. The celebration for St. Basil is more festive than Christmas in Greece. January 6, the day claimed to be the baptismal day for Christ, is celebrated with special religious ceremonies. Other holidays recognize St. John and Mary.

Literature. Pre-Christian literature includes the *Iliad* and the *Odyssey*, epic poems which tell of the great sea adventures of the early Greeks and are thought to have been written by Homer. Today these classics have been joined by the poems and novels of twentieth-century Greek writers such as George Seferis, although, for the most part, modern Greek literature does not reach the heights of the older writings.

Education. Greeks have always respected learning. However, as a result of poverty and frequent disputes over the last century, surveys of 1950 showed that 74 percent of the Greeks were illiterate. Today that figure is being changed by an education revival. Education is compulsory from ages six to 15. By 1986 nearly 98 percent of the students in this age range were in school. More than 70 percent of the young people continue on to secondary school. Illiteracy has been reduced to 10 percent.

Women. The traditions of the people have changed in other ways. The Greek gods and the Greek games, as well as the records of Greek writers and philosophers, reveal that the early Greeks held women to be equal to men in every endeavor—an attitude lost in history. Greek life today is a very male-centered society.

For More Information

Harrison, John and Shirley Harrison. *Greece.* New York: Rand McNally, 1981.

Mehling, Franz N., editor. *Greece: A Phaidon Cultural Guide.* Englewood Cliffs, New Jersey: Prentice-Hall, 1985.

Roux, Jeanne and George Roux. *Greece.* New York: Oxford University Press, 1965.

Wallbank, T. Walter, Alastair M. Taylor, and Nels M. Bailkey. *Civilization Past and Present*, Volume One. Chicago: Scott, Foresman and Company, 1965.

ICELANDERS
(ice' lan ders)

People of Iceland, who came originally from Norway, Sweden, and Denmark.

Population: 252,000 (1989 estimate).
Location: Iceland, an island in the North Atlantic just below the Arctic Circle.
Language: Icelandic.

Geographical Setting

Iceland is an island country in the north Atlantic Ocean about 200 miles east of Greenland and about 650 miles west of Norway. The island lies along the Mid-Atlantic Ridge, a line of geological change that includes active volcanoes. The island of Surtsey, just off the coast of mainland Iceland, was formed by volcanic eruptions between 1963 and 1967. Since the 1970s, volcanic activity has been plentiful, even destroying some towns and homes in Iceland. A total of 30 volcanoes have erupted on the island since it was settled in the ninth century A.D. Most Icelanders live in the urban area around the capital, Reykjavik, on the southwest coast. Part of the Gulf Stream flows around the southern and western coasts, warming the lowlands and keeping ports free of ice. The average high temperature in Reykjavik is 57 degrees Fahrenheit in July and 35 degrees in January. The lowland along the coast is the only place where Icelanders can grow crops or raise livestock.

Most of the rest of the country is barren plateau with an average altitude of about 2,000 feet above sea level. The country has more hot springs and sulfur stream areas than any other country. The geological activity includes some geysers that spout streams of water

Icelanders

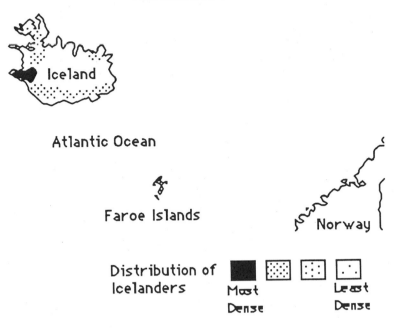

Atlantic Ocean

Faroe Islands

Norway

Distribution of Icelanders

Most Dense — Least Dense

into the air. In this land of geological variety, glaciers cover between one-eighth and one-quarter of the land.

Historical Background

Origin. At the end of the eighth century A.D., Celts visited Iceland and gave the island its name. But the history of the Icelanders begins at the time immigrants from Norway and the British Isles began to settle in Iceland about 874. Stories written a few centuries later identified the original settlers as Ingolfur Arnarson and his wife, Hallveig Frodadottir. They were followed by people from Norway, Scotland, and Ireland—all speaking the same language, the Old Norse of Scandinavia. Through years of relative isolation in their new home, that language evolved into today's Icelandic.

At that time, Norway was governed by a tyrannical king, Harald Haarfagr. To escape his reign, migration to Iceland was heavy, increasing the population to nearly 25,000 within the next 60 years. The large migration soon resulted in new settlements, and the settlers gathered periodically in a *Thing* to discuss their own affairs and dealings with the other groups. About 930 some Icelanders sent a delegate to Denmark to study government and develop a code of laws. Out of this need for collective government and the report of the delegate grew the Althing, the world's first parliament. Part of the Althing served also as a court in which to hear the code of laws—a code that was passed from person to person orally.

At the end of the tenth century, King Olaf I Tryggavason of Norway forced Icelanders to accept Christianity. While the Althing continued to meet and deliberate, Christian officials began to take an active part in the politics of the island.

Golden Age of Literature. In the 1100s and 1200s, much of the country's folklore and history was put into literature. The most famous collector and documenter of Icelandic history during that period was Snorri Sturleson. A poet as well as a historian and one of the strongest leaders of the Icelanders, he put into writing both sagas (tales of heroes) and eddas (stories of gods and heroes).

However, while a literate Iceland was creating its own culture, the government was finding difficult times. To settle a war with Norway, the Althing agreed in 1264 to accept the rule of the Norwegian king. Even so, Iceland was ruled separately from Norway and Icelanders continued to have a measure of independence. Under Norway, the country began a transformation into a trading nation, but trade by the Icelanders was severely controlled. Shortly, however, both Norwegians and Icelanders came under the rule of Denmark (1280).

In the early fourteenth century Norwegian ships began to visit Iceland to trade for the fish that were abundant in Icelandic waters. Through English merchants doing business in Bergen, Norway soon found out about the new food supply and began sailing to Iceland to trade for the fish directly. This trade made Iceland relatively wealthy. Norway and Denmark tried to stop the direct trade with the British. Lacking sufficient naval power, Denmark lost the battle of the seas. The struggle for trade with Iceland continued for many years. When a Danish governor was killed by the English in 1468, a five-year war erupted. Still Icelanders continued to prosper with their fishing industry, though their prosperity was interrupted in the early 1400s by volcanic activity and by the Bubonic Plague, which killed nearly two-thirds of the Icelanders.

Reformation and Danish power. The Lutheran Reformation, which changed the church in Denmark, came to Iceland in 1540, and at first met with great resistance. But after the capture of one Icelandic bishop and the execution of another one, the Reformation swept the island. By 1550, the Lutheran Church was firmly in place. After the Reformation, the Danish royal treasury took over lands owned by the monasteries in Iceland. The Danes tried to get more power over the island by throwing out German traders and substituting Danish merchants. Until this time, Icelanders had lived in small villages or tribal communities. But as the Danes created a bureaucracy to run the country, they centered it in Reykjavik. By 1800, this thriving town had about 300 residents.

Struggle for independence. The Danish rulers abolished the Althing in 1800. But in the 1830s, the Danish government relented and allowed representatives from Iceland to take part in an assembly of the whole Danish kingdom. The Icelanders opposed this arrangement and demanded the return of the Althing. This governing body was restored in 1843 but still under the control of the Danes. Not until 1904 was Iceland given a measure of home rule. Even with this limited independence, life began to change. Motors were installed in fishing boats, a telephone cable connected Iceland and Europe, and the University of Iceland was established in Reykjavik. Then, in 1915, women were granted the right to vote.

After World War I, Iceland became a separate state, but still under the Danish crown. The country was bound to Denmark in trade and foreign policy. However, during World War II Denmark was invaded by the Germans. The British took this opportunity to occupy Iceland and that country served as a military base for the Allies. Sixty thousand United States troops were stationed on the island, many at an air base near Reykjavik. This brought prosperity and temporary economic growth to the island. Toward the end of the war, on June 17, 1944, Iceland formally declared its independence.

Economic growth. Since the country became independent, the fishing-based economy has grown and with it the population. The number of Icelanders has doubled since the beginning of World War II. Technological changes keep the fishing industry expanding and the standard of living high, though most workers put in long hours at their jobs and many women have joined the work force. To preserve the prosperous fishing industry, Iceland has periodically expanded the waters it claims for its own. In 1991, after some dispute with

British fishermen, both countries agreed to respect a limit that allows Iceland control over the fishing within 200 miles of its border.

In 1949, Iceland joined the North Atlantic Treaty Organization (NATO) amid demonstrations against military alliances. Although the country has no army of its own, it was allowed into the military pact because of its strategic location. American forces have been stationed on the island since 1951.

Culture Today

A fishing country. The life of Icelanders is dominated by its geography: harsh climate, poor soil, and abundant fish in the surrounding ocean. Strong-willed Icelanders have learned to survive amidst snow, ice, wind, and volcanoes, and have even learned to harness the underground heat for their own purposes. About one-fifth of the work force is directly involved in the fishing industry, either working on boats or in fish-processing plants near shore. The fishermen work on large trawlers that drag nets along the bottom of the ocean, or in smaller boats using long lines that can stretch to 10 miles in length and hold as many as 20,000 hooks. Cod and capelin make up about two-thirds of the catch. It is difficult work, and because of its treacherous nature, a National Lifesaving Association makes daily radio checks of all ships at sea.

Icelandic names. Icelanders have no family names. Some names are so common that the telephone directory lists occupations as well as names and addresses in order to make identification easier. Icelanders use a first name, such as Gudni or Inga, and take as a last name the father's name, to which is added -*son* for boys and -*dóttir* for girls. Thus if Gudni and Inga's father's name was Asgeir, their names would become Gudni Asgeirsson and Inga Asgeirsdóttir. Women do not change their names when they get married, and Icelanders are properly addressed by their first names.

Food, clothing, and shelter. Lamb and fish are very popular foods in Iceland. Even hot dogs are made of lamb instead of beef or pork. Blood sausage and boiled sheep's head are considered delicacies. Dried or salted haddock and cod are staple foods.

During the winter, it is dark for long periods of time and Icelanders spend much time indoors. Houses were once built of turf and stone, but now reinforced concrete is preferred because of its durability during storms and earthquakes. Most of the Icelanders live in towns and villages—more than a third of them in Reykjavik. Natural hot water is piped into every town and village from local hot springs and serves as the heat source for the homes. Icelanders live like most Europeans, with almost all of the homes furnished with television sets, refrigerators, electric stoves, and other appliances.

Much of this comfort is part of a recent transformation in society, tied to location and technology. As recently as 1950, many more Icelanders lived on farms, cooked on coal stoves, and milked their cows by hand. Today, even farms are automated.

The change has brought European-style clothing to Iceland. Only on holidays do women wear the traditional black dress embroidered with gold or silver threads, or long, embroidered skirts, with blouses and an embroidered bodice. The men of Iceland have traditionally dressed in the heavy coats, trousers, and vests of seamen.

Folklore. Early in their life in Iceland, Norwegian Icelanders resumed the art of saga-telling in poetic form that had begun in Norway. Their work was so popular that poets from Iceland were popular visitors to Norway, Sweden, and Denmark by the tenth century. Snorri Sturleson, tribal leader, poet, and historian, recorded some of Iceland's customs and folk tales in the 1100s along with some of the rules of Icelandic grammar. For centuries afterward, writers concentrated on retelling the great sagas in Snorri's Edda and an earlier poetical edda. These accounts begin with stories of the ancient gods and goddesses, who were believed to have been related to the Swedish King Gylfi, and go on to tell about the great kings of Norway. The legends are filled with sagas of past glories and of *Huldufolk*, the unwashed children of Eve. According to Icelanders, God visited Eve in the Garden of Eden while she was washing her children. She presented just the bathed children, pretending they were all she had. This angered God, who decreed that the hidden children would remain hidden forever. These children are said to travel unnoticed everywhere bringing cheer, mischief, and even evil to those near them. A recent University of Iceland study found that 55 percent of the country's residents believe Huldufolk exist.

Literature, art, and music. By the tenth century, Icelanders had established a system of storytelling. Bards traveled from village to village recounting sagas and accounts of mythological characters. When, after a long time, the traveling bards disappeared, Icelanders substituted family nights, during which members of the family would repeat stories or read them aloud. Thus, Icelanders developed a love of the old sagas and of books. The literary tradition of the sagas underwent a revival in the nineteenth century, and many of the oldest tales were rewritten and elaborated. Almost all Iceland writers used their national setting, and a few have become internationally known. One of these, Halldor Laxness, won the Nobel Prize for Literature in 1955.

Part of the family night tradition was given over to folk dancing. The interest in music and dance has grown to support opera and classical music production in the National Theater. In Reykjavik, there are two professional theater companies, a ballet company, a symphony orchestra, an opera, and several art galleries, bookstores, cinemas, and museums.

Folk traditions remain strong in art, in part because it is a hobby that can produce extra income. Wool of all sorts is used to create clothing decorated with silver thread. Much early folk art is preserved in the Icelandic National Museum. Works of stone sculpture are exhibited in the Einar Jónsson Museum in Reykjavik. Einar Jónsson was one of Iceland's internationally recognized artists in the first half of the twentieth century, crafting stone sculptures that stand in many buildings and parks throughout the world—for example, in Fairmont Park in Philadelphia. The best known of Icelandic painters is Johannes Kjarval. He and most painters of Iceland portray landscapes and capture popular Icelandic activities such as fishing and skiing on canvas.

Education. Along with their interest in literature and art, Icelanders enjoy one of the highest literacy rates in the world. Children from seven to 15 are required to attend school, except in isolated areas. Even in these areas, teachers travel from farm to farm, staying for several weeks with each group of children. Others from rural areas ride buses to school or are sent to boarding school. After the mandatory schooling, youths are able to choose whether or not to attend a grammar school, a combination of high school and the first two years of American colleges. Successful completion of the grammar school leads to the University of Reykjavik. Other students go on from the primary schooling to vocational training schools and commercial colleges.

Government. With the world's oldest parliament, the Althing, Iceland is a republic. A president is the head of state but selects a prime minister who directs the day-to-day activities of the state and chooses a cabinet. The current president, Vigdís Finnbogadóttir, was elected to a third four-year term in 1988 with nearly 93 percent of the vote. Unopposed in 1984, she had won that election without a vote.

The Althing is made up of 63 members, whose first task when elected is to choose among themselves 21 members to serve in an Upper House and 42 to form a Lower House. In Iceland, when a proposal is approved by the Althing, it is submitted to the president. If the president disapproves, the proposal must be put to a vote of the people.

Welfare, education, health, road maintenance, and law enforcement are the responsibilities of local governments—provinces, districts, and municipalities. The towns are directed by councils elected for four-year terms.

Economy. In addition to fishing, Icelanders are likely to work in agriculture, manufacturing, or service industries. Agriculture is restricted to the lowlands (about one percent of the land), where about 5,000 farms produce sheep for wool, meat, and skins, cattle for dairy products, and hay. In the long hours of summer farmers grow great quantities of hay to feed their livestock in other seasons. Since the 1930s, farmers have also grown a wide variety of crops in greenhouses, which can be heated naturally using heat from the many hot springs.

Publishing and services are important business for Icelanders. Iceland prints more books per resident than any other country, and Icelandair is an important international carrier, bringing tourists to Iceland and operating as one of the least expensive of the transatlantic airlines.

Women play a large role in Icelandic economy, as was shown by a 1975 strike of women workers that shut down much of the country's industry. Banks closed and communications were snarled. The success of this strike is remembered among Icelanders. In 1985, a one-day anniversary strike kept this memory alive. On that day, even President Vigdís Finnbogadóttir stayed home.

Recreation. Icelanders love water sports, especially swimming. People swim throughout the year, indoors and outdoors as well in pools that are warmed by hot springs. Glima, a form of wrestling is nearly the national sport. A form of pony treking is very popular, as are other sports—basketball, handball, skiing, and soccer. Chess is a national passion.

Religion. Under the constitution of Iceland, there is complete freedom of religion. However, more than 95 percent of all Icelanders belong to the Evangelical Lutheran Church of Iceland, with its 284 parishes cared for by about 125 pastors. In comparison, the next-largest religious group is the Congregational Church of Reykjavik, with a membership of about 5,500.

Holidays. As is the case in Scandinavia and most of Europe, the holidays celebrated in Iceland are celebrations of Christian events. Exceptions that are non-religious are the holidays on June 17, commemorating the 1944 declaration of Icelandic independence, and a Bank Holiday in early August. Iceland culture has a long history, however, and some special occasions have been celebrated in the past, notably the celebration in 1930 of the thousandth year of existence of the Althing. Under this governing body, Icelanders have been one of the more progressive states of the world—the Althing proclaimed universal suffrage, the right of all adult citizens to vote, in 1920.

For More Information

Levathes, Louise E. "Iceland: Life Under the Glaciers." *National Geographic*, February, 1987, pp. 185–215.

Sigurdur, Nordal. *Icelandic Culture.* Ithaca, New York: Cornell University Press, 1990.

Tomasson, Richard F. *Iceland: The First New Society.* Minneapolis: University of Minnesota Press, 1980.

IRISH

(eye' rish)

Inhabitants of the island country of Ireland.

Population: 5,100,000 (1990 estimate).
Location: An island in the northeast Atlantic Ocean.
Language: Irish, English.

Geographical Setting

Ireland, the next largest of the British Isles after Great Britain, lies west of Great Britain in the North Atlantic. Physically, the island resembles a saucer, with coastal mountains or hills encircling a central basin. The highest mountains lie in the southwest, and though rugged they rise not much more than 3,000 feet above sea level. Ice Age glaciers carved lakes and valleys out of the coastal mountains. Much of the terrain is rocky and bare. In the interior, by contrast, the land is flat and fertile, though heavy rainfall has created large areas of marsh (called bogs) and many lakes. The very wet, generally temperate climate has encouraged the raising of livestock rather than tillage of the land.

Politically, the island has been divided into two parts of unequal size. The Irish Republic (population 3,500,000) comprises in its 26 countries most of the island's area, and is an independent state. Its capital, Dublin, lies on the east coast, across the Irish Sea from England and Wales. Westward from Dublin extends the "eastern corridor," a natural avenue through the mountains that historically has provided the main access to the interior from the sea. Northern Ireland (population 1,600,000), often called Ulster, consists of six counties and is a province of the United Kingdom (which also includes England, Scotland, and Wales, all on the island of Great Britain).

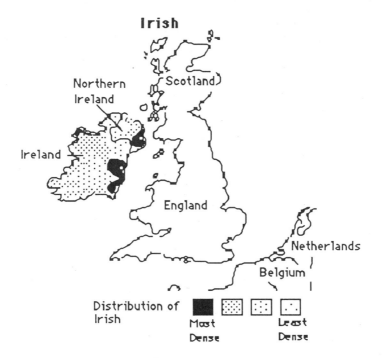

Distribution of Irish

Most Dense — Least Dense

Historical Background

Celtic society. Little is known about Ireland's inhabitants in the Stone and Iron Ages. Beginning about 500 B.C., Celtic settlers arrived, having previously occupied Britain and much of Western Europe (see CELTS). The tall, red-haired Celts absorbed the earlier occupants and established the Gaelic (gay lick) society that became the basis for Irish culture. The Celtic nobles feuded and warred among each other for land and cattle. The Celts founded no cities or towns. Their loosely structured society was based on small, scattered rural households. Though rural, the Celts possessed a sophisticated intellectual aristocracy. The nobles shared power with priests called *druids*, influential poets called *fili*, and learned lawyers called *brehons*. By the

400s, Celtic Ireland had been divided into five kingdoms: Ulster, Connacht, Leinster, Meath, and Munster.

Flourishing of Irish Christianity. St. Patrick introduced Christianity into Ireland in the A.D. 400s, and the new religion quickly took root. Celtic society especially suited the Christian institution of the monastery, a small religious "household" harboring a "family" of monks. By 700, over 70 monasteries had been founded, and abbots (heads of the monasteries) had become the most powerful Irish religious leaders. Irish monasteries became the greatest centers of learning in Europe at that time, while on the continent, Irish monks founded more monasteries and brought learning to European courts such as that of Charlemagne (see FRANKS).

Viking raiders, Norman invaders. About 800, Viking seamen began to raid Irish settlements, looting monasteries and burning libraries. Eventually they established their own outposts along the eastern coast, founding the first cities and towns. Most modern Irish cities, including Dublin, were such settlements at first. The Irish king Brian Boru defeated the Vikings near Dublin in 1014, ending the raids. The Viking settlers gradually assimilated into the Celtic population. In the late 1100s, another wave of invaders arrived, the Normans. Having conquered England 100 years earlier (see ENGLISH), the Normans came to Ireland at the request of an overthrown Irish king of Leinster. The Irish had no defense against Norman military expertise, and a small number of conquerors soon controlled the land. However, the independent Normans in Ireland soon unwillingly acknowledged their loyalty to the English-Norman king, Henry II. Like the Vikings, the Norman aristocracy eventually took up native ways, becoming (as the saying went) "more Irish than the Irish." These powerful lords maintained effective independence, subject to the English king in name only.

Plantation. The English Crown did not consolidate its control of Ireland until the 1600s, under Queen Elizabeth. The Protestant Queen and her successors pursued a policy of colonization of Protestants in Ireland, even though that country had stayed strongly Catholic. Most of these colonies, or "plantations," did not last. In Ulster, however, a large group of Protestant colonists from Scotland came and stayed. Following the establishment of the Ulster plantation, Oliver Cromwell dispossessed thousands of Gaelic and Gaelo-Norman landowners. By the end of Cromwell's rule (see ENGLISH) in 1660, some 3,000 mostly English Protestant landlords owned over 6,000,000 acres in Ireland. Some remained in England, but many others lived in Dublin or on their estates (where poor Irish tenants provided labor). Descendants of this powerful ruling class are called the "Anglo-Irish."

Rebellion and emancipation. In 1695, with English support, the Anglo-Irish Parliament imposed the Penal Laws, denying Catholics nearly all legal and civil rights. Catholics were not allowed to vote, for example, or to purchase land. The laws aimed to crush the Irish Catholic population and to root out the last of the Catholic aristocracy. Though the Penal Laws were gradually repealed, by the early 1800s Catholics owned less than 5 percent of Irish land. In the 1700s and 1800s, repeated but unsuccessful uprisings occurred, led by heroes such as Wolfe Tone and Robert Emmett. In 1828, a Catholic lawyer named Daniel O'Connell forced the repeal of the last Penal Law, which prohibited Catholics from holding office. O'Connell, called "the Liberator," achieved this by winning election to the Irish Parliament. He then organized a mass protest that forced Anglo-Irish lawmakers to allow him take his seat among them. The Irish refer to the victory as "the Emancipation."

Famine. In the 1840s, Irish potatoes—the primary staple of the peasants—were wiped out by disease for several years in a row. The crop failures brought severe famine to the people, and over 1,000,000 died of starvation or disease from 1845–51. Millions of Irish emigrated during and after this period, mostly to America, where they settled in northeastern cities such as New York and Boston. Emigration as an escape from poverty and hardship became an Irish tradition that has continued to the present. The population of Ireland declined from over 8,000,000 in the early 1800s to about half that by 1930.

Home Rule. Since the late 1800s, Irish patriots have attempted to end English control of Ireland's government. Charles Parnell led the Home Rule movement in the 1870s and 1880s; later, leadership passed to the Sinn Fein (Shin fain: "ourselves alone") party, under Arthur Griffith. The Easter Uprising of 1916, in which the Irish Volunteers seized buildings in central Dublin, ended in defeat and the leaders' executions by the English.

Partition. Eamon de Valera, a rebel commander who escaped execution, and Sinn Fein leader Michael Collins headed opposing factions after England implemented Home Rule in 1921. Collins, with the support of the new Irish Free State government, accepted England's retaining control of the six mostly Protestant northern counties. De Valera rejected this "partition" of Ireland, and civil war ensued between the two leaders' supporters. Collins died in an ambush in 1922, while de Valera joined Parliament in 1927. He formed the Fianna Fail ("soldiers of destiny") party and led the Irish government from 1932–59, proclaiming the Irish Republic in 1949. However, the six northern counties remain under direct British control, an issue that continues to cause division, unrest, and bloodshed among the Irish today.

Culture Today

Blarney. The Irish make an art of seeking and enjoying each other's company. Whether in the church, the home, the pub, or at an impromptu gathering outdoors, the Irish love to meet for conversation—and, perhaps, a drink or two. Most of Ireland's many tourists wish to kiss the famous Blarney Stone, and thus gain some of the Irish "gift of the gab." Ireland's geography and history have both tended to make the people tightly knit and sociable. Inside the coastal ring of mountains, few obstacles exist to easy movement from area to area. External cultural influences have been rare, owing to the island's isolation, and the people have turned to each other for amusement.

Catholic and Protestant concerns. The isolation of the Irish has decreased dramatically in recent decades. Television and movies bring the outside world to remote Irish villages, and travel has become cheaper and more comfortable than in the days of the great migrations. Today, many Irish go to England or the United States as visitors, to work for a year or two before returning home. In 1972, Ireland joined the European Economic Community, and in the 1990s looks forward with other EEC countries to stronger European unity. Yet the old tensions persist, particularly in Northern Ireland (Ulster), where Protestant descendants of the Scottish colonists still form a majority. Many in the south—Republicans, as they are called—wish to incorporate Ulster into the rest of Ireland. They point to the dominance of the Protestants over Catholics in the north, where the richer Protestants control politics and the economy. In cities like Belfast,

Catholic workers live in slums. For their part, the Protestants reject the Catholic religious doctrines that influence the Dublin government and fear losing rights that they value. Divorce, for example, is illegal in the Catholic south.

Terrorism. In the more than 70 years since Partition, no progress has been made in resolving the dilemma. Militants on both sides conduct bombing and assassination campaigns against each other and against the public. In the first two months of 1992, 27 people died in such terrorist attacks. All but one were civilians. The Irish Republican Army (IRA), the main Catholic terrorist group, conducts operations against both Ulster police forces and against the British Army, which has been stationed in Northern Ireland since 1972. The IRA has also killed British soldiers and civilians in attacks in Britain and Europe. The Dublin government has consistently attempted to stamp out the IRA terrorism, with little success. Ulster Protestants have also organized their own terrorist networks, which often carry out revenge attacks following those of the IRA. The tragedy of the situation is underlined by the character of the Irish themselves, a generous and warm-hearted people caught in the grip of an unfair past and a seemingly unchangeable present.

Food, clothing, and shelter. The Irish spend a lot of time outdoors (a tradition dating from Celtic times, when kings dined outside), and their favorite foods are usually hearty and filling. Main meals are breakfast and lunch. Breakfast often starts with porridge (boiled oatmeal with cream or butter), followed by eggs and bacon (or perhaps liver or grilled kidney). Strong tea rather than coffee accompanies the meal, as may a coarse brown bread or Irish "soda bread," made with baking soda and buttermilk. Lunch, usually the day's largest meal, might include a thick soup, a piece of beef or chicken, and vegetables— cabbage, peas, or the ever-present potato. Potatoes are eaten in many forms, often boiled or mixed with flour and fried in butter as potato cakes. They are also added to Irish stew, along with onions, carrots, and lamb or mutton. Dessert (called "sweets") or a savory cheese follows the meal. Supper is lighter, perhaps fish, sandwiches, or cold meat.

Irish clothing tends to aim for durability and comfort in the often wet outdoors. Best-known is Irish tweed, a thick cloth of woven wool used for pants, skirts, jackets, and hats. Wool also goes into sweaters, most famously those handmade by the Irish of the Aran islands in

A typical farmhouse in an Irish setting far from a city.
From the Library of Congress.

the west. Fine cotton lace has been made since the early 1800s, when women perfected the technique in the cottages of the south. Linen-weaving has long been a mainstay of Ulster's economy.

For centuries, Irish peasants lived in scanty dwellings of dried mud, sod (or turf, rectangles of grassy soil cut from the ground), and straw. Today, government housing programs struggle to keep pace with a quickly growing population. Many Irish live in "council houses," modest homes built by local governments.

Drink. Drinking, to the dismay of some, is widely considered a national pastime, and viewed as a valuable aid to the art of conversation. Three beverages command special affection. The most popular drink, Guinness stout, is a rich, brown beer brewed from roasted malt. Irish whiskey (the word *whiskey* comes from the Gaelic) takes a distinctive flavor from the peat (moss) used in distilling. Whiskey and Guinness are served in pubs, the neighborhood saloons that act as common meeting places. A secret but widespread and traditional practice is the illegal production of poteen, a potent liquor often distilled from potatoes.

Family life. Family values among the Catholic Irish are heavily influenced by religion. The Catholic Church forbids birth control, so families have traditionally been large. Emigration has dropped in recent years, so that the population now grows at a yearly rate of about 15 percent. Almost half the people are under 25. The Irish love children and lavish great affection on them, almost always bringing them along to adult gatherings. Women are today taking a more active role in a society that has traditionally been dominated by the men. The current president of Ireland is a woman, Mary Robinson. Many Catholic women quietly defy the church (and their husbands) by using birth control.

Religion. About 75 percent of the Irish are Roman Catholic; most of the remainder, who are Protestant, live in Northern Ireland. In the south alone, the proportion of Catholics rises to 95 percent. Both sections, however, view the entire island as a single spiritual province, and for both, the Archbishop of Armagh holds seniority as "Primate of All Ireland." Armagh, in Northern Ireland, was St. Patrick's headquarters in his campaign to convert the Irish Celts.

Holidays. The Irish celebrate the common Christian holidays—Christmas, Good Friday, and Easter much as they are celebrated in other English-speaking countries. To these holidays, the Irish add three bank holidays. The most internationally well-known Irish holiday is St. Patrick's Day, which falls on March 17 and commemorates the patron saint of Ireland. However, celebration of this holiday is more subdued in Ireland than among the Irish immigrants in the United States.

Language. Though Irish is the official first language of the Republic, most people use English in daily life. As the language of the ruling classes, English grew widespread in the 1600s and 1700s, though by

Creating beautiful works from lace is an important cottage industry in Ireland. *From the Library of Congress.*

the early 1800s, about half the population still spoke Irish. The Great Famine (1845–50) struck the rural, poor, Irish-speaking areas most heavily, however, and many Irish-speakers died or emigrated. The people associated the language with poverty and hardship, and fewer than 700,000 spoke it by the late 1800s. In the 1890s, the Gaelic League (*Conradh na Gaelge*) promoted Irish language and culture with considerable success. Today, students in the Republic must study some Irish in school, and all government jobs require knowledge of it. Beginning in the 1950s, the Dublin government has supported special Irish-speaking areas, called *Gaeltachtai*, mostly along the isolated and relatively poor western coast. Most Catholic Irish are familiar with the language; perhaps a third can speak conversationally.

The arts. Music, particularly singing, ranks high among Irish interests. Singers have long been popular figures in Ireland. On the pop music scene, fans worldwide enjoy the work of stars like Van Morrison and Sinead O'Connor. Most cities feature regular art and music festivals, and Dublin boasts a thriving theater community. Irish folk music bears some resemblance to American country music. Country musicians find interested audiences in Ireland and Irish musicians visiting America blend their music well with country music artists.

Literature. Ireland has produced some of the world's greatest writers, an achievement especially impressive given its small size. Its love affair with words goes back to Celtic times, when bards (oral poets) claimed a prestigious and influential place in society. Many of the best-known authors of "English" literature are in fact Irish, whether Protestant or Catholic: Jonathan Swift (1667–1745; *Gulliver's Travels*), Oscar Wilde (1854–1900; *The Picture of Dorian Gray)*, playwright George Bernard Shaw (1856–1950; *Pygmalion*), poet W. B. Yeats (1865–1939), James Joyce (1884–1941; *Ulysses*), and Samuel Beckett (1906–89; *Waiting for Godot*)—to name but a few. If one were to single out a particular work, it might be Joyce's *Ulysses*. This revolutionary novel, banned for many years in both Ireland and the United States, follows in minute-by-minute detail three people's lives during one day in Dublin—June 16, 1904. Joyce's earlier works also offer fascinating glimpses of Irish life, in an always masterful but more conventional style. The Irish revere their poets and other wordsmiths, at the same time viewing the writer's life in the same way that Americans might view a businessman's: as a mainstream, commonplace occupation.

For More Information

Birnbaum's Ireland 1992. New York: HarperCollins, 1992.

Foster, R. F. *Oxford Illustrated History of Ireland.* Oxford, England: Oxford University Press, 1989.

Neill, Kenneth. *An Illustrated History of the Irish People.* New York: Mayflower Books, 1979.

O'Brien, Conor Cruise and Maire. *A Concise History of Ireland.* London: Thames and Hudson, 1973 (rev. ed.).

O'Faolain, Sean. *The Story of the Irish People.* New York: Avenel Books, 1982.

ITALIANS

(ih tal' yuns)

Native people of Italy.

Population: 57,600,000 (1990 estimate).
Location: Italy, a peninsula in the Mediterranean Sea.
Language: Italian, a Romance language.

Geographical Setting

The terrain of the peninsula that makes up Italy is highly varied. Beginning in the north, the Alps Mountains fall abruptly to the great valley of the Po River and the plains of Lombardy. This northern region extends to the beginnings of the Apenine Mountains and contains some of the most fertile land of Europe. Grapes, fruit trees, rice, and other agricultural products grow in abundance, and cattle is successfully raised. Northern Italy is home to about half the Italian people. The climate throughout the peninsula is mostly warm, modulated by cool sea breezes. Central Italy has a climate moderated by the Apenine Mountains, which rise on the northwestern coast and gradually decline in height, forming a spine through the length of mainland Italy and into the island of Sicily. In the south, the land is poorer except along the coast, and the climate is hotter in summer.

Historical Background

Early inhabitants. Agricultural and pastoral settlements in Italy have been traced back to 1000 B.C. Over the 1,000 years following that date, some of the people established trading city-states along the coastline. The inhabitants of these city-states and the inland agriculturalists were finally united under the direction of the government

Italians

Distribution of Italians

Most Dense — Least Dense

of Rome in 89 B.C., when the right of Roman citizenship was extended to people throughout Italy. The Romans proceeded to fight for control of their territory against an internal division under which Mark Antony ruled part of the empire, then against Cleopatra, Queen of Egypt, who had enlisted the aid of Antony in an effort to take over the entire Roman territory. The A.D. 31 defeat of Mark Antony and Cleopatra, who had claimed one-third of all Roman land, marked the beginning of a Roman Empire that was to dominate the Mediterranean area for 300 years. However, in the fourth century A.D., pressures from both external sources such as the Goths (who had been given permission to settle in Roman territory) and disputes within the empire forced Emperor Constantine I to transfer half of the empire to Constantinople. By 476 the Empire based in Rome had disintegrated. Although it was no longer important as the political center for the

Old and new Rome stand side by side today. *Courtesy of Leah Cadavona.*

empire, Rome became the center of Christianity during this century, and the Pope emerged as a leader of the Roman people. By the late 700s much of Europe, including Italy, was again a Roman Empire, this time controlled by the Franks with papal sanction until the German King Otto I was crowned emperor of the Holy Roman Empire in 962. Meanwhile, the Italian cities had begun to act once more as independent units.

A pattern of city-states developed under the leadership of a merchant class grown wealthy through trade, banking, and industry. Florence, Genoa, Pisa, Milan, and Venice became independent states whose citizens fell under the rule of powerful families called *signori*. The Visconti family ruled Milan and the Medici family ruled Florence, for example. These signori remained in control of their own states and quarreled with their neighbors, enlisting the aid of paid mercenaries called *condottieri*. Under these conditions, the Italian city-states were in a state of constant skirmishing. The condottieri fought their counterparts from other states only halfheartedly. It was not in their interest to completely defeat a foe or to end a struggle, thereby putting themselves out of work. So disagreements continued for many years, but not at a level that would disturb developments of other interests by the signori.

During the fourteenth to sixteenth centuries, a period of great achievement known as the Renaissance, these signori were instrumental in advancing the cultural and civic life of the people by acting as sponsors for artists and people of letters. Florence became the center of the arts in all of Renaissance Europe. Great names in literature and art were supported by the signori during this period. Niccola Pisano (1220–1278), for example, gave birth to a period of great Italian sculpture when he was commissioned to design a pulpit for the church at Pisa. The signori sponsored schools taught by people known as *dictatories*—experts in grammar and rhetoric. The dictatories revived Italian interest in the old classics of Rome and Greece and developed an interest in current human activities as opposed to total concern with the church. This "humanism" was championed by Francesco Petrarca (Petrarch, 1304–1374), who lauded concern with the present world and human condition in a famous "conversation" with St. Augustine. This was accompanied by the work of Giovanni Boccaccio (1313–1375), who wrote in *The Decameron* comedic sketches told by people escaping the Bubonic Plague, which struck Florence with such impact that 60 percent of the people of the city were killed by the disease.

By the 1400s the Renaissance was in full bloom, with such great architects as Donato Bramante (restorer of St. Peter's Basilica) and masterful artists such as Leonardo da Vinci and Michelangelo Buonarroti creating works that attract tourists to Italy today. Perhaps because the city-states had established a policy of competition for sponsorship of the greatest authors, artists, and thinkers, many Italians of this era gained enduring fame.

However mild in comparison to wars elsewhere, the frequent wars between the city-states weakened their defenses against foreign powers. In 1494 France invaded Italy, and control by outside countries began. Spain conquered Italy in 1556 and the country was overcome by Austria (1714). The French general Napoleon Bonaparte invaded Italy in 1796 and ruled the people harshly until his forces withdrew in 1814, allowing the Austrians to regain control. At last Italians began to unify against foreign rule, led by the northern Italian state of Piedmont. Under the Risorgimento Movement, Italians initiated a series of revolutions that finally led to victory in 1859 under the leadership of Piedmont and the popular guerrilla fighter Giuseppe Garibaldi. A Kingdom of Italy was proclaimed in 1861, and Victor Emmanuel II of Piedmont assumed the throne.

The city-states had been unified, but under conditions that were unequal. For one thing, the states had distinguished themselves in different fields—art, music, business. For another, the pattern of taxes

In earlier days, prisoners were marched across this bridge, "The Bridge of Sighs," to prison and execution in the building on the right. *From the Library of Congress.*

in the various city-states varied. Also, residents of city-states in the north were wealthy while the standard of living in the south was poor. These inequities encouraged an atmosphere of banditry in the countryside. Conditions deteriorated to an even greater degree during and after World War I, a war in which Italy joined the Allies against Germany. As a result of their involvement, Italians suffered serious losses of men, material, and morale. The country after the war was ready for governmental changes and found them when Benito Mussolini was named prime minister in 1922. Mussolini abandoned civil liberties and outlawed all political parties except for his own, and became an absolute dictator by 1925. He then sided with Adolph Hitler as World War II loomed in the late 1930s. There followed a period of international Italian expansion. Already with a foothold in Africa through Somaliland, Mussolini sent his armies into Ethiopia in 1935, into Spain in support of the fascists in 1936–1939, and into Albania in 1939. Italy joined with Germany in World War II and became an occupied country. German armies resided in Italy until 1943, when King Victor Emmanuel III forced Mussolini to resign and the Germans were pushed out. However, by 1946 Victor Emmanuel III had abdicated his throne in favor of his son Umberto II. Umberto was in turn rebuffed when Italians voted to abolish the monarchy two months later. A new republic embarked on a period of rapid industrial expansion that brought a sharp increase in the standard of living. However, the political life of the republic has been unstable. More than 40 different governments have been in power since 1946.

A major thrust of the Italian government has been to combat crime. In the 1980s the national forces have been directed toward eliminating the organized crime group known as the Mafia. In 1987 and again in 1989 Mafia members were pursued and mass trials were held for them, with 400 or 500 Mafiosi imprisoned. This seems to have had little effect, however, since, in 1990, the Mafiosi were accused of the murders of some 2,000 Italians.

Some Italians of Great Accomplishment

Religious leaders
  Saint Francis
  Saint Thomas of Aquino

Politicians
  Lorenzo de Medici— powerful leader of Florence
  Nicolo Machiavelli—political manager and writer about political strategy

Artists
  Sandro Boticelli
  Benvenuto Cellini
  Leonardo da Vinci
  Michelangelo Buonarotti
  Raphael Santi
  Tiziano Vecelli (Titian)
  Donato Di Betto Bardi

Scientists
  Galileo Galilei—astronomer
  Allesandro Volta—physicist
  Guglielmo Marconi—telegraph developer

Military leaders
  Andrea Doria—admiral
  Napoleon Bonaparte—leader of France
  Guiseppe Garibaldi—general who united Italy

Musicians
  Gioacchino Antonio Rossini
  Giacomo Puccini
  Arturo Toscanini
  Guiseppe Verdi

Culture Today

Government. Italians elect their representatives to the two houses of government (the Senate and the Chamber of Deputies) for a period of five years. A president is elected separately each seven years (or less, depending on the popularity of the government). The election of the president illustrates one of the main attributes of the Italian—individuality. The people are represented in this election by the massive houses of parliament—315 senators and 630 deputies—to which 58 regional representatives are added to preserve Italian provincial self-interests.

In spite of this large central government, some of the isolation of the old city-states remains in that the people are more immediately affected by their regional governments. Each of the 20 regions of Italy is a self-ruling area. An area is governed by a regional council with lawmaking powers and a *giunta regionale*, or regional leader, invested with executive authority. Regions are further divided into provinces that are responsible for carrying out the policies of the central government and into communes that are responsible for police services, highways, and other local concerns.

There are eight major political parties in the country, promising government aid to communities and individuals in return for their votes. A coalition government, most frequently led by the Christian Democrat Party, with the Socialist Party as a junior partner, is the usual pattern. Controversial issues such as where a road is to be built and benefits such as old-age pensions are awarded on the basis of which party the voters support. This system of favors in exchange for votes encourages Italians to shift their allegiances from one party to another. Italians, on average, love their country but hold little faith in their governments. For stability the people look to the family as the unit that deserves unswerving loyalty. It has been said that the real government of Italy is the family.

Family life. While industry grows and art centers attract tourists, Italy still remains a strongly agricultural nation. The land of the south is mostly mountainous or hilly and is divided into large estates (*latifundia*) for grazing and wheat production. The peasants and day laborers who farm the large estates are generally the poorest group in Italy. In the north a share-farming system exists in which the landlord provides territory and capital in exchange for up to 50 percent of the crop from the tenant families. The typical farm is small (about 17 acres) and is devoted to raising crops mostly for subsistence.

Whether in the villages, farms, or cities, families are of primary importance to Italians. Loyalty to and support of the family ranks above respect for the nation or its laws—or any other aspect of life. The Italian concept of family is reflected in a novel by Ignazio Silone, in which a grandmother is arguing with her grandson's uncle to gain support for her criminal grandson:

> You are right in saying that he has committed wrongs, but you, my son, must admit that I am right when I say that, notwithstanding all of your allegations against him, he is nonetheless one of ours. No manmade laws can change his blood.
>
> Barzani 1967, p. 326

The Italian family is based on power. The most powerful or most wealthy male member of the family is the outward ruler of the family, regardless of his age. But more than in most other societies, the women rule the family because of their responsibility for producing and rearing the family members, and because of the man's preoccupation with gaining wealth and power. This preoccupation demands that many men take membership in a club or organization outside the family that promises support in their efforts to get ahead economically. However, few men would admit to domination by a female relative. Even the laws protect the male position. For example, a woman can be punished by law if she commits adultery; a man cannot.

Certainly, the roles of Italian country men and women are clearly defined. Males are responsible for earning the livelihood in Italian rural families. Women are responsible for the home and cooking. Only in very poor families do the women go out into the fields to participate in the harvesting. However, their roles and fortunes depend to some extent on their landlords and in parts of Italy on the Mafiosi of their village.

Food, clothing, and shelter. Wheat, rice, olives, and grapes are popular Italian food crops. The grapes are mainly used to produce wine for export and consumption. Raw eggs, bacon, cheese, and bread are breakfast foods. A midday meal (*pranzo*) is eaten about 2:00 p.m. and might include pasta, meat, or fish, a vegetable dish, salad, cheese, and fruit, with each dish being served and eaten separately. A lighter meal is served at 8:00 or 9:00 in the evening. The pasta—macaroni, spaghetti, fettucine, lasagna, or cannelloni—is cooked to a chewy consistency. Different regions tend to specialize in particular dishes; the city of Bologna features lasagna, for example. In the north, rice is frequently a substitute for pasta and butter for olive oil in such dishes as *risotto* (rice, broth, onions, saffron, and cheese) and *fonduto* (cheese, butter, milk, and truffles). When rice is a substitute for pasta, Italians generally prefer a hard form of it, and may supplement the dish with green tomatoes. Common meats or fish dishes are veal stew, roast lamb, octopus, tunny, and swordfish. Wine is an everyday beverage with meals. Central Italy is well-known for its fish soup, *boiabesa*. Southern Italian dishes include a great amount of tomatoes and peppers, and feature macaroni and spaghetti.

Italian farmhouses are built of stone or brick and roofed with tile. The farmhouse usually includes two stories, with an outside stairway to approach the upper story. The ground floor might be occupied by animals and equipment. Poorer peasant families in southern Italy live in one room that serves as the kitchen, living quarters, and a stable for the peasants' animals.

The center of the city dweller's existence is the quarter, a large block of flats that is a highly populated village within the city. Apartment houses are built on the pattern of the old Italian villa. An entrance arch leads into the ground floor, which is reserved for stores, offices, and stables. The other floors are traditionally reserved for living quarters. Marble is common inside the homes, as are Venetian blinds (known in Italy as Persian blinds).

Economy. In spite of its agricultural base, less than one-fourth of the Italian population is occupied in farming. The majority live in the city, where they operate small family businesses or are employed in industry. Italians produce motor vehicles, textiles, and a wide variety of consumer goods. Marble quarrying is an industry that has been highly developed by the Italians in the past. The sculptor Michelangelo visited marble quarries near the coast of Tuscany to select and cut his material personally. Sculpture and other arts and crafts continue to flourish among the Italians, with glass and pottery work, gold and silver ornaments, lacemaking, woodcarving, and straw goods now added to the Italian arts.

After the world wars, Italy became increasingly industrial. Today less than nine percent of the Italian workers are involved in agriculture and that once-dominant labor produces less than five percent of the nation's wealth. In contrast, 32 percent of the workers produce about one-third of the nation's income in industry apart from manufacturing and nearly one-fourth of the workers produce 27 percent of the wealth through manufacturing. Small-scale production by Italian artisans remains strong—one of the strongest fields of economic growth in the world since the 1960s. The additional third of the Italian work force earn their livings in services. Tourism is one of Italy's largest resources.

Religion. Although they are divided between the north and the south and by the specific region in which they live, Italians are united by religion, language, and education. Peasants, workers, and leading Italians are overwhelmingly Roman Catholic. The Catholic Church occupies a privileged position in Italian society, affecting family, education, and marriage legislation. The base of the church, the Vatican, is recognized as a separate country within Italy. In the past, priests taught in Italian schools and they still do today. But now, as a result of the decision in 1984 to abolish compulsory religious training in the schools, education is mostly government operated, and religious influence is declining.

Education. Secular education is compulsory from the ages of six to 14 and most children attend public schools. In higher education, the characteristic division by regions are again evident, with different areas of Italy specializing in certain fields. Italians might study law in Naples and medicine in Bologna. Florence has been a center of the arts. Italians who study and work there can build on a heritage created by artists such as Lorenzo Bernini, Antonio Canova, Donato Di Betto Bardi (Donatello) and Michelangelo Buonarotti. Italian authors add to a body of literature by writers such as Dante Alighieri, and musicians build on a tradition that includes composers such as Giacomo Puccini.

Holidays. Italians enjoy ceremonies, feasts, elaborate religious rites, and food. Their celebrations frequently include fireworks and loud noise. They are given to show. When Adolph Hitler visited Rome, entire buildings were erected of wood and cardboard (in the style of movie sets) to enhance the city while he was entertained there.

Italians celebrate the major Christian holidays, often with parades and great floral displays. In addition, each province or village declares holidays in honor of the patron saint or saints of that region. There are also three days of celebration of Italian nationalism: April 25, Liberation Day, a celebration of the Allied victory ending World

Rome preserved many parts of Greek culture. This Greek rites abbey is at Grottafornata. *Courtesy of Adn Kronos and the Italian Cultural Center.*

War II; May 12, Tricolour Day, a flag day; and November 5, National Unity Day, celebrating the unification of Italy in 1866.

Literature. In 1942, Count Carlo Sforza, then in the United States, began a series of lectures at the University of California about Italian culture. His lectures were the basis for a book published in 1949, after the count had returned to political life in Italy. The thesis of this book is that Italians in Italy feel inferior to their neighbors and thus neglect modern writing, art, and music. The reason for this inferiority complex, Sforza suggests, is ancient Rome. While this once-powerful city provided a sort of unity among diverse city-states

In the golden age of Italian art, support for artists came from the wealthy rulers and landowners. The result was exquisite art such as this on the ceiling of the Vatican. *Courtesy of Leah Cadavona.*

and allowed for developments in art, literature, and politics that are sources of pride to Italians today, the glory of ancient Rome, perhaps exaggerated through time, tends to be the standard by which modern accomplishments are measured. And, since the Roman Empire was really a collection of self-governing city-state units, Italians still tend to identify with a particular region, and they respect artists and writers who do likewise, rather than identifying with a "universal" Italian. Thus, the writer Allesandro Manzoni (1785–1873) was identified with Milan; Giovanni Verga (1840–1922), also with Milan; and, earlier, Giulio Cesare Cortese (1375–1621), with Naples. Poets Carlo Porta

Italians are fond of celebrations. Priests begin one procession by walking a floral path more than 220 meters square. *Courtesy of Adn Kronos and the Italian Cultural Center.*

and Gioacchino Belli wrote in the nineteenth century about Milan and Rome. The shadow of Rome, according to Sforza, was the cause of the gloomy writing of Dante Alighieri, who wrote *Divine Comedy* at a time of great liveliness and prosperity in Italy. (Some might argue, however, that Dante's point of view was more the result of his own misfortunes in life.)

Early in the twentieth century, Italian writers joined artists in a futurist movement—an attempt to reflect industrial changes in their society that was characterized by loud rhetoric such as that found in the novels of Eugenio Montele's *Salvator*. The 1920s brought a period of quiet followed by writings of social protest in the 1930s. An outstanding author of that time was Alberto Moravia, whose book *The Conformist* was the basis for a popular film. The 1950s and 1960s saw a resurgence of literary works in many forms. Caldo Levi, for example, illustrates a school of realism and postwar national introspection in his book *Christ Stopped at Eboli.*

Many writers and artists who are recognized today worked in a period known as the Rinovamento, which began in the nineteenth century. It was a period of renewed national spirit in Italy. Perhaps the greatest literary spirit of the twentieth century is Gabriele D'Annunzio, who wrote not only books such as *Il Trionio della Morte*, but plays and poetry. D'Annunzio's writings were greatly influenced by classic Greek and Roman styles. Natalia Ginzburg writes of middle-class life in Italy, and Italo Calvino creates works of fantasy, fairy tales, and science fiction.

Art. Similarly, recent Italian artists have carried on the tradition of sculpture and painting that was supported during the days of the glorious city-states by rulers of the states, who seemed often to be in competition for artistic sponsorship. Antonio Canova (1757–1822) and Pietro Teneri (1798–1869) continued to produce impressive works in stone and Pio Fedi became famous for his goldwork and engravings. Giovanni Dupré revived Italian interest in religious works. Twentieth-century artists are given credit for throwing off the cloak of antiquity and producing new patterns in art. Filippo Marinetti and others developed a style called *futurism*, in which they tried to create in plastic forms the speed, motion, violence, and technology of the new-to-Italy industrialization. After 1920 and throughout the age of fascism a new movement, *novocento*, called for more orderliness in paintings. Fortunato Depero was a leading figure in this movement. Since the war, Italian artists have experimented with their new freedoms in many forms of art. Mario Mafai represents abstractionists in modern Italy with his paintings of landscapes. Nino Longobardi experiments in monochromes from his base in Naples.

Music. Italian interest in classical music has produced few leading musicians as compared to neighboring France and Germany. Still, such earlier composers and operatic conductors as Giuseppe Verdi, Giacomo Puccini, and Alberto Franchetti have been followed by other Italian composers of opera in the 1900s. The adoration of classic music is illustrated by Gian Francisco Malipiero, who has adapted

The early Romans ended each aqueduct into the city at a fountain. Most of the original ones are now gone, but fountains such as Trevi are still popular. *Courtesy of Adn Kronos and the Italian Cultural Center.*

many classical pieces to modern sounds. Perhaps the leading twentieth-century composer of opera is Luigi Nono.

Unity and division. Italy is a land united by its past and by its present-day industrialization, along with efforts by the national government to strengthen the economies of poorer sections in the south and northeast. But some of the same factors have traditionally separated the country. People of Sicily still feel themselves to be Sicilians first; Florence, Florentines; and Naples, Neapolitans. This regional em-

The Fountain of Trevi was remembered by the song "Three Coins in the Fountain." *Courtesy of Adn Kronos and the Italian Cultural Center.*

phasis is reflected in the language, with each region holding to its own dialect of the common Italian. And the regionality has divided the country between a more industrialized and aggressive north and a nearly poverty-stricken south still clinging to the perceived glory days of settlement and rule by the Greeks. Of interest to economists is the difference between the home industries of the northeast that have now separated from the home and become more mechanized and the larger industrial organizations of central Italy. While the large industries fluctuate with good and bad times, these small industries seem to add stability to the Italian economy.

Some Nineteenth Century and Earlier Italian Composers and Their Operas

Pietro Cavalli	*l'Artemisia*
Alberto Franchetti	*Asraele, Germania*
Baron Ruggerio Lconcavallo	*La Boheme*
Pietro Mascogni	*Cavallera Rusticana*
Giacomo Orefice	*Gladiatore, Cecilia*
Angelo Orvieto	*Moses*
Giacomo Puccini	*Tosca*
Guiseppi Verdi	*Ernani, Rigoletto, Il Travatore*

For More Information

Coppa, Frank J. *Studies in Modern Italian History: From the Risorgimento to the Republic.* New York: Peter Lang, 1986.

Sforza, Count Carlo. *Italy and the Italians.* New York: E. P. Dutton, 1949.

Tannenbaum, Edward R. *The Fascist Experience: Italian Society and Culture 1922–1945.* New York: Basic Books, Inc., 1972.

LAPPS
(laps)

Native people, some of whom are reindeer herders, of far northern Scandinavia; the people prefer to be called the Saami.

Population: 40,000 (1990 estimate).
Location: Northern Scandinavia.
Languages: Lappish, Swedish, Norwegian, Finnish, Russian.

Geographical Setting

Lapland, a region rather than a separate country, takes in the northern parts of Norway, Sweden, and Finland, as well as Russia's Kola Peninsula. Home to hundreds of thousands of Scandinavians as well as to the relatively small number of Lapps, Lapland lies mostly above the Arctic Circle. About one-third the size of Alaska, it falls into three geographic regions, each with its own variation of a generalized Lapp culture. Coast Lapps occupy the jagged Arctic coast of Norway and the Kola Area, with its deep fjords (inlets) and river valleys; reindeer-herding Mountain Lapps have traditionally followed their nomadic lifestyle among the mountains and plateaus that divide northern Norway and Sweden; seminomadic Forest Lapps live among the low-lying woods and lakes of northern Finland and Sweden. Other groups are the Skolt Lapps of northern Finland and the western Kola peninsula, and the Kola Lapps of the peninsula proper.

Winters are long, dark, and very cold. Much of Lapland has snow for eight months or more—the sun disappears for weeks and temperature of -20 degrees Fahrenheit are not unusual. Though short, the summers offer correspondingly longer days and temperatures in the 70s. In the warm summers, the Lapps grow a few hardy crops, harvest berries, protect their reindeer from clouds of insects, and—

Lapps

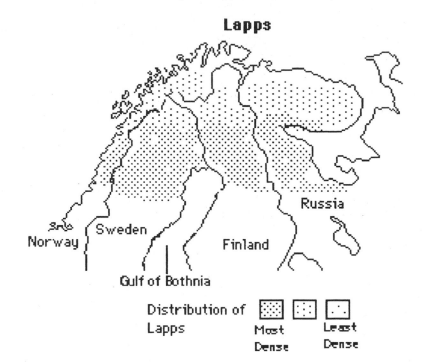

Distribution of Lapps — Most Dense / Least Dense

in recent years—sell goods to growing numbers of Scandinavian and European tourists.

Historical Background

Origin. It is uncertain exactly when the Saami—as the people refer to themselves—arrived in Lapland. Their traditions maintain that they have always been there. The ancient culture called Komsa, which flourished about 6,000 B.C. and left archeological remains on the Lappish coast, might represent the Lapps' ancestors. If so, they probably moved into Finland and surrounding areas as the ice of the last Ice Age receded. Scholars believe these early hunters might originally have come from central Russia or western Asia. Around 5000 B.C., ancestors of the present-day Scandinavians had occupied southern Norway and Sweden, and by about 1000 B.C. the Finns had moved into southern Finland from the southeast, gradually pushing the Lapps north.

Hunters on skis. The earliest account of the Lapps is that of the Roman historian Tacitus (about A.D. 100), who described them as

Lapps use domesticated reindeer to carry their goods and pull their sleds. *Courtesy of the Finnish Tourist Board.*

wild and very poor, without houses or horses, eating herbs, wearing fur, and sleeping on the ground. Both men and women hunted. Later historians also describe them as hunters, adding that they covered ground quickly by using skis. It is believed that the Lapps invented skis.

Domestication of reindeer. In addition to hunting and fishing, at some point the Lapps also began to rely on herds of domesticated reindeer. A Norwegian chieftan named Ottar (about A.D. 900) left an account showing that most of his taxes came from the Lapps. The taxes were paid in skins and other such goods, but Ottar also mentions his ownership of 600 reindeer, tended by Lapps. Over coming centuries, as Norwegian, Swedish, and Finnish settlers moved north, grazing grounds grew scarcer and wild herds shrank through over-hunting. Settlement was especially heavy along the Norwegian coast, where many Coast Lapps turned to farming and cattle-raising to supplement their subsistence. By the 1600s, Mountain Lapps had adopted the reindeer nomadism with which they would become so strongly identified, switching their herds seasonally between winter and summer pastures. Both Coast and Forest Lapps also migrated seasonally, but over smaller distances. They are usually described as seminomadic. All used domesticated reindeer to carry their goods and pull their sleds, for milking, as decoys to catch wild reindeer, and for meat and skin.

Christianity. Beginning around the 1100s, Norwegian, Swedish, and even Russian Orthodox missionaries began converting Lapps to Christianity. While some churches and monasteries were established in Lapp centers, the process was a slow one. Not until the late 1600s, under Norwegian auspices, did Christianity really begin to take root. During the early 1700s, the Norwegian missionary Thomas von Western, called "the Apostle of the Lapps," undertook the first systematic attempt to replace the old beliefs. He and his successors established the Lapp Seminary at Trondheim, Norway, built schools and churches, and spread church officials throughout Lapland. In the mid-1800s, a preacher named Lars Laestadius introduced a new revivalist Christian movement whose greater emotional content fit in with traditional beliefs better than the dry Lutheranism of the established church. Laestadianism, now incorporated into Lappish Lutheranism, remains an important feature of the people's religious life.

Imperial neighbors. Religious influence was closely tied to political control, as the Lapps' ambitious neighbors claimed Lapland's territory for themselves. Missionaries, local church officials, settlers, traders and trappers, exerting increasing influence over the lives of Lapps, acted also to "plant the flag" for their respective countries. Borders between Sweden (which at this time controlled Finland) and Russia were decided in 1595. Sweden and Norway fixed their border in 1751, but allowed Lapps to cross freely between the two countries, and Norway and Russia fixed theirs in 1823. During this period, Lapps paid heavy taxes to these states, often to two or even three countries at a time. Generally, they could not own land, but merely use it.

Modern times. During the 1900s, Lapps began taking a larger part in the economies of their home states. As more and more Scandinavians moved into Lapland, the region's industries and trade grew. Jobs in mining, forestry, fishing, and tourism all brought a measure of prosperity, but also often resulted in the loss of traditional ways.

Today's Lapps enjoy greater liberty, comfort and educational opportunities than in the past. And while some old ways have vanished, others have been integrated into the newer practices. The governments have sometimes attempted to make the Lapps into Norwegians or Swedes or Finns. Most Lapps don't resent such attempts, but prefer—despite centuries of limited interbreeding—to remain in a culture apart.

Culture Today

Reindeer. Reindeer nomadism, adopted by the Lapps as they moved north, has given way to changes. Yet the reindeer's importance to the Lapps, which existed before they adopted a nomadic lifestyle, has also survived its departure. In some ways, the animal's role is similar to what it was before nomadism became widely practiced (though, in fact, it was never practiced by the majority of Lapps). Large herds are still kept, but the people no longer use the reindeer so thoroughly nor rely on it so completely. Fewer than 10 percent of Lapps tend reindeer today, and those herders raise them mostly for slaughter. They are sold to wholesalers and then to butchers. Seasonal migrations with the reindeer, when they occur at all, are short. As often as not, the herders have comfortable cabins at both winter and summer pasture sites, rather than the portable tents of the past.

Food, clothing, and shelter. Traditionally, Lapps used every part of the reindeer, most of it for food and clothing. Reindeer milk is very rich, though little is produced. It is drunk with coffee or made into cheese. The meat is lean and high in protein and vitamins. The animals' blood is mixed with grain for porridge, with flour for pancakes, and with meat for sausages, which are encased in lengths of intestine. The stomach may be cleaned, turned inside out, and used to store food. Like reindeer meat, fish has remained an important food. Taken from Lapland's many lakes as well as from the sea, the fish are boiled, grilled whole, dried, smoked, salted, ground up, or eaten raw. Many varieties of berries grow wild, and are eaten fresh or cooked. Today, products such as white sugar, flour, and dried milk are bought in stores, as are other convenience foods. Some wheat, barley, and potatoes are still home grown, though most Lapps buy them. Lapps drink coffee during the day, though the Skolt Lapps show a Russian influence in their love of tea, as well as in the rye bread that they have traditionally baked. Supper is the main meal, and, in the past, was often the only hot food (aside from continual drinks such as coffee or plain hot water) consumed during the day. While a bowl of hot porridge or broth might be had at breakfast, cold foods like cheese or dried meat were simpler and easier. Only after evening camp had been set up would a complicated meal be prepared.

Reindeer skin can be used in all sorts of clothing. With the fur left on and worn inside, it makes an excellent heavy shirt that insulates without being hot in summer. Moccasins are also sewn from the skins, sometimes with a curved-up toe which keeps the foot in place in ski-bindings. Instead of socks, the moccasins are stuffed with soft, dry sedge grass, which insulates and can be replaced daily. The hides are dressed to make pants and boots. Sinew is used to sew the

A Lapp woman wearing the traditional dress and bonnet. *Courtesy of the Finnish Tourist Board.*

leather goods, as well as to hold together sleds and boats. The clothing not made from reindeer hide is almost always woven from brightly colored wool or felt. For the men, belted coats (the *kolts*) and distinctive hats feature intricate bands of bright red, yellow and white patterns against deep blue. Men's hats vary: in Norway and Finland, men have cylindrical hats with what looks like a small cushion in the shape of a four-pointed star dangling from the top. These are called "hats of the four winds." Swedish Lapp men wear caps of similar colorful material, with small bills and large, fluffy red pompoms on top. Women's dresses and aprons have similar patterns, with blue and red predominating. Women wear colorful bonnets with earflaps.

Family life. Jobs in the traditional family were sharply divided by sex. Men cared for the reindeer, hunted, dressed and prepared the meat, and made boats, sleds, tools, and utensils. Women prepared the material for clothes, spinning and dyeing wool, dressing the skins, and sewing the garments. They did the cooking, except for meat, which was preferably cooked by men. Both made silver ornaments for belts or necklaces, which were worn with other finery at weddings and special occasions. Weddings are festive affairs, with the wedding feast provided by the bride's parents. In Lapp families the youngest son has been favored, traditionally inheriting the bulk of the father's estate, particularly his reindeer. He is expected to look after his aging parents, while older brothers could be assumed to have married and made their way in the world.

Religion. Pre-Christian beliefs were largely animistic, with the chief gods being forces of nature such as the sun, the four winds, fertility, and disease. Western Lapps also adopted some Norse gods, such as *Tiermes*, their counterpart to Thor, the Old Norse God of Thunder. The gods were worshiped at sites called *seide*, open-air altars of stone or wood. Often these were situated near impressive natural landmarks: unusually shaped boulders, trees, or lakes. Lapps were famous for their sorcerers or shamans, called *noiade*. The noiade mediated between the spirit and human worlds, using magic drums to enter the spirit realm. They were believed to be able to enlist the help of animals, or actually to transform themselves into animals. Some of these old beliefs have carried over into today's Lapp version of Christianity.

In attempting to promote Christianity, the early missionaries persecuted the noiade, and destroyed many of the magic drums, though some have been preserved and are now found in museums. The Lapps also had an elaborate cult centered around the bear, with special rituals for hunting and killing the beast. Today many old practices have been given up in favor of Lutheranism, a Christian Protestant denomination. The Lapps' version of Lutheranism, however, called Laestadianism, incorporates a little of the old attitude. For example, early Laestadian meetings were known for their high emotional content, which has been compared with the ecstatic trances of shamanistic culture.

Language. Lappish is distantly related to Finnish, belonging to the Finno-Ugric family of languages. It thus falls outside the Indo-European group to which most European languages belong, and is very difficult for outsiders to learn. In fact, there are three separate and mutually incomprehensible Lappish languages (North, South, and East Lappish), as well as numerous local dialects. Most Lapps now speak North Lappish, however, which has become accepted as the standard form. The language reflects the culture's traditional outdoor world. For example, there are over 400 words to describe reindeer, dealing with the niceties such as color, size, antler spread, and texture of fur. Lapps increasingly speak the languages of the countries they live in, though Lappish is also taught in school.

Literature and the arts. Oral poetry and folk-tales have played an important part in Lapp culture. The poetry celebrates Lapland's natural beauty and the glories of the nomadic life. Two poems were translated in the late 1600s. Capturing the attention of European and American poets, most notably Henry Wadsworth Longfellow, these two poems brought international attention to Lapp oral literature. During the twentieth century, Lapp poets have continued in the tradition, writing poems that can be sung in the distinctively Lappish musical form called the *juoigos,* or (in English) "yoik." The yoiks are plaintive, humming songs similar to yodeling; sometimes the singers leave out words altogether and repeat standard sounds like *voia-voia* or *nana-nana.* Yoiks can be written down or made up on the spot, and employ subtle poetic effects such as alliteration, onomatopoeia, and internal rhythms. Lappish art consists mostly of crafts, in which geometric motifs are used to decorate tools and utensils. The implements are usually of wood, horn, bone, or silver, with the patterns engraved on them.

Outlook on life. Lapps are characteristically small in stature, but wiry, strong, lively, and congenial. Recent changes have presented some problems: tourist hunters kill much game, which Lapps still rely on for food; the continuing influx of settlers has raised land prices so that many Lapps cannot afford to buy land; and schooling has taught young Lapps about the outside world but threatened to create a generation gap. The Scandinavian governments have instituted programs to help the Lapps preserve their culture, however, and interest has grown among outsiders. Though some Lapps have suffered the apathy shared by other disrupted peoples, others have adapted. Most now work in such jobs as mining, medicine, engineering, teaching, or administration. Anthropologists have broken the Lapps into categories (Coast Lapps, for example). With typical humor, Lapps who hold "modern" jobs have placed themselves in other categories, such as "Office Lapps" or "Conference Lapps." Any one of them, however, is likely to spend the weekend camping or hunting in the beloved wilderness.

For More Information

Andersen, Sally. "Norway's Reindeer Lapps," *National Geographic*, September, 1977.

Collinder, Bjorn. *The Lapps*. Princeton: Princeton University Press, 1949.

Ingold, Tim. *The Skolt Lapps Today*. Cambridge: Cambridge University Press, 1976.

James, Alan. *Lapps: Reindeer Herders of Lapland*. Vero Beach, Florida: Rourke Publications, 1989.

NORWEGIANS

(nor wee' jans)

The native peoples of Norway.

Population: 4,250,000 (1991 estimate).
Location. Norway.
Language. Norwegian, a north Germanic language in two forms: Bokmöl, an older form used in 80 percent of the schools, and Nynorsk (new Norwegian, used in 20 percent of the schools).

Geographical Setting

Bounded by the North Sea, Arctic Ocean, Finland, Russia, and Sweden, the land of the Norwegians is mountainous and jagged. Mountain cliffs fall abruptly to the sea along the western boundary and are cut by countless indentations of the coastline called *fjords*. The mountains and the fjords interrupt the land so that the easiest way to travel from city to city is by ship. The ruggedness of the land is seen by its dimensions—1,100 miles from north to south, four to 70 miles east to west, but with a coastline that is 12,000 miles long. Nearly one-third of the land is within the Arctic Circle. Still, the climate along the west coast is moderate, with year-round temperatures from the high 20s to the 40 degrees Fahrenheit (and slightly higher in the south) tempered by the ocean's Gulf Stream. The Langfieldene range divides the southern portion of the country and the peaks of the Kjoelen Mountains separate Norway from Sweden. East of these ranges, temperatures are more varied, with colder winters and warmer summers, and rainfall is lower. Only four percent of the land of Norway is suitable for growing crops.

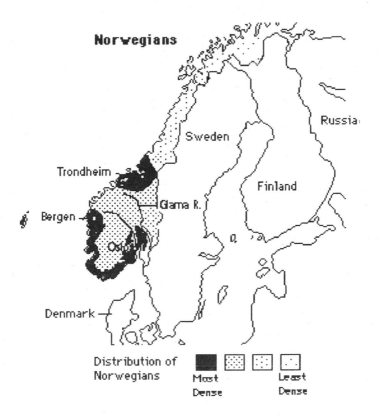

Distribution of Norwegians — Most Dense / Least Dense

Historical Background

Relics of ancient societies have been found in widely separated areas of Norway—at Kamma in Finnmark (the extreme north of Norway) and at Fosna in the northwest of the country. These relics indicate that people were living in this northern land as early as 8000 B.C. By 500 B.C., the beginning of this region's Iron Age, the people there were in contact with Celtic tribes and before the end of the Iron Age (about A.D. 400) the north people had had some association with Romans. However, the history of the people we know as Norse or Norwegians begins with the stories of the Vikings, people who were pushed by Germanic tribes to the edges of the seas and began a life of trade and raid, some believe in response to overcrowding on the poor agricultural soil of the region. From the Viking appearance to the twentieth century, Norwegian history is broken into periods of disorganization, union, and rule by others.

Vikings. Before the ninth century A.D. bands of hunters roamed the forests, living off the land and traveling among the fjords that broke the mountainous peninsula that would become Norway and Sweden. The rugged terrain separated them into small kingdoms ruled by jarls, kingdoms that soon learned to supplement their meager farming output by raiding their neighbors. In 863, Harold the Fair Hair managed to bring most of the small kingdoms under his rule. He ruled all of Norway until 933, when he was succeeded by his son Erick, who was soon driven from the throne by Hako I, a brother who had traveled to England and become a Christian.

These people had become expert shipbuilders by the 800s (see VIKINGS). In the next two centuries, they used their long, slender ships to travel as far as North America and the extremes of the Baltic and North seas. Some of these Vikings settled in Iceland. Others moved to France, then briefly dominated England. In writing about the Viking adventures in Europe, one author describes their style of fighting: "Headlong forward, foot and horsemen, charge and fight, and die like Normans" (Burchardt 1974, p. 75). However, by the year 1050, the Vikings had been defeated in Britain and their raids successfully resisted in other areas. The Holy Roman Empire and the Christian religion had spread across the sea to Norway.

Development of language. Before that time, the Norse language, had been mostly a spoken language. Interaction with Christian ambassadors from Rome brought the Vikings the Roman alphabet. This written language and their withdrawal from raiding as it became less

Stages in Norse History

Prehistory	9000 or 8000 B.C. to A.D. 800
Vikings	800 to 1030
Unification (the Saga Age)	1031–1319
Union with Sweden	1319–1537
Danish control	1537–1660
Independence	1660–1814
Rule by Sweden	1814–1905
Independence	1905-present

successful served to blend the Norse into one loosely knit group that began to sustain itself by a combination of fishing and farming. However, the geography of Norway separated the people into small units. Although they are unified by ancient tradition, Norwegians are physically separated into five divisions because of the waterways that dissect their country.

Danish rule. The geographic division of the country made it difficult to defend and to support its growing population. Norway found itself in alliance with or dominated by other Scandinavian nations—often through intermarriage of royal families. In 1319 such a marriage resulted in Norway's rule by the Swedish king Magnus Erikson. Shortly after, another royal family interaction resulted in rule by Denmark. For 500 years beginning in A.D. 1390, Norway, with its weakly united and poorer Norse people, was ruled by other Scandinavians, at first by the Danes in a union of Denmark, Norway, and Sweden, the Kalmar Union, and later, when Sweden withdrew from this union, by Denmark in a Norwegian-Danish Union. However, under this government the Norwegians were treated as second-class citizens. The union was dissolved under the Treaty of Vienna in 1814, and Norway then fell under Swedish control. Although the Norse leader, Christian Frederick, resisted Sweden's control and secured a vote of affirmation by the Norwegians, accompanied by a pledge by every voter to defend Norway's independence and sacrifice their lives and blood for the country, Sweden continued to rule. The 1814 action did, however, result in a conference at Erdavall at which a constitution was prepared that was to be the basis for Norwegian self-rule—creating a hereditary monarchy and a legislature, the Storting. Still, the Norwegians were ruled by the king of Sweden until 1905, even though they had, led by John Sverdrup, spoken for independence as early as the 1880s. Early in the 1900s, the Storting's image was enhanced by a Swedish industrialist, Alfred Nobel, who entrusted the awarding of the Nobel Peace Prize to that legislature beginning in 1901.

Independence. In 1905, Norway became an independent country in a bloodless separation voted by the Swedish Diet and the Norwegian Storting. This freedom from disinterested or sometimes suppressive Danish and Swedish rule gave the Norwegians impetus for progress in both Norway and Iceland. Under their own king, Norwegians began to expand the already developing industrial section, capitalizing on the abundant hydro-electric energy resources. Except for German occupation of the country in World War II and Germany's puppet government led by Vidkun Quisling, Norway has been a constitutional monarchy since 1905. In that year the Norwegians elected Prince Charles of Denmark to be their king. He was followed 52 years later by his son Olav V, who was succeeded by Harald V. But since 1914, Norwegians have been ruled under a constitution that provides for a legislature, the Storting, composed of representatives of the people. This Storting guides the king's choice of members of a council and prime minister.

The Icelandic Norwegians remained under Danish rule until 1944, at which time Iceland was organized as a republic under a president and a cabinet. The governments of both countries are designed to respect the traditional independence of individuals and to suspect any involvement with foreigners.

Culture Today

Family and the land. In keeping with the past, the Norwegians in Norway and Iceland are bound by family and land. They are generally suspicious of larger governmental units unless there is direct participation by the people in these units. Value is placed on individuality and self-dependence. A hereditary monarchy was chosen by the peo-

Small villages and towns are tucked along the shores of the many inlets and fjords that form the long Norwegian coastline. *From the Library of Congress.*

ple as their form of government. They then elected to manage the government through a parliament, taking care that each of 19 counties in the country is represented in a two-house system. With each county defending its own customs and needs, elections in Norway are heavily attended. About 85 percent of the voters exercise their right in each election. Seven major political parties and, occasionally, lesser ones energetically compete in these elections. One party, the Labor Party, has dominated most recent elections. The counties (*fylker*) and the divisions within the parliament are based on the five old regional divisions of the Norwegians.

Within these regions, Norwegians hold strongly to their ancient dependencies on neighbors and family. A common trait of Norwegians is the desire to suppress hatred or dislike. A disliked neighbor is the more respected—the day may come that this neighbor must be depended upon for aid. Along with this suppression of ill feelings, Norse life is filled with kindness and honesty. Norse people are sometimes misjudged because of their belief that one can say anything to any other person so long as it is honest.

Interdependence and equality is also seen in the family. Husbands and wives enjoy great equality within their prescribed functions. It is the mother's duty to take care of the children, the father's to provide the family income. But in the industrial world of the late twentieth century, many women work outside the family—an activity freely accepted by the husbands, who sometimes reciprocate by helping with household chores but rarely with supervising the children. Two neighborhood aids help the working mother with the children. Elderly women called *parktante*, employed by local governments, watch over very young children in community parks, and older neighborhood girls of ages seven to 12 earn spending money watching over younger children.

Local rule. Traditions of individuality and isolation along the small fjords are reflected by the Norwegian cities. The two large cities in Norway, Oslo and Bergen, are the ancient headquarters of the leaders of two of Norway's five regions. Government is inconspicuous in these cities. For example, there is only one large public building in Oslo, the city hall. Norwegian emphasis on local units of commerce and government is reflected in the highway system around Oslo. Most of the highways leading to the city extend along the fjord for only 25 or 30 miles. The independence of local groups is also seen in the legal systems of Iceland and Norway. Most issues of law are first given to city or town courts for resolution and are transferred to larger units of government only if the city cannot resolve the issues.

Economy. Norwegians and Icelanders pursue the ancient vocations of fishing and boat building. In Norway these occupations are often combined with farming as in the past. The Norwegians have combined these occupations with industry as a means of easier survival. Less than 15 percent of the land of Norway and Iceland can be farmed. Much of it is mountainous and rugged. Of the four percent arable land, less than one-third is used for crops such as barley, oats, and potatoes. The rest is used for forest materials that supply the large lumber and paper pulp industries. About one-fourth of Norwegian land is covered by pine forests. Most of the thousands of small farms in Norway include both food crops and forests.

About 70,000 families combine farming with offshore fishing, mostly for herring, while in Iceland 70 percent of the economy is dependent upon fishing. Fishing is a major element of the economy and caused some disputes with Norway's neighbors in the late 1980s. Norwegians and Russians quarreled over fishing rights in the Barrents Sea, and Norwegians and Swedes quarreled over a Norwegian ban on culling seal pups while seals were denuding the northern fishing beds.

In the far north, Lapps or Saami, depend heavily on reindeer for their livelihood (see LAPPS). Disaster struck this area with the 1986 Chernobyl nuclear plant explosion in Byelorussia. Radiation from this faulty plant made it necessary to destroy about 70 percent of the reindeer meat in 1986. Government officials estimated that one-third of all reindeer in Norway would have to be destroyed because of the radioactive fallout.

Industries based on plentiful hydro-electric energy in Norway and geothermal energy in Iceland are changing the ways people live. Most homes in Norway have reasonably priced electricity. The electrical energy has allowed Norway to move rapidly to develop the forest industry as well as industries built around aluminium production and iron alloys.

Since the 1970s, Norwegians have experienced new wealth and increased trading with other countries because of offshore oil discoveries in the North Sea. There is usually less than one percent unemployment in Norway. An elaborate welfare state protects the unemployed, sick, and elderly.

Literature. The Viking traditions are kept alive in Norwegian literature. Icelanders still enjoy reading tales of ships, ice-gods, and conquests written in the old language. A collection called the *Edda* is the most popular reading. Norwegians, too, recount the old stories. However, in Norway the old language gave way in the 1900s to a new people's language and then to a mixture of traditional and new languages. In these languages, Norwegian people have kept alive their interest in literature and in tradition through the writings of authors such as Camilla Collett (*The Governor's Daughter*), and Jonas Lie (*The Pilot and His Wife, The Visionary*). However, the two most revered Norwegian authors are still Henrik Ibsen and Björnstjerne Björnson. Both are winners of the Nobel Prize for Literature. Writing in the late nineteenth century, Ibsen kept alive Norwegian hopes for independence and vividly portrayed the depressed and suppressed Norwegians in such plays as *Peer Gynt* and *A Doll's House.* Björnson (1832–1910) wrote novels of the Norwegian life but is best remembered as author of the national anthem of Norway.

During the nineteenth and the twentieth centuries, Norwegians sought to find their own folk ways, without the influences of the Danes. Old folk art again became popular. Writers like Ashjoernsen and Moe collected folk and fairy tales that had been handed down orally and put them into written form. Sigrid Undset, considered the greatest of modern writers, wrote a trilogy about thirteenth-century Norway, *Kristin Lavrandsdátter,* that earned her the Nobel Prize for literature.

Art and music. Norwegians are proud of the ability of their most famous sculptor, Gustov Vigeland. On the edge of Oslo, this artist began to build a fountain but soon expanded it into a sculpture park of concrete, stone, and metal. The centerpiece of this sculpture is a 50-foot tower, elevated above the surrounding area and accessible by stairways—all enhanced by carvings of 121 entwined human figures. West of Oslo, Norwegians maintain a folk park in which are displayed some of the buildings of past days, including a wooden church with the ancient Viking at its peaks. In the twentieth century Edvard Munch became Norway's most noted painter through his development of expressionism. Edvard Grieg (1843–1907), Norway's most famous musician, composed melodies based on the old folk tunes. His work stands above all other Norwegian musicians.

Education. In Iceland, education is free and compulsory to age 16. Norwegians have had free and compulsory education for students from seven to 14 since 1860. After their elementary education, Norwegians may attend a three-year secondary school to prepare for a skilled job or a four-year grammar school in preparation for the university. Norway has two well-known universities at Oslo and Bergen. All education in Norway is free.

After 12 years of free education, every Norwegian man is obligated to serve 12 months in the military.

Religion. The ancient religion of the early Norse is kept alive in folk tales. It was a religion of many gods, who lived in a fortified city much as their earthling subjects. The chief god, Odin, left this earth when he was killed by a wolf, Fenrir. Odin is joined in the godly city by his wife, Frigg, Frey (the god of spring), Tir (an older chief god), Oega (god of the sea), and many others. When venturing forth to battle, Odin mounts an eight-footed Sleipnir and is escorted by three rows of nine maidens who form his guard, the Valkyriur, whose power is described in the ancient stories:

> Three troops of maidens, though one maid foremost rode.
> A white and helmeted maid.
> Their horses shook themselves, and from their manes there fell dew
> in the deep dales and on the high hills hail.
>
> Buchardt 1974, p. 103

Again in religion in the twentieth century, Norwegians have demonstrated their independent spirit. Long ago, under Danish influence, the people of Norway accepted the Lutheran religion. However, they developed their own Evangelical Lutheran denomination, insisted that their king be a member of this church, and empowered the king to appoint the church's ministry. The church is exclusively Norwegian, and all but 150,000 of the people of Norway are members. Ninety-three percent of Icelanders belong to their own form of this same Evangelical Lutheran Church.

Food, clothing, and shelter. Life in Norway is based on the family and the family home, stone or wood houses of one or two stories built on farm plots or gathered in small villages standing on the hillsides of riverbanks and fjords. Many of the farm homes stand beside wooden storehouses (*stubbin*) raised above the ground for protection against dampness. The upper floor is for storage, the lower one for the family's animals. Often the second floor storage area is accessed by stairways wrapping around the outside of the building.

More land is suitable for grazing than for crop raising, so the Norwegian diet depends heavily on dairy products. The abundance of fish makes this a staple of the Norwegian menu. One famous meal in Norway is the breakfast served to the children of Oslo before school. It consists of milk, bread, butter, jams and jellies, and fresh fruits and vegetables in season, along with cod liver oil.

Most people of Norway have adopted heavy Western-style clothing, but the Norwegians are proud of their past. In celebrations and other special occasions, they dress in the old costumes—for women a plain blouse decorated with jewelry and an ankle-length skirt. Often this dress is enhanced by a lace or fine cloth hat that sits on the back of the head. Men wear bibbed trousers or tight knee breeches, with embroidered vests, fancy buttons, and silver-buckled shoes, along with broad-brimmed hats.

Holidays. In the villages and on the farms, Norwegian people celebrate holidays with great feasts. Most holidays are religious celebrations: Maundy Thursday, Good Friday, Easter, Ascension Day, and Christmas. Other holidays are May Day, a Bank Holiday, and Constitution Day (May 17). Winters are cold and dark in Norwegian lands, so Christmas is a special event. Farmers and farmer-fishers spend weeks preparing special breads and wild berry jellies to accompany the hogs that provide traditional meals for the season. A special piece of wood, the Yule log, is brought in to be burned during the Christmas season.

Recreation. Winter sports are the most popular forms of recreation in Norway. Children learn to ski at an early age and cross-country skiing is enjoyed by many in the country. Easter week is a time for many Norwegian workers to take their families to the mountains for a skiing holiday. A section of the country in the south, between the cities of Stavanger and Krageroe, is dotted with small fjords sheltered from the open sea and winds. This is the Norwegian summer recreation region where vacationers come to enjoy sandy beaches, bright waterfalls, salt water swimming, and sailing.

For More Information

Burchardt, C. B. *Norwegian Life and Literature: English Accounts and Views.* Westport, Connecticut: Greenwood Press, 1974.

Henriksen, Joan Felicia. *Norwegian Politics.* Oslo: H. Aschehoug and Co., 1991.

Midgaard, John. *A Brief History of Norway.* Oslo: Tano, 1986.

PORTUGUESE

(pour′ chuh geez)

The native inhabitants of Portugal.

Population: 10,500,000 (1991 estimate).
Location: Portugal, on the west side of the Iberian Peninsula.
Language: Portuguese, a Romance language.

Geographical Setting

Lying between Spain and the Atlantic Ocean and bounded by the ocean on the west and south, Portugal is separated from Spain by its geology. Ranges of mountains, extensions of the Cantabrian Mountains, themselves extensions of the Pyrenees Mountains, which border Spain and France, cross diagonally from northeast to southwest or south and separate large fertile valleys inland. In the extreme north, the mountains give way to a highland plain that is an extension of the great plain of Spain. This plain is supplied with water by the Douro River, which originates in Spain and forms part of the northern border between the two countries. The central valleys are watered by the Tagus River and its tributaries. The capital city, Lisbon, is a major port at the mouth of the Tagus. In the south, the Guadiana River forms part of the border with Spain. The waters from its rivers, most of which originate in the mountains of Spain, allow for a good agricultural economy.

The climate of Portugal varies with the altitude and with the latitude. The north is cold and rainy. Centrally, Lisbon has about 25 inches of rain a year and moderate temperatures. The south has very hot summers.

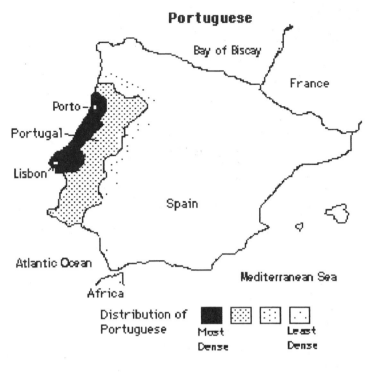

Portuguese

Distribution of Portuguese. Most Dense — Least Dense

Historical Background

Early settlers. Iberians, the earliest settlers of the Iberian Peninsula, inhabited the region that is now Portugal as early as 10,000 B.C. Part of the ancient land of Lusitania, they became subject to invasions by outsiders, beginning with the Celts around 1000 B.C. Romans conquered some of the area about 140 B.C., followed in the third century A.D. by the Roman soldiers of Augustus, in the fifth century by Alans and Visigoths, who swept through Spain to the Atlantic Ocean, and finally by Moors (Arabs), who conquered the area in 711. The current population known as Portuguese grew from the mixture of all the societies that have inhabited and traded in the region.

An independent kingdom. Muslims occupied the southern portion of the country for over 400 years, and had a profound influence on the land—an influence still reflected in some Portuguese architecture. However, by 1090, the Spanish kingdoms of Castille and Leon had again taken control over some of the land in the north and had placed Henry the Younger of Burgundy as its ruler with permission to rule any land south of the Tagus River that he could capture from the

Moors. There followed a century of war between the house of Burgundy and the Moors. Under Henry's widow, Theresa, the campaign against the Moors began to build a sense of national identity, which led to the formation of an independent kingdom in 1143 under her son Alfonso I.

Christians finally succeeded in driving out the Muslims from much of the country in the thirteenth century. One of the first Christian rulers, Diniz, was responsible for a number of advancements—the building of a university in 1308, the establishment of Portuguese literature, support for agriculture and shipbuilding, and the foundation of a navy. By this time, the northern portion of the country was settled by small farmers and the south became the province of large estate holders whose land was farmed by peasants.

Expansion. Henry, Prince of Portugal (Henry the Navigator, 1394–1460), led Portugal into an age of discovery and exploration. For many years he sent out ships to find a way around the fierce weather off the African coast. At Sagres he established a school for navigators and gathered around him explorers and navigators. The knowledge of the sea gained through Henry's work allowed Portugal to become an international sailing power.

These sailing ventures led to the development of international trade and to colonization. However, Portuguese leaders early recognized the limits of a small country's ability to establish large colonies and control far-off regions of the world. Affonso de Albuquerque (1453–1515) decided that the way to world power was to establish fortified positions controlling vital sea lanes. These forts established claims on territories without really taking control of the people there. De Albuquerque established a fort at Ormuz to control the Persian Gulf, at Socotra to control the Red Sea, and at Malacca, the Malay Archipelago, Ceylon, and the Bay of Bengal. For a time, these control points were effective. Portugal controlled trade in pepper, mace, nutmeg, cloves, silk, and lace.

Under King Manuel I, who assumed the throne in the fifteenth century (1495–1521), Lisbon became a great port of Renaissance Europe. Less tolerant than his predecessors, Manuel I expelled the Jews from the country in 1497. But this was a period of European expansion throughout the world and Portuguese navigators roamed the oceans, winning command of the spice trade and establishing overseas colonies in the fifteenth and sixteenth centuries. Regions such as Angola, Guinea, Mozambique, Timor (in Indonesia), Macau (near

China), and the Azores fell under Portuguese rule. However, these colonies were short-lived as Portugal pursued its policy of force and minimal colonization. In the Malay colonies, the Portuguese demonstrated their intolerance by first persecuting Muslims, then expanding its Inquisition to include Hindu practices. The result was the withdrawal of Hindus from Portuguese claims, Hindus on whom the Portuguese had depended for trade. In the middle 1500s trade had begun to fall and the Portuguese seamen had turned to the slave trade for income. Portuguese now built large fortifications along the coast of Africa that were stone walled and included drawbridges, auction rooms, and dungeons, which they felt were necessary to ensure effective trade. Portuguese seamen and businessmen also extracted products such as gold and diamonds from Brazil. Nowhere did the Portuguese win popularity among the people whose territory fell under their claims. The Portuguese role as a world power came to an end with the change in the structure of Europe, which saw the Dutch separate from Spain and begin to play a world role at the same time that Spain was moving to rule over Portugal. By the 1600s the Dutch East India Company had put Portugal out of business in Malay, India, and the Persian Gulf.

Union with Spain. In 1580 Portugal and Spain were unified under the rule of King Philip. However, this union lasted less than 100 years. The Portuguese regained their independence in 1668 through a rebellion led by John, Duke of Brugaza, and supported by England. The following years brought peace and prosperity from the agricultural and mineral wealth of the overseas colonies until another period of foreign interference interrupted Portuguese progress. Again the Spanish invaded in 1762, and Napoleon brought French forces into the country from 1807 to 1811. Under these rules overseas trade continued, and some nobles profited, but the peasants suffered under the burden of heavy taxes. They objected when overseas adventures began to exhaust the Portuguese treasury.

Rebellion, republic, and dictatorship. A peasant rebellion ended when King Carlos I was assassinated in 1908 and the monarchy abolished. A republic was soon established, and under it the Portuguese people experienced a stream of short-lived governments until 1926. Then Dr. Antonio de Oliveira Salazar, an economics professor, became dictator of Portugal and remained in power for 36 years, relying on military force and a secret police to exercise complete control. His successor, Marcello Caetano, was overthrown in 1974, and the Portuguese again took to the streets, staging demonstrations, political rallies, and public debates—activities that had been forbidden to them for over 40 years.

The loss of an empire. For much of the middle twentieth century, the overseas colonies of Portugal were agitating for independence. The people of Angola had begun a freedom movement by 1956; Guinea declared for independence in 1963; and Mozambique, in 1964. In 1974, Portugal officially abandoned its overseas empire and the country suddenly became deluged by a half million *retornados*, refugees from the colonies. The retornados included both natives of Portugal who had lived in the colonies and disgruntled colonial natives. Since then Portugal has struggled to support a burgeoning population. In an area slightly larger than the state of Maine in the United States, the Portuguese must support a population that is nine times as large as the population of that state. Added to this economic burden is the commitment to aid now-separated colonies such as Angola. In 1988, Portugal abandoned its claim to the last of its overseas empire with an agreement to turn Macau over to the Chinese in 1999.

Twentieth-century rebellion. Most of the twentieth century has been marked by rebellions as the Portuguese people struggled with overpopulation and declining assets. A rebellion of 1908 resulted in the assassination of the king and the demise of the monarchy. A republic was formed, which itself was subject to a rebellion in which the president was arrested and exiled (1917). The constitution of the country was rewritten in 1976 to reflect a movement toward socialism, revised in 1982, and again in 1989—this time to eliminate aspects of Marxism from the law. So widespread were the Portuguese overseas holdings and Portuguese migrations on their release, that the governing legislature, the Assembly with 250 members, provided for four members to represent Portuguese citizens living overseas.

Culture Today

A mix of peoples. The first Portuguese were an Iberian people. Over the years Celts, Romans, Jews, Moors, and others migrated into the area and combined to develop a people with unique physical characteristics. The Portuguese typically have brown eyes, dark wavy hair, and an average height of 5 feet 5 inches among males.

Economy. Located on a peninsula, the Portuguese people are isolated from the rest of Europe and this has affected their economy and slowed cultural changes. The largest number of Portuguese workers continue in the traditional lifestyle as fishermen and peasants who farm using the ancient methods of the ox-cart and hoe. Their principal crops are wheat, maize, potatoes, tomatoes, and grapes. A few might still be found stomping the grapes with their feet to produce port wine, for which the Portuguese are world-famous. The fishermen mainly catch sardines, which are canned by the industrial labor force of the country.

Clothing, shelter, and food. While Western-style clothing has come to Portugal as it has to other European nations, agricultural workers can still be found wearing traditional dress: berets, loose-fitting shirts, and trousers for men; long dresses and shawls for women. The *capucha*, a hooded cape, and the *pathocas*, a rain cape made of reeds, are also worn in certain areas.

Peasants and fishermen live in small villages, often without electricity. Older-style homes feature latticed windows, orange tile against whitewashed clay, and graceful arches leading to an inner courtyard with lemon and almond trees. In their kitchens, women cook the traditional midday meal—soup, fish or eggs, and meat with pudding. The poorer people typically dine on a thick vegetable broth, a bean stew, or rice with sardines. Fish is the staple of the Portuguese diet; *bacalhau* (dried salt cod) is a national dish. Other dishes reflect regional differences: for example, nearly every town specializes in a particular cake. Belem favors cinnamon-flavored custard tarts and Madeira honeycake. Spring water or mineral water drawn from the Portuguese spas is a popular beverage. Coffee houses are a common sight in the city, but their patrons are mostly men since the older Portuguese still regard the home as the proper place for women.

Women. Today Portuguese women have gone outside the home, excelling as writers, painters, and university professors in present-day Portugal. Yet their role in the household is still considered of primary importance, for the family is viewed as the basic unit of Portuguese society. Relations between parents and children are generally close; in families with parents who migrate to other countries for work, grandparents and relatives become guardians. Portuguese children tend to live at home until marriage, and most are married in gath-

Women do much of the buying and selling in markets in Portugal. *Courtesy of Leah Cadavona.*

erings of the family and friends at one of the many Catholic churches of Portugal.

Religion. Most Portuguese are adherents of the Roman Catholic faith, and most of their celebrations are religious. Traditional pilgrimages, or *romarias*, to shrines outside a town or village are among the most important events of the Portuguese year. Families normally camp out in the open shrine, where they roast sardines for food and hold candlelight mass devotions at night.

Holidays. Exept for July and September, the Portuguese celebrate at least one occasion each month—the great majority of these holidays

Forted towns such as this guard the coastline of Portugal. *Courtesy of Leah Cadavona.*

being religious ones. Other than these Christian celebrations, Portuguese in Portugal celebrate the founding of the republic in 1910 on October 5 and the restoration of that independence on December 1. Portugal Day (June 10) and Liberty Day (April 25) have to do with the takeover of the Portuguese government by the military in 1974. In addition to these celebrations Carnival Day and special days for local patron saints are the occasions for dressing in elaborate costumes and joining parades accompanied by music and the perfume of flowers strewn along the way.

Education. Aside from its religious role, the Church plays a major role in the education and health care of the people. All children must attend school from the ages of six to 14. Many elect to do so in the several hundred private church-run schools rather than in the overcrowded public schools. Technical training schools provide education for ages that approximate grades 10 through 12 in American schools. Ninety-one percent of all Portuguese of these ages attend school. Beyond this level, admission to colleges and universities is limited by quotas set each year for each subject and each school.

Health. The government covers 80 percent of the costs of a patient's hospital visits in the cities. However, health services supplied to the people by the state are insufficient. The government can provide only one doctor for every 150 people, and many have died of tuberculosis. Therefore, the church supplies health services to supplement those provided by the government.

Government. The Portuguese elect their president and legislators. Even those Portuguese who work abroad are represented in the National Assembly. A prime minister and council of ministers is appointed by the president to carry out laws peaceably, but Portuguese politics has been marked by violence in recent years with strikes over economic reforms that included employers' rights to lay off workers and terrorist bombings against members of the major political parties and against installations of other nations inside Portugal.

Recreation. Portuguese economic and health conditions are poor, but families are close and the people still enjoy leisure time activities. Portuguese bullfights are distinguished by their lack of violence. The bulls' horns are sheathed to avoid injury to the horses, and the bull is not killed in the ring. Football and dancing are national pastimes. Almost every village has a floor made of beaten earth for the lively fandango and other folk dances. Portuguese singers specialize in the *fado*, a sad, throaty musical form that has been compared to the blues and is said to reflect the bittersweet nature of life in Portugal.

Arts. Festivities might be held in older buildings of Portugal, distinguished by their Manueline architecture—a style that became popular during the reign of King Manuel I and reflects a passion for the sea. The columns of Manueline churches are twisted to form wavy spirals and their arches are decorated with nautical cables and mariners' knots. Windows and doorways might be covered with branches of laurel leaves, corn cobs, pearls, ropes, and anchors. The building material is likely to be a form of decorated tile work known as *azulejos* (probably derived from earlier Moorish styles). Featuring tiles in blues, yellow, purples, and greens, azulejos have also been used to decorate fountains, benches, and living rooms with geometric designs or scenes of landscapes and hunting. Poetry is the great strength of Portuguese literature and dates back to *Os Lusiadas* by Luiz de Camoes, a long epic poem praising Portugal's triumphs and heroes. Poets and prose writers of the twentieth century (e.g., Fernando Pessoa, Ferreira de Castro) use the experience of being Portuguese as a common subject of their works.

Change. Since the 1960s, there has been a major exodus of people from the land as Portugal struggles for an industrial economy. The Portuguese have become Europe's foremost manufacturers of cork. Textile and appliance industries have also developed. Still the country is among the poorest in Europe, and many emigrate elsewhere to support their families. In Paris there is a community of over one half million Portuguese workers, some of whom return home to see their families only once a year.

For More Information

Camara, J. Mattosa, Jr. *The Portuguese Language.* Chicago: University of Chicago Press, 1972.

Munes, Maria L. *Becoming True to Ourselves: Cultural Decolonization and National Identity in the Lives of the Portuguese-Speaking World.* Boulder, Colorado: Greenwood Press, 1987.

Payne, Stanley G. *A History of Spain and Portugal,* Volumes 1 and 2. Madison, Wisconsin: University of Wisconsin Press, 1973.

SCOTS

(skawts)

People of Scotland, a northern country in the British Islands.

Population: 5,100,000 (1991 estimate).
Location: Northern Britain.
Languages: English, Scots, Gaelic.

Geographical Setting

Scotland occupies roughly the northern one-third of Britain, an area about the size of Maine. The nation's major geographical feature has also been its most important cultural one—the distinction between the southern lowlands and the northern highlands. The fault line separating the two runs diagonally from just north of Glasgow to just south of Aberdeen. Two-thirds of Scots live in the lowlands, which contain the two largest cities, Edinburgh, the Scottish capital, and Glasgow. Not all the lowlands are low; in the southeast the land rises to the Cheviot Hills, which mark Scotland's border with England. The border region, with its forests and other unspoiled areas, is lightly populated. Most of the lowland population lives in the broad midland valley that includes Glasgow and Edinburgh.

    Northeast of this strip, the Grampian Highlands rise between the Moray Firth to the north and the Firth of Tay to the south. Here are more mountains and rolling heath and coastal cities such as Dundee and Aberdeen, center of the thriving North Sea oil business that arose in the late 1970s. The Northwest Highlands lie north of a second fault running from Inverness southwest to Fort William. Three lochs (lakes), the most famous among them being Loch Ness with its fabled monster, are connected along this fault by the Caledonian Canal. The rocky highland hills and long narrow valleys include vast wilderness

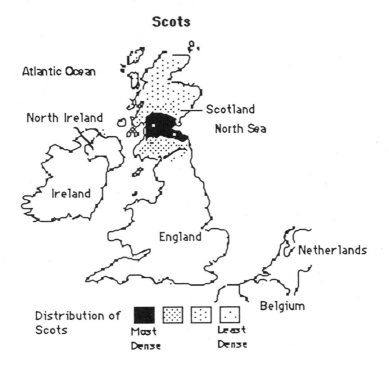

Scots

Atlantic Ocean

North Ireland

Scotland

North Sea

Ireland

England

Netherlands

Belgium

Distribution of Scots

Most Dense

Least Dense

areas whose beauty attracts tourists and hikers from around the world. Scotland's east coast faces often-bitter winds from the North Sea; the west coast, with its picturesque Hebrides Islands, enjoys a temperate climate brought by the north-flowing Gulf Stream. The Gulf Stream's influence makes the west generally warmer and wetter than the east. Glasgow and Edinburgh lie only 40 miles apart, for example. Yet Glasgow's rainy climate compares to that of Seattle, whereas Edinburgh's is more like San Francisco's—still moist but less rainy.

Historical Background

Early history. The earliest recorded history concerning the Scots comes from the Romans, who controlled southern Britain (see EN-

GLISH) in the first century A.D. In A.D. 84, the Romans defeated the tribal armies of Scotland in battle, but they were not able to conquer the people. The Roman emperor Hadrian built a massive stone wall to isolate the fierce "barbarians." Visitors can still see the remains of Hadrian's Wall, running across what is now northern England just south of the Scottish border. By the 600s, four tribal groups had emerged: the Angles of the southeast, related to the Germanic tribes settling England at the time; the Britons of the southwest, a Celtic people related to the Welsh (see WELSH); the Picts, also Celtic, who dominated the Highlands; and the Scots, a Celtic group who settled the western islands and coast from nearby Ireland. Christianity, brought by missionaries such as St. Ninian and St. Columba, spread slowly among the tribes beginning in about 400.

Kings, clans, and feuds. Following Viking invasions of the 800s and 900s, the four tribes gradually united under Scottish kings such as Kenneth MacAlpin. MacAlpin, who brought the Scots and Picts together in 843, is often called the first king of Scotland. His descendants succeeded in gaining limited control over rival kings and the feuding clans (groups of families related by blood). One king who briefly unseated the dynasty was Macbeth of Moray, who killed Duncan, a descendant of MacAlpin, in 1040. (Macbeth, who ruled for 17 years before being killed by Duncan's son, seems to have been a wiser monarch than Shakespeare's version of him in the famous play.) Eventually, the Scots gave their name to the land and all its people, but the kings often ruled in name only. Especially in the remote Highlands, local clan leaders in practice kept their independence.

Rivalry with England. In 1066, Norman invaders from France gained control of England. The powerful new English rulers (like Edward I, called "the Hammer of the Scots" in the 1200s) gained influence over the Scottish kings, thus helping to shape culture in the lowlands. Still the Scots resisted English dominance, often by allying with England's enemy, France. One brief period of glory came with Robert Bruce, a noble who gained the Scottish crown and wiped out an English army at Bannockburn in 1314. Every Scottish child hears how Bruce learned patience (while hiding out in a cave from the English) by watching a spider weave its web. Bruce's daughter married Walter the Steward (steward was a high office of the royal administration). This led to *Stewart*, later spelled *Stuart*, becoming the name of Scotland's royal house. Over the next few centuries, Stuart kings and queens rarely died in bed; 13 of them were killed by the English or while fighting rebellious subjects. Most famous is Mary Queen of Scots, beheaded by order of Queen Elizabeth in 1587.

Prickly partnership. The English and Scottish royal houses had become closely connected through marriage. On Elizabeth's death in 1603, Mary's son James, already king of Scotland, succeeded to the English throne as well. The Catholic Stuart monarchs faced trouble in both England and Scotland, as religious disputes among Catholics and Protestants wracked the land. James' son Charles I was executed in 1649 by Oliver Cromwell's Protestant regime, James II, after the Stuarts' restoration to the throne, was replaced in 1688 by his Protestant daughter Mary and her husband, William of Orange. While rebellions would continue in Scotland, the union of crowns marked the beginning of an increasing (yet not always comfortable) bond between Scotland and her more powerful neighbor. The Treaty of Union (1707) formalized the political connection, by incorporating Scotland's government into that of England. This created the United Kingdom and laid the foundation for the British Empire—to which Scots would contribute greatly in coming centuries.

Rebellion and enlightenment. Scotland in the 1700s experienced contrasting extremes of political turmoil and cultural brilliance. On

An ancient castle overlooks Edinburgh, Scotland. *Courtesy of Amy A. Trenkle.*

the political side, James Stuart, son of James II, led rebellions in the early 1700s, backed by France and Spain, England's Catholic enemies. The most important of these "Jacobite" (from Jacobus, Latin for James) campaigns occurred in 1715 and in 1745, when James's son Charles also shook Britain by invading from Scotland. The attempts, though failures, engendered a vast body of romantic legend, particularly around the figure of Charles, called Bonnie Prince Charlie or the Young Pretender (claimant to the throne). The Jacobites found support more among the fiercely independent highlanders, who had remained largely Catholic, than among the stern Protestant lowlanders.

Yet amid this political trouble, rooted in the past, Scotland surged into the modern age with remarkable commercial and intellectual vigor. This movement, called the Scottish Enlightenment, was led by thinkers such as philosopher David Hume and economist Adam Smith, both of whom profoundly influenced Western thought. Merchants and (by the late 1700s) industrialists brought prosperity to cities such as Edinburgh and Glasgow. The age had its dark side, however, in the "Clearances" by which ambitious landowners evicted their tenants in order to raise livestock. The cities grew enormously as landless peasants fled the countryside to become workers in city industry.

Scottish or British? By the 1800s, the Scots' story had seemingly become the story of Britain, the island on which the Scots, Welsh, and English are found. Yet Scots retained their distinctive character, even as they contributed to Britain's prosperity and worldwide power. They often led the way in technology and science. James Watt developed the principles of steam power, thus earning the title "Father of Industry"; John Macadam gave his name to the material used in paving roads; Scottish-born Alexander Graham Bell invented the telephone; and James Clerk Maxwell devised equations that unified the forces of electricity and magnetism, thus setting the course of modern physics. Scottish generals and soldiers fought and won Britain's wars. Scottish politicians helped lead Britain and her possessions the world over. Also, Canada's first two prime ministers were Scots. Scots emigrated in huge numbers, many south to England, others to Canada, Australia, or the United States.

Finally, mighty shipyards in Glasgow and arms factories in Falkirk provided the hardware that saw Britain through two world wars. The rise and decline of industrial centers such as Glasgow made the

Scottish worker a potent force in British politics, and the Labour Party in Scotland has been more radical than its English counterpart. During the Thatcher years (1979–1991), Labour consistently won in Scotland, although Conservatives continue to hold power in England—and thus over Scotland as well. The growing powerlessness of the Scottish voter in national elections has led to the renewed calls for political reform and for some form of self-rule for Scotland.

Culture Today

Clash of the Tartans. The Scot has become a romantic figure in popular imagination, a highland warrior draped in colorful cloth with crisscross pattern (tartan), carrying a huge sword (Claymore), and marching to the stirring sound of bagpipes. Ironically, this picture was created almost entirely by one man. Sir Walter Scott (1771–1832) wrote his highly popular novels after those very symbols had been banned (until 1782) by the British government, and after the highland way of life had been changed forever by the Jacobites' defeat and the Clearances. Yet Scott's works (*Waverly, Ivanhoe, The Lady of the Lake,* among many others) sparked a Scottish rage in British fashion. All over England (and America) people suddenly "discovered" Scottish ancestors and claimed their tartans. Weaving houses in Scotland were deluged with orders for the woolen cloth. They wove the traditional patterns and invented new ones to satisfy customers without a claim to an old one. The fad reached its peak when Queen Victoria and Prince Albert bought an estate, Balmoral, in the highlands in 1858, and Prince Albert designed a "Balmoral" tartan. Yet "tartanitis" continues to fascinate Scots, their descendants, and others worldwide.

Literature. Aside from Scott, Scottish authors include Robert Louis Stevenson (*Treasure Island, Kidnapped, Dr. Jekyll and Mr. Hyde*), J. M. Barrie (*Peter Pan*), and Sir Arthur Conan Doyle, creator of the immortal Sherlock Holmes. Scotland's best-loved writer, however, is without doubt the poet Robert Burns (1759–1796). Burns' poems celebrate the underdog and glorify the lost cause, themes dear to the Scottish heart, with its dethroned monarchs and Jacobite rebellions. Many Scots can quote long passages of Burns that they have learned in school, and Burns Night (January 25) is a festive occasion for Scots (as for the Burns societies and clubs around the globe). Scots have also made major contributions to scholarship, producing many classics of the academic world. David Hume (*Concerning Human Understanding*) and Adam Smith (*The Wealth of Nations*), mentioned above, revolutionized philosophy and economics in the 1700s; Thomas Carlyle's *French Revolution* was one of the most influential historical works of the 1800s. Poet Hugh MacDiarmid (1892–1979) is perhaps the best-known modern writer. Like Burns, he wrote in Scots, a lowland English.

The arts. Scots have a strong interest in arts, such as painting, architecture, and music. Allan Ramsay and Sir Henry Raeburn were famous portrait painters of the 1700s, and Alexander Nasmyth founded a tradition of landscape painting about the same time. In the 1800s, Sir David Wilkie specialized in rural and historical scenes. Robert Adam, with his sons William and John, developed the neo-classical look that distinguishes buildings of the late 1700s in Edinburgh. The Adam family designed many London buildings also, and their style was adopted throughout Europe. Charles Rennie Mackintosh designed buildings in and around Glasgow in the late 1800s, developing a style that helped originate the *art nouveau* look. His furniture and decorative designs created the "the Glasgow style," which (like the Adams' work) was copied worldwide. Scots enjoy their rich tradition of folk music, often sung with the fiddle. Songs like *Annie Laurie* and *Auld Lang Syne* are favorites through the English-speaking world. The famous bagpipe remains the typically Scottish instrument, often associated with a military context, but played on many public occasions in the country.

Language. In the past, highlanders spoke Gaelic, a Celtic language, and lowlanders spoke Scots, an old form of English influenced by Gaelic, Dutch, and French. Scots, the language of the old nobility, suffered when the king and his court moved to London in 1603. Today, most Scots speak English, but always with the distinctive Scottish accent. Scots survives, still spoken among the Scots themselves—though often watered down by English—and of course read in the poetry of Robert Burns. Scots words are expressive and colorful, as in "Ah'm fair farfochen" (I'm exhausted) or "the bairn's a wee bit wabbit" (the child's a little tired). Gaelic survives only in isolated areas of the Highlands.

Religion. The Presbyterian Church of Scotland—"the Kirk" in Scots—was founded by John Knox (c. 1514–1542), a Scottish leader influ-

Bagpipes are the musical symbol of Scotland. This bagpiper is playing in front of the National Gallery. *Courtesy of Amy A. Trenkle.*

enced by the strict Protestant theology of the Swiss reformer John Calvin. The Kirk, puritanic and democratic, has done much to shape Scottish character. To the Presbyterians, all are equal in the eyes of God—a dangerous belief to the class-conscious English. Though the Kirk's influence has lessened in recent times, its values—hard work, thrift, humility, and a certain grimness of outlook at which Scots themselves often poke fun—remain, especially in the lowlands where the church is strongest.

Clans. Traditional family structure, especially in the Highlands, centered around the clan. There are about 90 original clans. Many of the clan names are prefixed by "Mac," meaning "son of." Thus, clan MacGregor look back to its founder, a man named Gregor. The clans have loosely defined territories, and feuding (prolonged wars, often spanning generations) were once common between clans. The most famous feud was that between the Campbells (who supported the English) and the MacDonalds (Jacobites). Even today there are MacDonalds who will not speak to Campbells and vice-versa. Large clans enrolled smaller ones as allies, and the alliances also became traditional.

Food, clothing, and shelter. The Scots' diet reflects their agricultural roots. Main staples are oatmeal, barley, and potatoes. Oatmeal is made into porridge, a thick, hot breakfast cereal traditionally seasoned with salt. Barley is used primarily in the distillation of Scotch whiskey, now a major source of export revenue. Potatoes ("tatties") are most often eaten mashed. Brave tourists sample haggis, for which the heart, liver, and other organs of a sheep are chopped with onions and oatmeal, then stuffed into a sheep's stomach and boiled. This unique meal, served with tatties and "a wee dram" (small portion of whiskey), has taken its place with the tartan and bagpipes as a national symbol. Scots also enjoy rich vegetable soups. Seafood in many forms, but often smoked, is popular; beef is the favorite red meat.

The famous Scottish kilt, a knee-length skirt of tartan pattern, was created by an Englishman, Thomas Rawlinson, who lived in the 1700s. The older kilts were larger rectangles of cloth, hanging over the legs, gathered at the waist, and wrapped in folds around the upper body. The blanket-like garment served as a bed-roll for a night spent outdoors. Aside from the kilt, fancy "highland" dress includes a *sporan* (leather purse on a belt), stockings, brogues (broags shoes), dress jacket, and a number of decorative accessories. (The plaid is a length of tartan cloth draped over the shoulder, and does not properly refer to the pattern, which is the tartan.) Women's fancy dress is simpler, though elegant, consisting of white cotton blouse, perhaps with embroidered patterns, and a silk tartan skirt. Her version of the plaid, a tartan also in silk, is hung over the shoulder and pinned in place with a brooch. This finery, like the tartans, is mostly an invention of the modern age but has become traditional and it is taken quite seriously. The tartan shows up elsewhere, commonly worn on ties, caps, and shirts—even on cars and in the costumes of young "punk rockers" in Edinburgh and Glasgow.

Before the Clearances of the late 1700s and after, most Scottish peasants lived in turf and stone cottages. Such cottages still exist in some Highland areas. Most Scots today, however, are town- or city-dwellers. In the 1800s, many lived in poor, crowded city tenements, because the influx to the cities happened quickly. Housing became a growing concern of local government beginning as early as the 1800s. After World War II, "council houses" (provided by local councils) became widespread. The multistory blocks contain small, rented apartments. Almost 60 percent of Scots live in such housing, as compared with only about 30 percent of the English.

Holidays. Most Scottish holidays are those celebrated throughout Great Britain (see ENGLISH). However, two holidays are unique to Scotland: Scottish Quarter Day, celebrated 40 days after Christmas, and the commemoration of St. Andrew, patron saint of Scotland, on November 30.

For More Information

Bell, Brian. *Insight Guides: Scotland.* Singapore: APA Publications, 1991.

Daiches, David (ed.). *A Companion to Scottish Culture.* London: Edward Arnold (Publishers) Ltd., 1981.

Finlayson, Iain. *The Scots.* New York: Atheneum, 1987.

Fodor's 91 Scotland. New York: Fodor's Travel Publications, 1991.

SICILIANS
(sa sil′ yuns)

Native peoples of the Italian island of Sicily.

Population: 5,200,000 (1990 estimate).
Location: The largest island in the Mediterranean Sea, two miles from the southern extremity of the peninsula of Italy and 60 miles from Tunisia in Africa.
Language: Italian.

Geographical Setting

The Apenine Mountains, the spine of Italy, extend through the toe of the peninsula to the island of Sicily, where they commence nearest the mainland with the active volcano, Etna. The mountains then extend around the edge of the island, leaving an interior plain and other regions of rolling hills that break the mountains on the southeast and at the western tip of the triangular land mass. The coast in the south is cluttered with salt marshes. But most of the level parts of the island and the rolling hills are covered with a rich red soil on which the Sicilians grow many crops, but chiefly grains, citrus fruits, and grapes. Temperatures on the island vary with altitude but are mostly moderate. In April and September fierce winds blow across the Mediterranean Sea from Africa, the sirocco winds. These winds are capable of much damage since the forests that once covered the hills and mountains have been denuded in many places. Sicily is an area of frequent earthquakes.

The strategic position of the island, guarding the Mediterranean Sea and providing an approach to the European mainland, made Sicily a place of great importance to the early Mediterraneans.

Sicilians

Distribution of Sicilians

Most Dense

Least Dense

Historical Background

Greek settlers. Sicily has long been a mixing ground for the many peoples of the Mediterranean area, and the people and land today reflect that varied history. Before 2000 B.C. the island was inhabited by a people (*Sicanians*) who are known today only through the rock carvings they left in the western part of the island. Shortly after that date, immigrants, possibly from the direction of Greece, drove the Sicanians inland and settled along the craggy coastline. These *Sikelians* also left their marks on the land in the form of tombs in terraced hills and monuments. In 734 B.C. settlers from the African trading center of Carthage settled on the eastern shore and built a seaport there used for carrying out trade and for war with Athens. This city, Syracuse (Siracusa), became for a time the most important city on the island. It was the subject of tyrannical rule for much of its early history. Still in the 700s B.C. Greeks settled along the west coast of Sicily and began to expand to other parts of the country, first fighting the Syracuse. The Greeks expanded their territory but were never able to command the whole island. By 480 B.C. Carthaginians had gained command and began a period of prosperous trade and building. The island became involved in the Peloponnesian Wars when Syracuse defeated Athens in 413. Seven thousand Greeks in Sicily were rounded up and starved to death during this struggle.

Romans. Still, there was little unity among the various peoples of the island until 298 B.C., when Pyrrhus of Epirus (northwestern Greece) was able to conquer most of the island and subjugate the people. Thirty years later, the island was a loosely united collection of city-states. Two of them, Messina, located near Mt. Etna, and Syracuse, a bit farther south, were at war. The Messinans sought help and found it in the legions of Rome. Roman soldiers responded in a war with Carthage and Syracuse fought on Sicilian soil. Unsuccessful in shutting off ships from Carthage, Romans built a fleet of their own and emerged victorious over the forces of Carthage. For six centuries following this victory in 227 B.C., Rome was in command of Sicily. Under the Romans, Sicilians built great public buildings, expanded trade, and became involved in art in a period some call the first Golden Age of Sicily.

Vandals, Goths, Byzantines, and Arabs. The invasions were not ended, however. By 400 A.D. Vandals had reached the island by sea, and they were followed by Goths and then Byzantines. Sicily became the western outpost of the Byzantine empire. In the late 600s, a new wave of rulers had come to the island from Africa, the Arabs crusading in the name of Islam. By 878 the Arabs had defeated the stronghold at Syracuse and the island had become a Muslim land. But Arab interest lagged and the island fell into near anarchy. One threatened leader again looked for help and found it among the Normans of what is now France.

Normans. Led by Roger de Hautville, the Normans conquered the island and established a single kingdom there. The second king, Roger II, led the land into 50 years of growth and prosperity known as the second Golden Age. Again foreign intervention disrupted the tranquil life. In 1187, the weak king William II died, leaving a kingdom again on the verge of anarchy to his wife, Constance. Constance remarried, this time to the Holy Roman Emperor from Germany, Henry VI.

Germans. Germany became the ruling power in Sicily. A strong ruler, Frederick II, was followed by Manfred, who was disliked by the Roman Catholic Church. The Holy See, then powerful throughout Europe, replaced Manfred with Charles, Duke of Anjou, and French feudalism came to the island.

The Sicilians were, however, not disposed to trade their old, more democratic ways for feudalism. Struggling until 1282, the Sicilians gathered at the sound of the first bell of Easter at the Church of Santo Spirito in Palermo. In the "Sicilian Vespers" they advanced on the French rulers of the city and drove them out. In the process, 8,000 French people and Sicilians who had cooperated with them were killed.

Spain. Again, the Sicilians needed help to protect themselves from the angry French. They found it this time in Peter III of Aragon and Sicily became a Spanish satellite. Under various leaders, mostly vice-roys assigned by Aragon, Spain ruled the land until 1712. The island, however, did not lack for interest from other nations. In battles between Dutch and British navies, the British found Sicily an attractive base and invaded the island. The Treaty of Utrect in 1712 included a British decision to give the island to Savoy. The next in the succession of owners was Austria, its emperor claiming the island in 1718. Sicilians were not happy with this management and by the mid-1800s were prepared to seek freedom. This time the people of Palermo turned toward Italy. General Garibaldi, the uniter of mainland Italy, crossed into Sicily in 1860. His rule of the island was generous and benevolent, such a change from past experiences that the Sicilians and the people of Naples, with whom they had been loosely associated in a nation of "Two Sicilies," voted to become parts of Garibaldi's Italy. Except for a brief period (1943–1946) when American military commanders took charge of the island, Sicily has been part of Italy since the time of the great general.

Italian rule. Italy itself was and is a divided country with a prosperous, heavily inhabited north and a poorer, less densely populated south. Sicily is part of the less prosperous south. In the 1980s the Italian government undertook to improve health and educational services to the south. But serious economic issues arose as the projects for improvement did not result quickly enough in economic growth. In the 1990s, Sicily is still developing, but relies for nearly one-fourth of its income on the trade in tourists eager to view the relics of its varied past.

Culture Today

Variety. Few of the invaders of Sicily were eliminated completely from the island. The result is a people of mixed descent and with customs and characteristics unlike their mainland partners. The various heritages have come together in a Sicilian people that distrusts foreign visitors—a distrust growing from past experiences—even though a major portion of the Sicilian income depends on visitors from other lands. One Sicilian author describes Sicilians as living in a "wall of silence" and, when among foreigners, unable to remember the road to their own homes, even when the roads and homes are in sight.

In contrast to Italian neighbors reputed as often loud and boisterous, the typical Sicilian is reserved.

Shelter and clothing. Variations are seen everywhere: in the division of the population among very rich and very poor; in building styles that include ancient ruins, large palaces, masses of shacks, and ugly villages; and in relatively new cities like Messina, destroyed by earthquake in 1909, rebuilt, destroyed by war in 1943, and rebuilt once more. The rich can be seen living in hilltop mansions, while nearby are small stone houses with tile roofs, or, in the cities, tightly packed block houses and apartments from which washed clothes are hung across the narrow alleys and streets. Stone is the building material of Sicily, and some farm homes are little more than shaped and stacked stones with wooden doors and thatched roofs.

Sicilians in the 1990s dress in Western-style trousers, shirts, and dresses, usually of dark colors. Only in festivals and shows do the women wear the traditional dress—a light-colored blouse with flowing sleeves and a bright, richly embroidered, long skirt with a matching vest and small head cover. In the 1990s, Sicilians dress for practicality. Fishermen often go barefoot; the warm weather encourages the male workers to wear pants and undershirts and peasant women are often seen in loosely fitted dresses.

Economy. Even though the island has a budding petroleum industry, poverty is common in Sicily. Nearly 50 percent of the working-age population might be unemployed at any given time. Fewer than half a million people work in industry, mostly in shipping, construction, and production of such items as fertilizers and sulfur. Others work in the oil fields, in the vineyards of the famous wineries, on fishing vessels, or as small businessmen. Six hundred thousand Sicilians are farmers of small individual plots or workers in larger citrus or wheat farms.

Mafia. Although thought to be descended from an early military organization established to protect Sicilians from the endless wave of invaders, the idea of mafia (the tactic of violence) originated among the Sicilians in the nineteenth century. At that time, the government attempted to break large estates into parcels that would be redistributed to the peasants who worked them. Mafiosi were recruited from the peasantry to provide large estate owners with armed forces to control the central government and other, more restless, peasants. This group was officially disbanded by General Garibaldi in 1860, but the power of the Mafia continued. Presently the Mafiosi are less powerful than they have been in the past. Criminal activities continue to exist, but today they are not restricted to the old Mafiosi groups, nor to Sicily. More than a thousand leading Italian citizens belong to a secret masonic lodge (Propaganda Due) that has been associated with political scandals as well as terrorism.

Arts and literature. A rich variety in art attracts tourists to the island. Relics, Greek temples, and Roman stadia are mixed with Moorish brick and stone work and sculptures throughout the major cities, revealing the range of societies that have lived and worked on the island.

A remnant of the past, but still functional in the 1990s, is the two-wheeled, mule-drawn small wagon, which shares the streets with larger farm wagons and automobiles and is a moving example of Sicilian art. Large wheels with painted rims and decorated spokes support seats and cargo beds brightly colored in yellows, blues, and reds. A typical cart seems to bear framed paintings of the landscape or of family scenes all around its body. The mule adds to the decoration, with harness enhanced by tufted feathers. Although a popular tourist attraction, these carts are utilitarian, helping to carry goods from market to market or market to home.

The literature directly attributable to Sicilians is limited. Among the writers who chose the history of Sicily or life on the island as their themes, three are internationally known. These authors wrote mostly from a perspective of the earlier attitudes of Sicilians, who for centuries firmly believed in the richness of their country and the superiority of their lifestyles as opposed to life in mainland Italy.

Pirandello wrote directly to this issue, contrasting Sicilian life to life in the newly industralized Italy. Earlier, Guiseppi Tomasi, a prince of Lampeduca, wrote about Sicilian life in *The Leopard*, as did Vitaliano Brencati in *Don Juan in Sicily* and *The Handsome Antonio*.

Religion. Another venue for artistic expression is religion. Most Sicilians are Roman Catholics while a smaller group are Greek Orthodox. They practice these religions with a myriad of processions. Leading many of these religious parades are sculpted or carved holy figures. Religion provides the themes for paintings and for dramatic productions. A favorite play often tells of the historic battles between Christians and Moors—ending with the massacre of the Moors. The many influences on Sicilian architecture can be seen in such magnificient structures as the Cathedral of Palermo. Fine tile work, dome-shaped towers, Gothic arches, richly carved eaves, and delicately decorated arcades enhance this large church that bridges a narrow road in the city.

As in many other societies, church attendance is mostly carried out by women, men stay at home tending to the farms or gather at the village cafes to sip coffee and talk about events of the day.

Education. Before 1864, nearly all Sicilians were illiterate—living in small villages and tending small farms where reading and writing were not vital. Garibaldi began to alter that statistic, establishing schools and wedding Sicily firmly to the rest of Italy. Italian-style schools were added to the island, and eventually three great universities arose—at Palermo, Catania, and Messina. The efforts succeeded with the help of new demands for literacy by the industrial-commercial developments. In the 1990s there is a high degree of literacy in Sicily.

For More Information

Finley, M. I., et al. *A History of Sicily*, New York: Viking-Penguin, 1987.

Séballeau, Pierre S. *Sicily.* New York: Oxford University Press, 1968.

Smith, Dennis, M. *History of Sicily*. Berkeley, California: University of California Press, 1982.

SPANIARDS

(span′ yurds)

Native people of the country of Spain.

Population: 38,500,000 (1991 estimate).
Location: Spain, a peninsula shared with Portugal and islands in Southern Europe between the Atlantic Ocean and Mediterranean Sea.
Language: Spanish, a Romance language.

Geographical Setting

Most of the land of Spain is highland, 1,000 feet above sea level in the southwest and rising to a central plateau that reaches to 5,000 feet before falling in the northeast, then rising again to the Pyrenees Mountains. The Pyrenees separate Spain from France and extend through a region known as Galicia on the coast of the Bay of Biscay. Other ranges form a broken ring around and across the central plateau. In the south the Sierra Range and the Gaetic Mountains separate the inland table from the dry and rugged coast of the Mediterranean. The Iberian Mountains arc northwest to southeast below the Ebro River, separating the ancient kingdoms of Aragon and Catalonia from the rest of Spain. The extensions of the Pyrenees Mountains along the northern coast of the Bay of Biscay separate a narrow coastal land from the interior table and isolate two more regions of Spain— Asturias and Cantabria. Three-fifths of the country is the high tableland that once formed the nations of Castile and León. In this region, the capital of Spain, Madrid, lies in a valley carved in the southern edge within view of a southwest to northeast range of mountains, the Sierra de Guadarrama.

Spanish

Distribution of Spanish — Most Dense / Least Dense

Historical Background

Early history. Ancestors of modern humans, the Neanderthal and Cro-Magnon people are known to have inhabited the Iberian Peninsula as early as 200,000 years ago. But the peninsula takes its name from people known as Iberians who occupied Spain approximately 5,000 years ago, sailors and traders from the Mediterranean area. Spain was long a trading center in this sea; Phoenician traders established posts along the Iberian coast about 2000 B.C. During the next 4,000 years various groups immigrated to the region as conquerors, settlers, or traders. About 900 B.C., Celts from the north settled in present-day Spain. They were later joined by the Greeks and Carthaginians seeking trade bases in the western Mediterranean.

Romans claimed the peninsula from 133 B.C. until they were replaced by Visigoths in A.D. 405. These invaders were, in turn, joined by Arabs carrying the new religion of Islam (these Moors settled in the southern Iberian peninsula beginning in 711) and Jews. Spanish ancestry is shaped by a mixture of the groups.

Moors. The rule of Abd al-Rahman III (921–961) marks the height of economic and cultural growth during the reign of the Muslim (Moor) leaders, under whose rule Spain (a country the Moors called Al-Andalus—"of the Vandals") became a land of prosperous cities whose citizens took an active part in trading glass, paper, leather, metalwork, silk and other goods. Science and medicine flourished, and the presence of Christians and Jews was tolerated in Muslim Spain. Under the Moors, great scholars, both Arabs and Jews, established Al-Andalus as an intellectual center.

Interest in scholarship was to continue through the Muslim and Christian eras. In 1130 Alfonso VII established a school for scholars (who were mostly Arabs or Jews) at Toledo, and by 1243, a university had been established at Salamanca. These actions spread the ideas of Arabs, Jews, and Greeks throughout Europe.

Catholics. Meanwhile the Christian Catholics struggled to keep their kingdoms from the hands of the Muslims, driven by warriors from Castile, an independent country in the central plateau area of present-day Spain. El Cid Campeador was one of the most reknowned Castilian warriors of the reconquest. In 1094 he led his troops south and east from Castile to capture the southeastern coastal area known as Valencia and hold it against the Moors for five years. The ballad of his adventures became a classic in Spanish literature and Castilian Spanish would became the language of the people. A new wave of Muslims entered the land from North Africa in 1146, but the Christians continued their conquest of all of Spain, replacing the Moorish governments in region after region until 1492, the year in which the team of Ferdinand and Isabella began to unite all of today's Spain under one rule. Their rule was at once famous and infamous. Under them Spain became a strong world force, and sent explorers such as Cortés and Columbus throughout the world. On the other hand, their Christian zeal led them to rule with an iron hand, including interrogating citizens who might be Catholic heretics and expelling Jews with the view of Christianizing them. These activities became known as the Spanish Inquisition.

Perhaps the most famous of the Moorish buildings in Spain is the massive Alhambra in Granada, with a surrounding wall that was two and a quarter miles around. This is the Hall of Embassadors in the Alhambra. *From the Library of Congress.*

Some of the great Arab and Muslim scholars of Spain	
Ben Gabriol	1012–1058
Rabbi Ben Ezra	1092–1167
Averroës	1126–1198
Moses Maimonides	1135–1204

Inquisition. In the same year that the expeditions of Columbus were financed by Isabella, the new Spanish kingdom began a program of uniting the country under one religious banner. Jews and Arabs were compelled, often by force, to leave the country or to become Christians through the act of Christian baptism. Many Moors were "christianized," and many others were evicted—from Castile in 1502, Aragon in 1526, and all of Spain by the year 1609. Many Jews were also "christianized" although many of those undergoing baptism put up a front of Christianity while retaining their own religious beliefs. This turn of events was of considerable distress to the Spanish rulers; Jews were interrogated and tortured to test their real religious beliefs. Jews were restricted in the types of work they did. Since the Spanish felt that handling money was disdainful, Jews were often relegated to the positions of moneylenders and small merchants. Forced upon them, the association with finance established a stereotype that has endured to today.

Imperialism. Exploration of the New World began with Columbus and and continued into the sixteenth century, making Spain the greatest European power of the age. Hernán Cortés and Francisco Pizarro are two explorers of the age whose discoveries led to Spanish colonies in the New World and an influx of gold and silver from them. The colonies made Spain one of the richest countries in the world. The discovery of the silver mountain Potosí in Bolivia (1545) brought the Spanish crown more silver than had been found in all of Europe for the preceding 100 years. But this wealth did not satisfy the demands of the royal family and, by the end of the 1600s, Spanish power had declined. Throughout this history, the divisiveness of Spain was reflected in the many cities in which the seat of government was placed—Toledo, León, Burgos, Seville, Valladolid, Segovia, and finally, in 1561, Madrid.

French rule. The next century brought the defeat of the Spanish in the War of Spanish Succession (1701–1713). England and France had become concerned over Spanish holdings in the Netherlands. The great Spanish Armada (navy) had been defeated in 1588 and Spain had begun a long decline in world power. The War of Succession stripped the country of many of its overseas possessions and placed the Bourbon king Philip V of France over Spain. Never more united than a collection of separate kingdoms paying allegiance to the throne of Castile and León, Spain now became a number of provinces ruled by France. Napoleon occupied the country with French forces from 1810 to 1813.

Independence. Spain regained the throne in 1814 and a period of political turmoil began that saw the government change from a monarchy to a republic, then to a monarchy once again. Revolts became commonplace. A wave of strikes and terrorism descended upon the cities. In 1923 General Miguel Primo de Rivera became the dictator of Spain but was forced to leave in 1930. The people became polarized into two groups. On one side were the Church, landowners, and the army, including General Francisco Franco. On the other side were workers, peasants, and intellectuals. Their differences erupted into Civil War in 1936 and, by 1939, General Franco's army had won a hard-fought victory in a war that had cost approximately a million lives. Franco, an economics professor, became dictator of Spain and remained in power for the next 36 years. The nation grew peaceful and stable once again but the liberties of the Spanish were restricted. Franco's Nationalist party was the only legal political group in Spain.

Early in his rule, Franco declared his intent to return the government to a constitutional monarchy and nominated Juan Carlos, a royal heir, to succeed him. A powerful military leader, Admiral Luis Carrero Blanco, was Franco's choice to be Juan Carlos's prime minister and to ensure a peaceful transition. However, this plan failed when Blanco was assassinated by Basque separatists. After Franco died in 1975, King Juan Carlos did become head of state, himself strongly leading Spain into a new era. Spain changed from a dictatorship to a democratic monarchy. In 1983 regional governments were set up in 17 areas of Spain, giving the people of each area the power of self-rule. However, this action did not appease those who looked for separation of the various segments of Spain, particularly the Basques and Catalans who live in the prosperous borderland with France. In recent years, violent action, particularly by Basque rebels, has resulted in a great deal of disruption in Spain.

Meanwhile, Spain has built a new economy, much of it based on tourism. The low prices and promise of good weather in the south of Spain attract as many as 50 million tourists a year. But as the economy has improved, prices have risen, threatening the tourist industry. Two great events of 1992 were planned to revive the sagging economy—the Olympic Games in Barcelona and a World Fair in Seville.

Culture Today

Village life. Whether in densely populated, fertile growing areas or scattered on the broad semiarid central plateau, Spaniards tend to live together in small villages. This sometimes proves difficult, since the Spanish farmer must then often travel considerable distances to reach the piece of land to be farmed. The Spaniards who live in the traditional lifestyle of *el pueblo* (the village) leave their homes after sunrise, traveling on foot or in donkey carts over dirt roads to work the land. Many are day laborers who hire out their services for wages. They plant or harvest, taking a short break for lunch, and go back at night to the pueblos.

For many centuries, farming was the way of life for most Spaniards, but today only about 15 percent of the population are agricultural workers. On large estates (*latifundias*), on small irrigated farms (*huertas*), and on meager plots, these farmers grow typical Spanish crops—wheat and other grains, vegetables, and citrus fruits. Rice and cotton have become common as well. Livestock generally includes goats, sheep, and pigs. Pig-killing is a traditional ceremony. Other Spanish workers have migrated to the cities and larger towns to find work in manufacturing or in the large tourist trade.

In some areas, particularly agricultural areas, hostility is the central theme of Spanish culture. In these areas there is a fierce loyalty to the *pueblo*, or village community. Most every village has a rival pueblo to which it bears hostility. The hostility is often openly expressed on festivals of the local patron saint of a community.

City life. The standard of living in the country is far lower than that in the city, a contrast that has fueled a mass exodus of people from rural to urban regions since the 1960s. There has been a steady growth of Spanish industries; chemicals, machine tools, ships, and appliances are typical manufactured products. The automobile industry is the

A Spanish girl in festival dress.
Courtesy of Leah Cadavona.

country's largest employer, and the fishing industry is another major employer. The Spanish operate the largest fishing fleet in the world.

In city offices and retail shops the workday of the people is interrupted by an extended lunch period. Office hours are from 9:00 a.m. to 2:30 p.m. A worker normally goes to lunch and returns to work from 5:00 p.m. to 7:30 p.m. A walk (*paseo*) and the evening meal, which is eaten as late as 10:00 or 10:30 p.m., complete the typical day. This pattern has changed in some regions with the advance of industry. The people of Barcelona, for example, no longer break for the long afternoon "siesta."

Shelter and clothing. The poorest people in Spain, such as the farmers on the plateau or in Galicia, live in one-story houses built of stone, wood, and clay. The Spanish civil war destroyed many of these towns, and the homes were rebuilt as apartment buildings. The structures, single-family homes or apartments, are covered with whitewashed plaster and topped with gently sloping tile roofs. Windows are often covered with iron grillwork, protecting a family of six or eight members, who might sleep together in a single room. More prosperous families live in a traditional two-story house that is built around a patio with awnings, shrubbery, and possibly fountains.

Rural men wear traditional dress—white cotton shirts, black trousers with a sash, and black, round berets. Rural women wear plain dresses or full skirts and blouses. Living without the modern conveniences of the city, these rural women might scrub the household wash outside in an open trough.

Almost all city dwellers wear Western-style clothing, and live in apartments where they enjoy conveniences such as refrigerators and washing machines. During festivals, they can be seen in traditional clothing. Men may wear the short jacket, tight trousers, and wide-brimmed hat (*sombrero de ala ancha*). Younger women wear spotted and flounced cotton dresses while older women are clad entirely in black. Such costumes are worn during nonreligious fairs (*ferias*) and religious festivals (*fiestas*). During the fiestas, carved images of religious figures are clothed in brocades and velvets, covered with jewels, and mounted on wooden platforms to be carried through the streets.

Family life. Courtship between boys and girls often begins at age 15 and generally continues until age 18. Groups of boys and girls wander across city squares in opposite directions to meet. A couple might exchange glances that lead to an introduction. Then courtship is carried on in public view, either at the window or doorway of the girl's home. The family of the girl pretends not to notice. The suitor (*novio*) finally calls on the girl's father for his blessing of the union. This is followed by a visit from the suitor's mother to the girl's mother, who persuades her husband to give his blessing. Approval from parents is largely a formality, however; young people generally choose their own partners. The newly married couple lives in their own home and typically raises a family that includes from two to three children. It is common for the couple to set aside a portion of their earnings for the support of older relations when necessary.

Spanish food. While some foods are common throughout Spain, the regional complexion of the land results in regional variations in the diet. The cold soup *gazpacho* is made of strained tomatoes, olive oil, and spices, then sprinkled with bread cubes, chopped cucumbers, onions, and tomatoes. In addition to wine, a common Spanish beverage is hot chocolate, eaten with deep-fried strips of dough called *churros*. Popular fish dishes are squid, crab, sardines, and fried baby eels. Meats, eaten mainly in the cities, are chicken, goat, lamb, pork, and rabbit. Round or oval loaves of white bread are common at various meals.

Regionally, veal is more popular in Basque country, *zerzuela*, a fish casserole, in Barcelona, and fine stews in Galicia. *Paella*, a typical

Spanish dish, is most common in Valencia. It might include shrimp, lobster, chicken, ham, and vegetables all combined with rice and cooked with saffron flavoring.

Recreation. Bullfighting is a popular event throughout Spain. Not to be classed as a sport, but as a competition, the Spanish bullfight is more akin to a ritual dance or ballet. Spaniards attend bullfights to admire the movements of the matadors and toreadors. These Spanish bullfighters follow a traditional pattern of stylized movements. The most highly regarded matadors are those who stand closest to the paths of the horns and make smooth passes with their capes before killing the bull. Although bullfighting is still a popular pastime, it now competes with soccer for the leisure time of the people.

Religion and holidays. Roman Catholicism was declared the official religion of the land in 1853, and most Spanish affirm their belief in this religion. However, the church is attended more by women than men, and many Spanish only reveal their religious affiliation at the baptism of infants and weddings. Still, each village or town has its patron saint and stage elaborate celebrations in his or her honor each year—each town celebrating in its own way. Streets are decorated, bonfires built, traditional dances (the bolero, the fandango, the flamenco) performed, and bullfights staged. In Pamplona during the festival of San Fermin, bulls are turned loose in the streets. Young men run ahead of the animals to the bull ring where amateur bullfights are held.

Education. The education of children begins with a requirement to attend school from the ages of six to 14. Private schools administered by the Roman Catholic Church are responsible for the education of over 30 percent of Spanish children, and these schools along with public schools are subsidized by the government. Secondary education is available for 14- to 16-year-old students. Those who don't pursue secondary education are obligated to undergo vocational training at the ages of 15 and 16.

Music and arts. Theater, music, and art are popular among the Spanish, who enjoy the works of past and modern playwrights (e.g., Lope de Vega, Alfonso Sastre), listen to recordings of Pablo Casals on the cello, or enjoy the paintings, sculptures, and ceramic pieces by masters such as Francisco Jose de Goya and Pablo Picasso.

Flamenco dancing is popular throughout Spain.
Courtesy of Leah Cadavona.

The golden age of art and music in Spain came in the affluent 1500s and continued into the period of declining wealth in the 1600s. Doménico Theotocópuli—El Greco—born in Crete and educated in Venice, moved to Toledo and became one of Spain's best-known painters. Velásquez and Estaban Murillo, both born in Seville, left scenes of the Spain of their time as well as religious pieces that are admired today.

The golden age also produced excellent musicians, some of whose creations are to be found in the *Palace Song Book* preserved from that time. Antonio de Cabezón became the "Spanish Bach," known for his organ compositions. But the most popular musical instrument even then was the *vihuela*, known today as the guitar. In the twentieth

Aspiring bullfighters begin their training at an early age. *Courtesy of Leah Cadavona.*

century, Andrés Segovia recharged Spanish interest in this instrument and in the country's most popular style of music, flamenco, a style that has its roots in the old folk songs of Andalusia.

During the reign of Generalisimo Franco, much work in all the arts faded. Many of the most talented artists, writers, and musicians had been loyal to the old government and fled Spain during the revolution. Spain's greatest composers, such as Luis de Pablo, Cristobal Halffter, and Juan Hidalgo continued to work in music by spending many years outside of Spain. De Pablo, for example, produced some of his greatest works in Berlin. Orchestral music returned to some excellence through the work of López Cobos. Flamenco music declined after the Franco era except for the work of Antonio Mairena, who sang pure flamenco songs and has organized many flamenco festivals. The popularity of flamenco was described by José Maria Caballero Bonald:

> All of a sudden the notes coincide with the beginning of a song and someone utters the preliminary wails. The singer clears his throat and searches for the beat. Everyone maintains a respectful, religious silence. At length, the lyrics emerge. Hands begin to clap miraculously in time with the guitar.
>
> Hooper 1986, p. 160

Rock music is now rising in Spain, championed by such performers as "The Child of the Combs" and "Frasco, the Coloured One."

**The Spanish create great sculptures for their
parents. This is for El Dia de San José in Valencia.**
Courtesy of Leah Cadavona.

Literature. The long literary tradition of Spain begins in the thirteenth
century, handed down in such works as *Poemas de Mio Cid* (1205)
and *La Razán de Amor*. *Don Quixote*, a two-part work by Miguel de
Cervantes, has endured since the early 1600s, and became the basis
of a popular musical, *Man of La Mancha*. It reflects the depression
of the declining glory of Spain through the eyes of an elderly warrior
who prefers madness to the reality of his day.

Spain's fall from grandeur produced a body of Spanish writing
of the 1800s that questioned the future of the country. By the end of
the century, these authors writing sadly of their own country had
turned out such volumes of literature that one of them, José Martinez

Ruiz, named them the Generation of 1898. The most famous of the writers of the twentieth century was born in 1899. Federico Garcia Lorca wrote poetry about love tragedies (*Bodas de Sangre*) and political introspection that led to his execution by Franco supporters at the outbreak of the civil war. Novels by writers such as Juan Goytisolo provide stories of life among the Spanish of the post-war generation.

Literature, too, fell into decline under Franco, or reverted to a drab "social realism" as in the Soviet Union. Novelists of the Franco era became associated with the oppressive management; so, after Franco's death, the revival of the novel was slow. Juan Benet is creating a series of novels about the civil war, and a younger author, Julian Rios, has undertaken to develop five novels in a new style that he hopes will set a style for Spanish writers. The first of these, *Larva*, was published in 1984 after ten years of work.

For More Information

Castro, Américo. *The Spaniards: An Introduction to Their History.* Translated by Willard F. King and Selma Margaretten. Berkeley, California: University of California Press, 1985.

Crow, John A. *Spain: The Root and the Flower.* Berkeley, California: University of California Press, 1985.

Defourneaux, Marcelin. *Daily Life in Spain in the Golden Age.* Translated by Newton Branch. London: George Allen and Unwin Ltd., 1970.

Graham, Robert. *Spain: A Nation Comes of Age.* New York: St. Martin's Press, 1984.

Hooper, John. *The Spaniards, A Portrait of the New Spain*, New York: Viking, 1986.

SWEDES

(sweeds)

Scandinavian people who are natives of Sweden.

Population: 8,600,000 (1991 estimate).
Location: Sweden, the easternmost of two countries sharing the peninsula above the Baltic Sea.
Language: Swedish, a northern Germanic language derived from Old Norse.

Geographical Setting

Sweden, a long, rather narrow country in Europe, along with Denmark and Norway forms a northern peninsula that is known as Scandinavia. It is a region of cold temperatures, tempered along the coasts by the flow of the Gulf Stream of the Atlantic Ocean. Traditionally, Sweden is thought to be made up of three regions: Norrland, Svealand, and Götaland—bands of land paralleling each other and running east to west.

The northern area, Norrland, is known for the large rivers that flow from the mountains bordering Norway into the Baltic Sea. It is a region of hills and many lakes, surrounded by pine forests. The horizontal strip south of Norrland, Svealand, includes the country's capital, Stockholm and is the best agricultural land. It has been farmed since before the Vikings. Four large lakes in this central region include Mälaren, which meets the Baltic Sea at Stockholm. Built on 14 islands, the capital city was established in the thirteenth century and has a population of more than 650,000 people.

Most Swedes consider the southern portion of Sweden, Götaland, to be composed of two distinct regions itself: Skäne, in the west, and Småland. Both regions have more mild climates than the rest of the

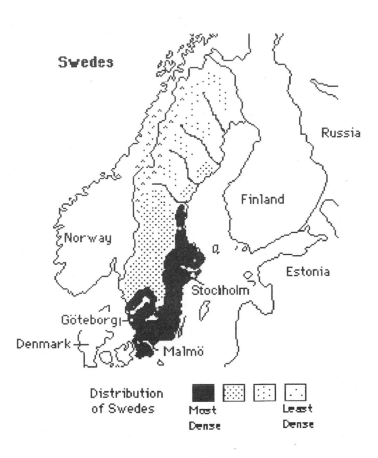

Swedes

Russia

Finland

Norway

Estonia

Stockholm

Göteborg

Denmark

Malmö

Distribution
of Swedes

Most
Dense

Least
Dense

country and most of the country's food production takes place in and around Skäne, where the land is flat and fertile. Eastward, Smäland is the heart of Sweden's important lumber industry.

Historical Background

The first Swedes. At the end of the last Ice Age, people moved north from the continent of Europe as gradually as the ice that covered much of Europe melted. By about 8000 B.C., the southern tip of Scandinavia was free of ice, and hunters arrived there from the area that is now Germany. Five thousand years later, farming was underway and people had migrated much farther north—into much of the land we call Sweden. These tribes included the Svear, after whom today's Swedes are named. The various tribes spread throughout

Scandinavia and established farming and fishing communities that traded with the Romans when those soldiers reached the Baltic Sea about 50 B.C.

Sagas. The early history of the Swedes is told, truthfully or fancifully, in the old folk stories, or sagas. According to these stories, early Swedish history is much intertwined with the rest of Scandinavia. The first kings of Sweden and Denmark were said to have been descended from the god Odin. At any rate, Sweden and Denmark were united under one major king about A.D. 630. That king was Ivar Widfadm of Denmark. Throughout its early history two major groups vied for control of the region that is now Sweden—Goths and Swedes.

Vikings. The Norsemen along the Swedish, Danish, and Norwegian coast may have found themselves too numerous and on too poor soil to support their numbers. Those on the coast learned to build ships and became excellent sailors. At first using their ships to raid one

Viking writings can still be found on rocks and monuments in Sweden. *Courtesy of Monica Gyulai.*

another, they eventually traveled as far south as the Black and Caspian seas, trading slaves and fur for gold, silver, and other goods. Eventually Swedish and Danish Vikings would colonize present-day Russia and Ukraine and establish governments there. Throughout this period, the ancient chronicles list rival kings of various parts of Sweden, Norway, and Denmark. But at the beginning of the 1000s, King Olaf was the dominant king in Sweden and he established Christianity in the region. Following him, the list of rival kings continues until the next century. In 1056, the Swedish king was killed and replaced by one of the Goths, King Stenkil. Not until 1129 were the Goths displaced by a new Swedish king and then only with an agreement that Goths and Swedes would alternate as rulers of Sweden.

Union of Calmar. Swedish activities were then directed to closer neighbors. After conquering much of Finland by 1249, Swedes were sometimes ruled by Germanic people. One of these, Albert, attempted to form a league with German cities, a move unpopular with his own people. The Swedes invited assistance from Norway and Denmark, who under a common queen, Margarethe, united the three states in 1397 under the Treaty of Calmar. Though serious struggles took place between supporters and opponents of the Union, it remained in place until 1523. In that year a Swedish noble fanned the flames of revolution that had earlier led to the near breakup of the Calmar Union. This noble, Gustavus Vasa, became king of an independent Sweden. Under his rule, Sweden supported the religious reforms of the German Martin Luther. The religion of Sweden became Lutheranism and remains so today. In addition to centralizing the government, influencing the economy, building the army, and expanding industry, Gustavus Vasa established a hereditary monarchy.

Thirty Years War. In the late sixteenth century, the Swedes again focused on conquering and controlling the regions that surrounded the Baltic Sea. After warring with Denmark, Russia, and Poland, the Swedes joined the Thirty Years' War, a Protestant-Catholic conflict, under King Gustavus II Adolphus. Leading German princes against Ferdinand of Prussia, Sweden became a powerful force in Europe. Following this war, fighting again broke out with Denmark, Russia, and Poland, and Sweden took many possessions in Europe, holding them until Peter the Great of Russia forced the Swedes to retreat in 1709.

Parliament. In 1720, Swedish members of parliament passed a new constitution, which shifted the majority of the king's powers to the parliament. This distribution of power is similar to the current political structure but, in the 1700s, lasted only 50 years. From 1772 until 1975, power was again wielded by the king. And during these two centuries, the Scandinavian countries continued to swing between independence and union with one another. During the Napoleonic Wars of the early 1800s, the rule of Sweden fell to Jean Baptiste Bernadotte, a French general and one of Napoleon's marshalls. Bernadotte was elected king of Sweden. King Carl XVI Gustav, the king of Sweden in the 1990s, is a descendant of Bernadotte.

Industry and labor. The 1800s saw increases in population that were far more rapid than increases in the food supply. Many Swedes moved from Sweden to the United States in search of food and jobs. However, industry grew in Sweden, and many Swedes preferred to take jobs on the new railroads and in the mines rather than emigrate. Their labor in iron, steel, and other industries transformed Sweden into a significant industrial nation. As in other parts of the world facing change and industrialization, however, Swedes found working conditions unfair and even dangerous.

Workers formed trade unions, demanded the right to vote, and struggled for higher wages. Out of these laborers' struggles grew an organized labor movement, along with freedom and equality in voting and the growth of the Social Democratic Party in politics. This party and the labor unions remain strong forces in Swedish politics today.

Culture Today

Government. Though the Swedish constitution recognizes a king or queen, this position is now primarily ceremonial. Legislative and executive powers of government are held by an elected prime minister, a cabinet, and the parliament. The Swedish parliament consists of 349 members elected by popular vote. The parliament, in turn, elects the prime minister and approves his cabinet. Thus the makeup of the cabinet reflects the political sentiments of the parliament.

While there are no rules declaring that political parties must be represented in the Cabinet in proportion to their election to the parliament, the Cabinet's membership must be approved by the parliament and must be supported by parliament in their policies or resign.

This rule is intended to assure that the Cabinet always represents the will of the majority of Swedish citizens.

In another effort to protect Swedes from corruption and unwanted use of power, Parliament appoints ombudsmen. These spokespeople for the average citizens investigate all sorts of complaints against the government, including consumer affairs, equal opportunity, and legal issues.

Economic life. Swedes are known for their high standard of living and severe income tax structure. Most Swedes live in comfortable houses or apartments, eat well, and are able to enjoy vacations and recreational facilities. In fact, it is a goal of many Swedes to own either a small weekend-and-summer house or a large sailboat—and a great number are able to achieve their goals. However, taxes in Sweden are high.

Swedes pay up to 50 percent of their earnings to the government in taxes. This support gives Swedish residents free education, low-cost health care, and financial support when unable to work or when aged. Roads are well-maintained and public transportation is available and easily accessed in most areas.

The economic prosperity of the Swedes is partly explained by the low population density. As more immigrants arrive from nearby countries that are less stable, Swedes fear for the stability of their economy and are concerned about changes necessary to accommodate foreign residents. They reflect this fear in racism and public protests against the immigrants.

The greatest fear brought on by immigration is job security. Most jobs in Sweden are in the service sector but with a significant number of employees in industry and manufacturing. Steel is an important manufactured product, as are cars (Volvo and Saab are Swedish car makers), but most Swedes work in education, government administration, and health care, and as miners, farmers, and fishers. Since a large portion of the country is covered with forest, there is a large lumber industry and a widespread use of wood pulp to manufacture paper.

Food. The Swedish diet reflects the country's geography. Swedes are known for their crisp, dark bread, sold as Wasa bread around the world. This dry, hard bread has its roots in the need to bake a bread that could keep through the winter. Breakfast usually includes this crisp bread or rye bread with butter, cheese, and tea or coffee. Hard-boiled eggs with caviar are weekend treats. Swedes consume more coffee per person than any other group in the world.

Fish is very popular, especially herring, which may be eaten pickled, in a mustard sauce, with sour cream, or in many other ways. Salmon is often eaten with dill sauce, or poached or cured into a dish called *gravlax*. The English term *lox* for "smoked salmon" comes from Swedish. Also popular is reindeer meat and meatballs made from ground beef. Boiled potatoes are common with most meals, as are salads of shredded white cabbage. Meals may be completed by a princess torte made by layering white cake, whipped cream, and raspberry jam and draping it with marzipan.

Shelter. In and around cities, Swedes often live in apartments, while in the countryside almost all have houses. All these structures tend to be rather plain on the outside. Often square or rectangular with angled roofs, homes are decorated on the outside with little other than rectangular windows, which are often three-panes thick for insulation against the cold, wet weather.

Neatness and cleanliness mark the small towns of Sweden. *Courtesy of Monica Gyulai.*

The street level of Swedish houses is frequently the second story, with a basement or subterranean level being the first. This tradition is both functional and aesthetic—it provides good insulation and keeps buildings from being too tall and cluttering views in residential areas. Swedish homes, both apartments and houses, always have an area dedicated as an entry way. Here, jackets may be hung and shoes removed (even by visitors), as people rarely wear shoes other than slippers indoors. Inside, the homes are often beautiful, yet simple. Floors are wood, cork, or tile, and cabinets are built-in. The style referred to as "Eurostyle" today is representative of modern Swedish homes and offices. Carl Malmsten and Josef Frank are famous Swedish furniture and textile designers.

Religion. Ninety-two percent of all Swedes claim membership in the Church of Sweden, an Evangelical Lutheran denomination. The king of Sweden is required to be a member of this faith, even though religious freedom is acclaimed in the laws of the country. About 180,000 Swedes are members of other Protestant denominations and 140,000 are Catholics. Between 15,000 and 20,000 Jews practice their faith freely in Sweden.

Education. One of the results of the Swedish tax system is that schooling is free not only at the elementary and high school levels but also at the professional, vocational, and university levels. From the age of seven until 16, children are required to attend school in Sweden, and some go to kindergarten earlier. While attending primary school, all children receive free lunches daily.

In addition to those skills emphasized in Western formal education—reading, writing, and arithmetic—Swedes are taught practical activities such as home economics. An eighth grader may be given an assignment requiring setting up a budget or planning for a new home. Sewing, woodworking, and other shop skills are also taught for several years in addition to cooking. Swedish youths are taught laundering techniques, how to plan meals, ways to shop for food, and even the proper way to iron clothes. Both boys and girls learn the basics of childcare. Swedish education has long avoided gender biases in classwork and textbooks.

One educational outcome that is very striking among Swedes is their command of foreign languages. English is almost always a second language, and Swedish students begin to learn this second language in the fourth grade. Many movies and television programs seen in Sweden come from the United States and England; the popular exposure results in a bilingual population. Many students continue to study other languages. French or German may be studied in the seventh grade, and a fourth language such as Spanish studied in the ninth grade.

Arts and literature. In the world of art, Swedes may be best known for their furniture designs and for their hand-blown glass creations. Glass-blowing workshops dot the forested countryside throughout the region of Småland. The cities of Orrefors and Kosta Boda are best known for their crystal-making studios. Swedish glass blowers are almost always men, and the craft is passed from father to son through many generations. Young men begin as apprentices and join teams to create fine glassware. A team of ten men may be involved in making a single wine glass.

Some Swedes are internationally acclaimed writers and performers. Children around the world read the stories of Astrid Lindgren and watch movies about the adventures of Lindgren's heroine, Pippi Longstocking. August Strindberg is a world-renowned playwright, novelist, and poet who lived a hard and troubled life and recorded much of his struggle in plays such as *The Red Room* and *Miss Julie.* A director, scriptwriter, and producer, Ingmar Bergman continues to make obscure, symbolic, and intense films characterized by

A wooden horse decorates a park in Sweden. *Courtesy of Claes Andersson.*

Many beautiful buildings of Sweden are made from the most abundant building material—wood. *From the Library of Congress.*

contemplation of morality and religious faith. *The Seventh Seal, Wild Strawberries,* and *Fanny and Alexander* are among his acclaimed productions. Also well-known in the motion picture world, Ingrid Bergman was a Swedish actress best remembered for her role in the movie *Casablanca.*

Science and invention. The system used today for classifying all living things was developed in the eighteenth century by Carl von Linné, a Swedish botanist and physician. The Linnean system assigns each organism to a kingdom, phylum, class, order, family, genus, and species. Linné's garden was arranged in sections that corresponded with his classification system and is carefully tended to this day.

Swedes invented the zipper, the modern adjustable wrench, and safety matches, as well as dynamite, a discovery of Alfred Bernhard Nobel. Nobel, a chemist, is remembered for establishing a fund to give prizes for great accomplishments. The Nobel Prizes for chemistry, economics, literature, medicine, and physiology are presented in Stockholm's city hall every year. Other Nobel prizes are awarded at different sites. Members of the Swedish Academia participate in choosing the honorees.

Recreation. Swedish athletes make full use of their northern climate. Skiing, both downhill and cross-country, are common winter activities, along with ice-skating and ice-hockey. Ingmar Stenmark and Gunde Svan are well-known skiers of the 1990s. Börje Salming, a Swedish hockey player was drafted by the National Hockey League after playing well in international competitions. Most Swedish communities have hockey teams for old and young. Aside from the champions in winter sports, Bjorn Borg became an international tennis star in the 1970s and 1980s.

In March, thousands of Swedes cross-country ski in the 55-mile Vasa Race (*Vassloppet*). The course runs from Sälen to Mora and follows the legendary route that Gustav Vasa is said to have skied, rallying Swedes to support efforts to free Sweden from the Danes.

As soon as the sun melts the ice, people take to sailing. As children, many Swedes learn to sail in small boats and race on their own or with classmates. The Swedish passion for sailing often continues into adulthood, with excursions among Sweden's more than 40,000 islands.

In the middle of summer, there is sunlight almost 24 hours each day. Swedes use this special time of year to explore the country's forests on foot, searching for tasty berries and edible mushrooms. This activity is so popular that some Swedes carefully guard the secret of their collecting area.

Holidays. December 13 is Saint Lucia Day. Girls and boys all over Sweden dress in white robes before dawn, bringing their parents breakfast and participating in processions through their communities. One girl in each procession is chosen to represent Saint Lucia and wears a crown of lights (candles) on her head—the holiday is sometimes called the Festival of Lights. The representative for Saint Lucia is followed by girls with garland crowns who carry candles and boys carrying stars and wearing tall conic hats. The children and adults join in singing traditional songs and enjoy buns seasoned with saffron.

Later in December, Christmas Eve is celebrated around decorated pine trees. Families gather for meals of fish, ham, and glögg (a warm red wine and aquavit spiced with cinnamon), and to exchange gifts. The Santa Claus legend has its counterpart in Swedish lore in which a Christmas gnome travels by sleigh and reindeer to deliver gifts to children.

In August, when crayfish are plentiful, Swedes gather to dine on these shellfish, drink vodka, and sing. Many carry wooden traps to nearby lakes and streams to collect their own fresh crayfish. Among popular songs at these festivities are those written by Swedish poet Carl M. Bellman, who lived in the eighteenth century.

The long days of summer provide a great cause for celebration in Sweden. On Midsummer's Eve, the day of the year with the greatest period of sunlight, people gather outdoors to sing and dance around Maypoles decorated with birch leaves and flowers. The dancing and celebrating continues late into the day and night, as does the sunlight.

For More Information

La Fay, Howard. *The Vikings.* Washington, D.C.: National Geographic Society, 1972.

Mead, W. R., et. al. *Scandinavia.* Amsterdam: Time Life books, 1985.

Olsson, Kari. *Sweden: A Good Life for All,* New York: Dillon, 1983.

Scott, Franklin D. *Sweden: The Nation's History.* Minneapolis, Minnesota: University of Minnesota Press, 1977.

SWISS
(swiss)

Descendants of Romanized Celtic and Germanic settlers of the
Alps and Alpine plateaus and valleys.

Population: 6,800,000 (1991 estimate).
Location: West-central Europe.
Languages: German, French, Italian, Romansch.

Geographical Setting

Landlocked and mountainous Switzerland, deep in west-central Europe, is bounded (clockwise from the north) by Germany, Austria, Italy, and France. About twice the size of New Jersey, the country falls into three geographical regions: the Jura Mountains of the northwest border-area with France; the Mitteland, a central plateau amounting to about 30 percent of the total land, where most Swiss industry and agriculture take place and which contains the major cities of Geneva, Zurich, Berne, and Lausanne; and the Swiss Alps, whose mountains and high plateaus cover the southern 60 percent of the land. The Alps extend east, west, and south of Switzerland, running from eastern France through the Swiss border regions with Italy into Austria.

Switzerland has over 1,000 lakes. The largest ones—Geneva, Constance, and Maggiore—lie on the French, German, and Italian borders respectively. A ring of middle-sized lakes lies in a rough circle around the Mitteland communities of Neuchatel, Zurich, Lucerne, Brienz, and Thun. The Rhine River flows along the Austrian and German borders, through Lake Constance. It turns north at the Swiss city of Basel, from which it is navigable to its outlet on the North Sea. Other rivers fed by the Alpine watershed include the Rhone,

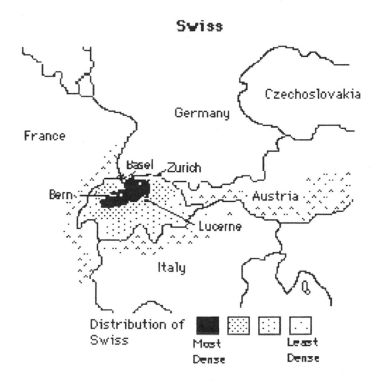

Swiss

Distribution of Swiss — Most Dense — Least Dense

flowing south through the Alps to Lake Geneva and on to the Mediterranean, and the Aare, flowing north from Lake Thun to join the Rhine. Much of the high Alpine land is covered with glaciers.

The Swiss climate varies with the terrain, but is mostly temperate outside of the Alps. Summers can be cool, with frost in the mountains. Winters are cold and often snowy, especially in the Alps, where famous and fashionable resorts attract skiers from around the world.

Historical Background

Celts and Romans. Little is known of Switzerland's inhabitants until about 100 B.C., when the region began to come into contact with Romans. In 58 B.C., the Roman legions (army units) of Julius Caesar mobilized against a Celtic people called the Helvetians, who are thought to have settled between the Rhine and the Alps some 50 years earlier. The Helvetians wished to migrate south of the Rhone. In provoking Caesar to turn them back, they unwittingly brought about the historic Roman conquest of Gaul (as the Romans called the parts of Europe north of Italy). The Helvetians returned, giving their name to the region later called Switzerland. Because the Rhine formed the Roman Empire's northern border, Helvetia became essentially a military outpost. It prospered under about 300 years of Roman rule, with its various Celtic groups enjoying the order and trade brought by the legions stationed there.

Germans and Burgundians. During the 200s A.D., as the western Roman Empire began to disintegrate, a Germanic tribe called the Alemanni invaded Helvetia repeatedly from across the Rhine. For some 200 years they burned and sacked Helvetian towns. In the 400s, with Helvetia weakened, they occupied the northern part of the region permanently. At the same time, a Gallic people called the Burgundians settled in the area of Lake Geneva. These events decided the future Swiss linguistic boundaries: German-speakers in the largest central area; French-speakers descended from the Burgundians in the west; Italian-speakers in the Ticino, the part of Switzerland that juts southward into Italy; and speakers of Romansch, the Latin tongue of the Romanized Celts, in the far east of Switzerland. The Romansch-speakers were isolated in the Rhaetian Alps by the German settlers, who stuck to the valleys and plateaus.

Frankish rule. In the 500s, the Alemanni and the Burgundians were conquered by the Franks, who introduced Christianity, founded or rebuilt cities, and established a feudal social system. The Franks exerted political control, but did not settle the region. Several important monasteries were founded in Switzerland during the period of Frankish rule, which lasted until the 1000s. The Burgundians and Alemanni then were ruled by the (German) Holy Roman Empire, which was controlled by the house of Habsburg beginning in the 1200s.

Beginnings of unity. The Habsburgs had made enemies of three forest communities around Lake Lucerne: Uri, Schwyz, and Nidwalden. When the first Habsburg ruler died in mid-July 1291, the popular assemblies of the three communities seized the opportunity to rebel from Habsburg control. On August 1, they formed the "everlasting alliance" among themselves, which became the basis of the

Swiss Confederation. (The name "Swiss" comes from the largest of these original "cantons," Schwyz.) During the 1300s and 1400s, more communities joined the confederation, and a series of victories over the Habsburgs affirmed Swiss independence. In 1499, the empire recognized this independence with the Treaty of Basel, and by 1513 the number of cantons had grown to 13, taking in most of present Swiss territory.

Protestant Reformation. Swiss church leaders played major roles in the Protestant Reformation, and in the subsequent religious conflicts that swept Europe in the 1500s-1600s. Ulrich Zwingli, a Protestant preacher, led a movement to make a Protestant Zurich the leader of a Protestant Switzerland. Opposed by the central "forest" cantons, which continued to embrace Catholicism, Zwingli died in battle when the Catholic cantons marched on Zurich in 1531. A few years after Zwingli's death, a French reformer named John Calvin led a similar but more successful movement in Geneva. Next to Martin Luther, the German minister who initiated the Reformation, Calvin emerged as the most influential proponent of Protestant views. Calvinism took deep root in Geneva and in other Swiss cities, such as Zurich, Basel, and Berne. Its influence spread throughout Northern Europe (see, for example, SCOTS). In contrast to the cities, the rural majority of the cantons remained Catholic.

Absolutism and revolution. Strife between rural peasants and city rulers over economic and political issues lasted into the late 1600s. By the 1700s, the ruling class had gained the upper hand. Swiss democratic institutions became stifled by this powerful, wealthy class. Switzerland fell under the influence of her powerful neighbor France; the Swiss (who had been serving as mercenaries for European armies since the 1500s) supplied France's kings with soldiers and a personal guard. The French Revolution (1789) changed Swiss rule. Over the next 60 years, the ruling class that had been supported by French royalty was overthrown in some Swiss cities as part of the revolutions that swept Europe. During this period the Swiss provided refuge for large numbers of revolutionaries from other countries and experienced a liberalization of governmental institutions. A final spasm of religious conflict resulted in the Sonderbund War in 1847, in which Catholic attempts to secede from the confederation were defeated. New constitutions in 1848 and 1874, similar to that of the United States, strengthened the federal government.

Unity from diversity. Over the last 150 years, the Swiss have focused on achieving a balance among their various religious and social groups—a balance they have seen as necessary to preserving their independence. Surrounded by ambitious and often aggressive neighbors, the cantons have relied on compromise and cooperation with each other. A national policy of neutrality (see below) allowed growing prosperity to continue through two world wars that devastated the rest of Europe. Despite their democratic traditions, the Swiss remain socially conservative. Swiss women could not vote in federal elections until 1971; not until 1990 did women win the right to vote locally in the last canton to allow them to do so, Appenzell.

Culture Today

The cantons. The Swiss Confederation today comprises 23 cantons, three of which are divided into half-cantons. A bicameral legislature, like that of the United States, chooses a seven-member Federal Council. Its president, who serves for one year, is succeeded by the vice-president. The federal government controls foreign policy, mail, currency, and railroads; areas not allocated to the federal government by the constitution are regulated by the individual cantons.

While some cantons take their borders from differences in language, others are multilingual. German is spoken in the large central cluster of cantons, taking in about 70 percent of the Swiss population. French is spoken in a western band, along a north-south line drawn just west of the cities of Basel and Berne that includes the Lake Geneva area and the cantons of Jura, Fribourg, Vaud, and Neuchatel. Of the large southern canton of Valais, the western half speaks French and the eastern half, German. The canton of Ticino, geographically and historically linked with Italy, is separated from the German-speaking north by the Alps; the Ticinese proudly maintain their Italian language and ways. The largest canton, Graubunden, between Austria and Italy, is home to German- and Italian-speakers, as well as to the one percent of Swiss (about 30 percent of Graubunden's population) who speak Romansch ("Roman"). These descendants of the Romanized Celts, living in the mountainous region's isolated valleys, have survived as a linguistic snapshot of Switzerland's past.

Language As a result of the Alpine geography, German, Italian and Romansch have been spoken in a variety of dialects. The main German dialect is *Schwyzerdutsch* ("Swiss-German") now used by vir-

Switzerland is well-known as a clock and watch manufacturing country. This clock tower is in Zurich. *Courtesy of Amy A. Trenkle.*

tually all German-speakers. Schwyzerdutsch evolved as a spoken language, with a breathtaking number of subdialects, most of which are mutually comprehensible. For German-speakers, each dialect reflects local characteristics. Like its people, for example, Zurich's dialect is regarded as "aggressive" or "harsh," while Berne's *Barndutsch* reflects the friendly, congenial reputation of the Bernese. Schwyzerdutsch evolved and even today exists mostly in spoken form; high German has traditionally been used for writing. The Ticinese speak their own dialect of Italian, while similar dialects are spoken in areas of Graubunden. Romansch has been standardized in a single form, but is still widely spoken in five distinct dialects: depending on which valley one is in, one might hear the same drinking vessel called a *cuppina, scadiola, scariola, cuppegn,* or *tazza.* The canton of Graubunden ("gray league"), formed in the 1300s to throw off Habsburg rule, reflects in its very name the Swiss mixture of cultural colors—in French it is *Grisons,* in Italian, *Grigioni,* and in Romansch, *Grischun.*

Neutrality. Neutrality in international conflicts grew out of military defeat by France in 1515, when Swiss cultural diversity threatened the Confederation's survival. The Reformation followed shortly thereafter, adding religious divisions to political ones. Had the Swiss not valued their independence so highly, the German- and French-speakers might easily have chosen to be absorbed by their powerful neighbors, with whom they shared linguistic and cultural backgrounds. Yet they did not, choosing instead neutrality as a way of avoiding being torn apart in conflicts between these neighbors. Neutrality brought benefits other than internal stability. Swiss businesses have profited, particularly banking, in which the Swiss are world leaders. Swiss banks have been protected by strict laws regarding the privacy of account-holders, who are identified by number rather than name. The "numbered Swiss account" became a mainstay of the Hollywood crime movie, though the laws were changed in 1971 to allow governments to obtain the identities of suspected tax evaders.

Far from preoccupying them with their own affairs, the neutrality of the Swiss has allowed them to play an important and balanced role in world politics. Geneva was world headquarters for the League of Nations and is European headquarters for its successor, the United Nations. (The Swiss have declined membership in the United Nations, because it might infringe on neutrality.) Geneva also hosts a number of other international organizations, including the International Red Cross, and is the site of the Geneva Convention, which regulates the treatment of civilians, prisoners of war, and the wounded in wartime.

Food, clothing, and shelter. Predictably, Swiss cuisine varies according to ethnic influences. Another historic division is equally telling, however: that between country and city. Thus, two dishes eaten today by all Swiss are the simple cheese fondue (pieces of bread dipped in a melted combination of Gruyere and Emmental cheese) eaten for centuries by Swiss peasants, and veal with a sauce of white wine and cream, formerly enjoyed by sophisticated city dwellers.

Much of Switzerland is mountainous. Villages dot the Swiss Alps. *Courtesy of Dieter Bauer Meister.*

Cheese, however, is king: not only in fondue, but in almost any form imaginable. *Raclette,* the famous dish of the French canton Vaud, consists of a wheel of cheese cut in half, melted before a fire, then poured and scraped onto a plate, and eaten with pickles and roast potatoes. *Kaseschnitte* (*croute* in French) is a casserole of slabs of bread topped with grated cheese and butter, baked with wine, ham, mushrooms or eggs. In the Valais, pieces of cheese are coated in egg and bread crumbs, then deep fried to make *Kasechuchli.* Aside from cheese, the Swiss are famous for chocolate, the export of which provides a major source of national revenue.

As for other regional cuisine, German areas favor pork, often accompanied by *rosti,* a dish of diced potatoes mixed with herbs, bacon or cheese and fried to a golden brown. Ticinese dishes include *gnocchi,* a type of pasta made from potatoes, risotto, or rice mixed with meat, onions and herbs, and *polenta,* which is made from corn-meal and is similar to American grits. French-speakers enjoy such Gallic specialties as meat stews flavored with wine, organ meats like tripe, liver or kidney, thick steaks with various sauces, and lake trout coated in flour and fried in butter.

In the past, Swiss peasants wore regional costumes, which in Alpine areas often featured the leather shorts (*lederhosen*) found also in the Austrian Alps. The shorts were worn with sturdy leather boots. Today, more conventional work clothes are worn, though the costumes may still be seen in local parades. In the towns and cities, the Swiss tend to be formal in dress, with jackets and ties common for men and dresses for women.

Traditionally, houses have most commonly been built of wood, especially in Alpine and forest areas. In mountain villages, they are set close together across narrow streets, as protection against cold and heavy snowfall. Stone was often used to reinforce corners and roofs, and stone or masonry would encase the kitchen area to prevent fire. Swiss cities each have a different architectural flavor, blending modern architectural trends with monasteries, churches, and towers from the medieval past. Berne, for example, is famous for its elegant arcades, which seem influenced by Turkish or Asian styles. The Swiss value architecture, and they have produced one of the most influential architects of modern times, Le Corbusier (Charles Edward Jeanneret, 1887–1965).

Family life. Swiss family life is well-regulated and conservative. Few women hold careers outside of the family, and young people tend to be cooperative and well-behaved compared with their European or American counterparts. Education is rigorous and strict; children from America and elsewhere are often sent by well-to-do parents to Swiss boarding schools.

Literature and the arts. Children everywhere have read and loved *Heidi,* the story of a young Swiss girl and her love for the mountain countryside and for her grandfather. (And for cheese, which she eats with a devotion approaching the fanatical.) Written by Johanna Spyri (1827–1901), *Heidi* remains for many the most typical Swiss story. Yet it actually is not typical of Swiss literature, the most influential of which has been academic or scientific. Famous writers include

Geneva-born philosopher Jean-Jacques Rousseau, who profoundly influenced political thought in the eighteenth century. In the nineteenth century, the ideas of the writer Ferdinand de Saussure originated and continue to dominate the files of modern linguistics, as did the work of historian Jacob Burckhardt in art. Carl Gustav Jung was, with Sigmund Freud, one of the two giants of modern psychology. His idea of the "collective unconscious" continues to hold interest for modern readers. Among many Nobel Prize winners was the naturalized Swiss citizen Albert Einstein (1879–1955), who worked as an office clerk in Berne while composing ideas that would revolutionize modern physics. Swiss artists have been most renowned in modern times. Best-known are painter Paul Klee and painter-sculptor Alberto Giacometti, whose distinctive, elongated figures brought him a worldwide audience.

Religion. Since the conclusion of conflicts following the Reformation, the Swiss have placed a high value on religious freedom as a way of maintaining civil harmony. Today, of the 19 German-speaking cantons and half-cantons, 10 are mainly Catholic and nine, mainly Protestant; of the six French-speaking cantons, two are mainly Protestant and four, mainly Catholic. Ticino is mostly Catholic. Nationally, the numbers are about equal between the two faiths. There are about 20,000 Swiss Jews.

Religious tolerance brought Switzerland perhaps its most famous industry. French Protestants, persecuted in France, settled in Geneva in the 1500s and among them were skilled craftsmen who helped found the local clock-making industry. Swiss timepieces soon set the standard for the world, and continue to be a major export.

Holidays. The Swiss celebrate few national holidays, and these are the religious holidays common to Christianity. May 1 is Labor Day and August 1 is National Day. As might be expected in this country of diversity, there are more holidays that are celebrated on a regional basis.

For More Information

Bonjour, E. et al. *A Short History of Switzerland.* Oxford: Oxford University Press, 1952.

Coons, Nancy. *Fodor's 92 Switzerland.* New York: Fodor's Travel Publications, 1991.

Sorell, Walter. *The Swiss.* New York: Bobbs-Merrill Co., Inc., 1972.

Steinberg, Jonathan. *Why Switzerland?* Cambridge, England: Cambridge University Press, 1976.

Thurer, George. *Free and Swiss: The Story of Switzerland.* Coral Gables, Florida: University of Miami Press, 1971.

WALLOONS

(wah loons′)

A Romance-language speaking people of Belgium.

Population: 2,700,000 (1989 estimate).
Location: Southern Belgium, particularly the provinces of Haimant, Liege, Namur.
Language: Walloon, a Romance dialect similar to French.

Geographical Setting

The Meuse River passes through a neck of France projecting into Belgium and then continues north into that country as far as the city of Namur, where it turns abruptly almost eastward before facing north again toward Holland. South and east of the river, the Meuse valley rises gently in rolling hills to form a higher plateau on which stands the densely wooded Ardennes Forest. Water is plentiful for agriculture in this region, and the temperature is moderate. Oats, rye, wheat, and sugar beets grow well in soil that is in some places rich and in others marginal for crop bearing. Agriculture was long the major economy of the region and accounts for the congregation of its population in small towns and villages. Nevertheless, Walloonia is a densely populated region averaging about 450 persons per square mile.

Historical Background

Origins. By 850 B.C. various Celtic tribes began to move westward and southward to inhabit the land that is now Belgium. One of these tribes, arriving perhaps 600 years later, came to be known as Belgics. The Belgics inhabited the land between the Rhine and the Seine

Walloons

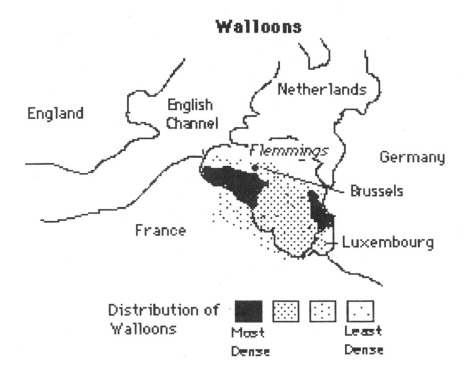

Distribution of
Walloons

Most
Dense

Least
Dense

Rivers in what is now France, Belgium, and Germany. When Roman legions arrived in this territory, they found it inhabited by three groups of people surviving by clothmaking, wool preparation, iron-working, and agriculture. One of the three groups was called Belgea by the Romans.

Romans. Romans ruled the land from 57 B.C. to 431 A.D., using the coastal region as a base from which to attack and control Britain and enlisted the Celtic inland people as soldiers in this endeavor. During this period, the Romans encouraged the iron industry and established Latin as the language of commerce.

Franks. Following the Romans, Franks took control of the region and held it until 987, although not as part of the Frankish Holy Roman Empire after 833. The Frankish soldiers followed the path of the Meuse River northward into today's Belgium for a short distance and surrounded the region of the Ardennes Forest. Thus, the Franks established the border between Dutch-speaking Flanders and the Walloons. Little interested in exploring the Ardennes Forest and its many streams, the French ignored the people there except to exact tribute. By the fifth century A.D., the Walloonians of the area near the Ardennes Forest had adopted the French language, lacing it with words and sounds from their own version of Latin.

After Charlemagne. When Charlemagne died in 814, the great Holy Roman Empire was divided among his three sons. Two of the sons inherited large bodies of contiguous land, the portions that became France and Germany. The other inherited a crazy-quilt pattern of lands that included the lowlands of Holland and Belgium, and part of Spain and Spanish islands. This area was to undergo several different rules during the next 1,000 years and force many alliances upon the people of Walloonia, which was then known as Litharingia.

Spain. From 1384 to 1555, all of Belgium was under the house of Burgundy, a French ruling family. But in 1555, Spanish people claimed their older heritage, and Belgium became a satellite state of Spain. While the Netherlands remained under Spanish rule, some dissatisfied people of both north and south Belgium sought protection and rule from the Prince of Orange. Against this union, the Walloons rose up to defend their Catholic ancestry and claim ties again with the Netherlands. The Union of Utrecht (1618) added the cities of the south of Belgium to the northern provinces of the Netherlands. Spain then began to use the agricultural and industrial production to support the heavy costs of the Spanish Navy. Over the next 100 years, Spain weakened, until, in 1713, the Spanish Netherlands were taken over by Maria Theresa of Austria. That rule was plagued with dissent, and, in 1790, rebellion had grown into revolution (the Brabant Revolution), after which the Independent United States of Belgium was formed.

Napoleon. Shortly after, Napoleon invaded Walloon land, which he ruled for nearly 20 years. Following his defeat, the land was briefly organized as defined at the Congress of Vienna into a kingdom of the Netherlands. By 1830 William of Orange had become ruler of this kingdom and had installed Dutch as the official language. Opposed to the language change, the workers in the south protested. A separate Kingdom of Belgium was established in 1830 when King Leopold took the throne. Sixty years later, the right of the nobility to choose its ruler was expanded to other landed men and wealthy Belgians began to enjoy some political freedom.

World War I. That political freedom was interrupted in 1914 when German forces entered the land and held it for four years. During that time, important battles of World War I were fought on Belgian Walloon territory, including the famous battles of the Ardennes Forest. At the end of the war, the Belgians found themselves with two administrative units—Fleming and Walloon. The division among Belgians was most conspicuous in the army. The Walloons had been progressive industrialists (albeit of small industries) since the time of Rome and had become prominent landowners. From this group arose elite officers of the army who were French-speaking. These French officers frequently had no way to communicate with their own troops—most of whom spoke Dutch. The language confusion of the Belgians was recorded in this bit of poetry of the period:

> French in the parlor, Flemish in the kitchen
> You speak the language of the man whose bread you eat.
> It is necessary to cease being Flemish in order to become Belgian.
> Wickman 1984, p. 94

Nevertheless, the people of Belgium were united under one government that was strong enough to form economic pacts with France, Scandinavia, and the Netherlands. It was also able to take the stride to freedom with the allowance of universal male suffrage in 1919.

Language. The Franks had established the linguistic boundary between Dutch and Romance languages more than a thousand years earlier. And the advent of the Spanish into the Netherlands had fomented religious differences. Finally, when Belgium was formed, it was by agreement on religious grounds: the Catholic people of the combined lowland countries agreed to unite in spite of the language problems. Both religion and language issues remained before the people as the structure of Belgium changed. The old southern commercial center of Brugges began to fade and with it the earlier industrial development of the south. In its place arose the northern port-city of Antwerp, around which new industry began to grow.

By 1884, the Dutch-speaking Flemings had gained control of the government and would hold it until 1914. In 1902, Albert du Bois had recognized the fading condition of Walloonia and spoke for unity with France in his *Catechism Wallon*. By the beginning of the first World War, the concerns of Walloonians had resulted in French-speaking independent segments of the political parties of Belgium. The leader of the Parti Ouvrier Belge, Jules Destrée, had in 1912 expressed this concern in a letter to King Albert I. Translated into English, this letter reads:

> Sire, let me tell you the truth, the grand and horrible truth, there are no Belgians
> ... You reign over two people. There are in Belgium Walloons and Flemings—
> there are no Belgians.
>
> Wickman 1984, p. 62.

Destrée felt that the idea of incorporation with France was impossible and proposed that a constitutional government be developed that would guarantee Walloonian rights. In 1947 a caucus of Walloonians found 486 of 1,048 delegates favoring separation from Belgium and union with France, but Belgium compromised by forming separate governments for Walloons and Flemings.

Equality? Destrée's ideas were incorporated in a Belgian consitution revised between 1967 and 1971. This provided for a federation of two separate units, with two separate governments and a central government that provided proportional representation of Flemings and Walloons. Over the years following, separate school systems using Walloon (French) and Flemish were established and these were further divided among church schools and state schools.

Division between Walloons and Flemings in the 1950s and 1960s found a new ground. The ruler during World War II had been Leopold III, who had very early capitulated to the Germans—some Belgians felt too early. During the war Leopold was forced to give up his rule. After the war, Walloonians found themselves with a more rapidly declining economy and higher taxes under the Loi Lanque, which they felt was unjustly imposed. The dissention resulted in a split in the Belgian trade union and the formation of the Mouvement Populaire Walloon. When the question of reinstating King Leopold arose, Walloonians were not receptive to the old form of government. Although Leopold was reinstated by popular election, Walloons voted against this action.

The fate of Walloonians remains in question, with recent government action (1986) requiring that Dutch be offered as a second language in all Walloon-language schools, and eventually be a required course. Meanwhile, the economy of Belgium has shifted to an industrial economy based in the north, and a commercial and political base in Brussels. Brussels, also the political capital, is a separate bilingual section of the country that forms a self-governing island in the Flemish northern sector.

Liège is the largest French-speaking city in Belgium. *Courtesy of the Belgian Institute for Information and Documentation.*

Culture Today

Language. It is the language of Rome and France that separates the Walloons from their northern Belgium neighbors, the Flemings. This language of the Walloons is, in fact, several dialects—western, central, and eastern Walloon Picard Goumais—that are related to but different from French. The language of the Walloons, for example, pronounces no unaccented "e's," does not use "q" or "qu" as the French do, and has no "x," "ph," or "th" sounds. A romance language, the language of the Walloons differs greatly from the Germanic languages of their Dutch, German, and eastern Belgian neighbors.

Walloon history is marked by the difficulties of language. In 1917, Wallonians were still the dominant group in Belgium, even though they were in the minority. Most of the officers in the military were Walloon-speaking leaders of Dutch-speaking soldiers. In 1986, a Walloon-speaking mayor was elected for the town of Vorren, which had recently been transferred to the Dutch-speaking province of Limburg. The debate over his right to remain in office because he was unable to speak Dutch eventually spilled over into the national government and caused that government's resignation.

Village life. Once Walloonia was the economic backbone of Belgium, with small industries manufacturing basketry, milling grains, preparing syrups and preserves, creating ironworks, and quarrying stone. It was, and remains, a land of small villages. And these villages, although changing today, reflect the region's history. One reporter studied a village of about 900 citizens and found there, in the 1950s, a near caste system that was led by a nobility inherited from the Knights Templar and the days of the German Holy Roman Empire. The true Walloonians were led by this nobility of Germanic people. Another legacy of the days of the Knights Templar, to whom much of the land was given, is the high position of the Catholic clergy. Below the nobility and clergy, landowners who possessed coats of arms, then professionals, then farmers of larger tracts and politicians, and finally laborers formed the societal levels in the village.

The typical village, containing a few stores and neat rows of brick houses, remains in spite of modern industrialization. While village life continues, mining, quarrying, and manufacturing provide more than half the jobs for Walloonians and require a great deal of commuting to larger towns with their factories and ports. Diamond processors, food processors, chemical manufacturers, and iron and steel refiners are major production employers in all of Belgium, while another large percentage of the population of the cities and the villages works in the many offices dedicated to commerce—local and international.

A major location in each village is one or more cafés, where the villagers gather in the evenings to drink beer, eat, and talk. In most Walloon villages these cafés do not fully open until the work shifts have ended in the evening.

Farm life. The most common farm pattern is a single family operating a small farm of 100 to 200 acres on which sweet potatoes, rye, wheat, and other grains are grown and on which a few cattle are tended. Often, the day-to-day care of the farm is left to the women while the men travel to and from work in the new factories in the east. Belgium and especially Walloonia are not large regions, so workers can board one of the many narrow gauge trains to commute to the large towns and cities in Walloonia or Flanders to work, and then return in the evening to do the heavy work of the farm. Farm women are nearly always responsible for dairy work and for maintaining the small, immaculately kept brick farmhouses.

Family life. More important than the village to most Walloonians is the family. This consists of a nuclear family (husband, wife, and children) and other nearby relatives. The members of the family work together and share common goals and interests. In some places, the family once served as a bank, with family members pooling their incomes to buy land, houses, and other necessities. In the 1990s Walloonians, like other people, are being affected by industrialization. Individual members are becoming less dependent on the family structure as they move away or commute some distance to jobs in manufacturing.

Although the Walloon family is male-dominated, eventually it is the older women who have much to say about the activities of the family and the nature of the home. These women have much influence in such events as weddings. The young couples of the 1990s, as did their ancestors, form bonds without the intercession of family or matchmakers. Older women still act as counselors in these matters, but the family is not as much involved in arranging marriages as in the past. In the early part of this century it was common practice for a male suitor to call on the family of the prospective bride accompanied by a set of his friends. Invited in, he and his friends would be plied with liquor until it was time to leave. If the young men behaved well under the abundance of liquor, the older woman of the family would signify approval by offering coffee before the visitors left.

Food. Walloon peasants eat four or more times a day beginning with an early morning breakfast of slabs of bread and butter, fruit preserves or cheese, and coffee. Dinner is the noon meal and may include one of many soups, bacon or ham, vegetables in season, and always fried potatoes (french fries may be a Belgian creation rather than a French one). A mid-afternoon snack is made up of *tartines*—bread, butter, and preserves such as that eaten as part of breakfast. A typical late supper consists of fried potatoes, bread and butter, bacon, eggs, sometimes rabbit, a delicate pastry, and *charcutene*, pork sausage with head cheese.

Recreation. Some of the popular recreational activities of the Walloons have bases in the past. For example, an old Wallonian game involved mounting live ducks on slowly rotating wheels. Participants would throw metal blades at the ducks in hopes of beheading them. Winners took home the duck for dinner. This sport is no longer played but is remembered in the popular celebration of the Feast of the Beheading of St. John the Baptist, commonly known as the "day of the cock," and in the current attachment with birds seen in the sport of racing pigeons. Pitching iron quoits is drawn from the older game of horseshoes.

Meeting for hours in the cafés to talk about politics, work, and families is the most popular leisure-time activity in the Walloon villages and towns. But the national Belgian passion is British-style football. Fans turn out in great numbers for football events, and avidly take sides in the contest. A riot at one 1985 football game in the city of Garmash resulted in such heated debate that it nearly brought down the Belgian government.

Education. Walloons have their own separate government under the national government at Brussels. This government operates a separate Walloon-language school system under the Belgian system, which demands full-time school attendance from age six to 16 and then part-time attendance for an additional two years. But Walloonians are more and more finding it necessary to commute to Brussels, a bilingual city, or to factories in Dutch-speaking areas. In 1986, the federal government decreed that Walloonian students should be given the option of learning Dutch as a second language to prepare them for the growing business, industry, and commerce opportunities in the north. Many students also learn German, a language also spoken in some parts of Belgium. Students may continue to study in colleges, technical institutes, and universities. The University of Liege is one of the oldest European seats of learning.

Religion. Almost all Walloons are Christians, and most are Roman Catholics. But the isolation in the past that found much of the region surrounded but neglected by the Frankish rulers left many remnants of the earlier Druid religions. The Evil One still haunts the forest regions, and various methods of healing reflect blends of early Christianity and Druidism. *Toucher*, healing by touch, is still practiced in some villages. This is accompanied by Druidic incantations called *seignai* or in some settings is replaced by a more precise touching called *ri'pougui*, in which the injured part of the body is encircled with thumbs and forefingers.

Still, most Walloons celebrate Christian ceremonies and rituals, with days for recognizing the saints; times of particular celebration and feasting.

Art and literature. During the period of Spanish rule and even before, all of the lowlands that is now Holland and Belgium was united as the Netherlands and then the Spanish Netherlands. In this period, a great tradition in art and literature developed in the northern part of the Netherlands. During the Spanish rule, this interest in art and literature was much suppressed, but after the 1830 independence of the area, there was a strong movement toward recalling the work of the writers and artists of Flanders. At the same time that Walloons were gaining strength through industry, that strength was being challenged by Spanish pressure to move commerce from Brugges in the south to the better port at Antwerp. Walloon industrial growth was finally destroyed during World War I, and the leadership of Walloonia became dominated by the Germanic nobility. The result is that much of the literary and artistic heritage of Belgium is based in the north and related to the literature and art of Holland. For an account of this artistic and literary heritage see DUTCH and FLEMING.

For More Information

Irving, Dr. R. E. M. *The Flemings and Walloons of Belgium:* Report #46. London: The Minority Rights Group, (not dated).

Turney-High, Harry Holbert. *Chateau-Gérard: The Life and Times of a Walloon Village.* Columbia, South Carolina: University of South Carolina Press, 1953.

Wickman, Stephen B. *Belgium, A Country Study.* Washington, D.C.: American University, 1984.

WELSH
(welsh)

People of predominantly Celtic descent who live in Wales.

Population: 2,900,000 (1990 estimate).
Location: Western Britain.
Languages: English, Welsh.

Geographical Setting

Wales, homeland of the Welsh, occupies an area of western Britain just slightly larger than New Jersey. (Wales, England and Scotland together make up the island of Britain [see ENGLISH and SCOTS]. Britain plus the island of Ireland [see IRISH] comprise the British Isles.) Wales is shaped roughly like a rectangle with a bite taken out of the west side. The bite is Cardigan Bay, facing Ireland across the Irish Channel. North of Cardigan Bay the island of Anglesey and the Lleyn peninsula jut westward; to the south, also stretching west, lies the larger Pembroke peninsula. Bounded by water on three sides, Wales itself constitutes a peninsula, with its eastern border formed by England. Much of the terrain is mountainous in the northwest, the rugged Snowdonia range is named for Mount Snowdon, at 3,560 feet the highest in Britain south of Scotland. Lesser mountains and hills run south through central Wales into Pembroke and the famous coalfields of South Wales.

Principal cities and towns lie mostly along the coast. From these busy seaports Welsh sea captains carried ore and slate from Welsh mines and quarries. Notable seaports spread from Cardiff, Wales' capital and largest city, which lies on the Bristol Channel in the south, to Caernarfon (car nar vin) and Bangor opposite Anglesey in the north. The Welsh climate is temperate and wet.

Welsh

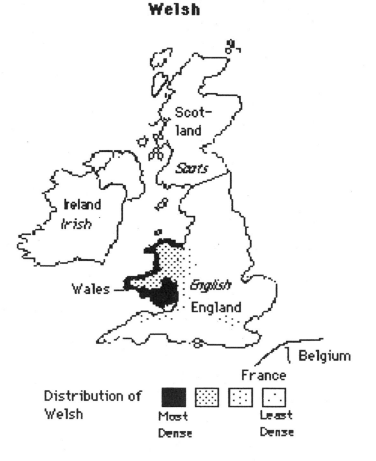

Distribution of Welsh

Most Dense   Least Dense

Historical Background

Celts and Romans. Little is known of the peoples who settled Britain before 1000 B.C., about the middle of the Bronze Age. They left their mark, however, in the massive stone structures (such as Stonehenge) found throughout the British Isles. Toward the end of the Bronze Age (from about 1000–200 B.C.), Central European peoples known collectively as Celts expanded westward into Italy, Spain, France, and the British Isles. With their iron weapons and tools, the warlike Celtic tribes brought the Iron Age to northern Europe. In Britain, the Celts absorbed the previous population. Beginning in A.D. 43, the Romans gained control of southern England and Wales. They built roads, forts, and military camps, traces of which remain today. By A.D. 400, after more than 350 years of such occupation, the Celts of southern Britain had adopted some aspects of Roman culture, though Wale's remoteness meant that Celtic ways remained strong there (see CELTS).

Coming of the English. With the collapse of Roman power in the 400s, Germanic tribes from Northern Europe began settling in south-eastern Britain. Most numerous were the Angles and the Saxons, related peoples who became the English (the word "English" comes from the name of the Angles). The Celts resisted this long influx of alien settlers, but were gradually pushed west. By about 800, they occupied only Britain's remotest reaches, where their descendants live today: the Highland Scots, the Cornish of the southwest coast, and the Welsh. The Irish are also Celtic.

Over the coming centuries, the Welsh, isolated from other Celts, developed their own distinctive culture. However, their identity would always be shaped by the presence of their powerful English neighbors. The names of the land and the people in English both come from the Anglo-Saxon *wealas*, or "strangers." It was in the 600s, when the borders of modern Wales had been established, that the Welsh first referred to themselves as *Cymry*, "fellow-countrymen," the term still used in Welsh today.

Norman castles. In 1066, William the Conqueror defeated the English and, with his French-born Norman nobles and knights, took power in England. England's new rulers quickly grew determined to subdue the unruly Welsh. Over the next century, the Normans built a series of wooden forts throughout Wales, from which Norman lords held control over surrounding lands. In the late 1100s, they replaced the wooden strongholds with massive, turreted stone castles. From about 1140–1240, Welsh princes such as Rhys ap Gruffydd and Llewellyn the Great rose up against the Normans, capturing some castles and briefly regaining power in the land.

English conquest. After Llewellyn's death in 1240, Welsh unity weakened. The English King Edward I (died 1307) conquered Wales in the late 1200s, building another series of massive castles to reinforce his rule. (By the 1200s, the Norman rulers of England are usually considered to be English, although French was still the language of government [see ENGLISH].) Under Edward and his successors, Welsh revolts continued against the English. Most important was the rebellion of Owain Glyndwr in the early 1400s. Despite his ultimate failure, Glyndwr strikes a heroic chord in Welsh memory as the last great leader to envision and fight for an independent Wales.

Union under Tudor monarchs. During the 1400s, the Welsh increasingly became involved in English affairs. In particular, they took part in the War of the Roses, in which the noble houses of York and Lancaster contested the English throne. In 1485, a young Welsh nobleman named Henry Tudor (whose mother was a Lancaster) won the Battle of Bosworth Field against King Richard III, thus securing his claim to the English throne. The Welsh rejoiced at having a Welshman as king of England. King Henry VII, as Henry Tudor was called, restored many of the rights that the Welsh had lost under English occupation. Under his son, Henry VIII, Wales and England became unified under one political system. Elizabeth I, daughter of Henry VIII and the last Tudor monarch, died in 1603. By that time, English language, law, and customs had become entrenched in Welsh life. Since that time, the history of the Welsh people has been closely tied to that of their English neighbors. The land of the Welsh people has become a highly industrialized and mining section of the United Kingdom of Great Britain. About four of five Welsh people have adopted English as their language. Yet the Welsh remained a people apart, proud, independent-minded, and always conscious of their own national character.

Culture Today

Industry. From Roman times, mining has been a part of life in ore-rich Wales. Gold, silver, lead, and copper could be found with relative ease. In the 1800s, as the Industrial Revolution gathered speed, large-scale mining of these metals, along with massive amounts of coal and slate, provided many Welsh families with their livelihoods. Slate quarrymen (those who dug the hard, gray stone from the ground) and coal miners—each a dusty, hard-working, close-knit group—became one version of the "typical" Welshman to the outside world. Entire towns of these working men and their families sprang up, in areas such as the Rhondda Valley in South Wales. By 1911, the South Wales coalfields employed over 200,000 people. With the Great Depression of the 1930s, however, these industries died, never to recover. Today, environmental damage remains in some areas. Social attitudes continue to be shaped by what many Welsh regard as past exploitation of the working people by rich (and often English) industrialists.

Religion. Like the Industrial Revolution, a religious revolution swept through Wales for a century or so, then moved on, leaving Welsh society deeply changed in its wake. While the Welsh had been converted to Christianity before the arrival of the Anglo-Saxons, the people had never been especially religious. For years, the Anglican (English) Church represented English attitudes, leaving the Welsh lukewarm. From the mid-1700s to the mid-1800s, however, the Methodist Revival blew through the Welsh countryside, displacing the conservative, English-dominated Anglican Church. The fiery Methodist preachers advocated social equality, education, and personal salvation to ecstatic crowds of Welsh peasants. This "Nonconformist" version of the Protestant faith became the people's religion, practiced in small country chapels rather than grand churches, emphasizing personal faith rather than social class. Though the religious enthusiasms have largely faded in recent years, such social attitudes remain firmly rooted in the Welsh character. Methodism, with its rollicking hymns and religious songs, also left its mark in the deep Welsh love of singing.

Cymreictod. The Welsh and the nearby Scots and Irish descend from different branches of the Celtic family. Scots and Irish are from the Gaelic (gay lick) branch, while the Welsh, the Cornish and the Bretons (breh tunz) of France descend from the Brythonic (brih thon ick) branch. Thus, while they cannot understand an Irish or Scottish Gaelic-speaker, Welsh-speakers can get by in conversation with a French-born speaker of Breton. Only about 20 percent of the population speaks Welsh (and they are bilingual in English). Still, the Welsh speakers are viewed as somehow "more Welsh," members of a special core in society, a center to which others anchor their own feelings of *Cymreictod*, or Welshness. All road signs are written in both Welsh and English, television and radio shows are often broadcast in Welsh, and Welsh is offered in school.

Legend and symbol. Much of Cymreictod derives from colorful legends of the Celtic past. Magic and mystery abound in these ancient tales. Best-known is that of King Arthur and his Knights of the Round Table. It is believed that, if he actually existed, Arthur was a Celtic king from about 500, who fought against invading Anglo-Saxons. His tale has been embroidered through the centuries, after being popularized by an imaginative Welsh writer of the 1100s, Geoffrey of Monmouth. Visitors to Wales today may be shown the site of the Round Table, as well as the window at which Geoffrey wrote his tales—while appreciating that both sites occupy the realm of legend, not fact.

Arthurian legend also supplied the Welsh national symbol, a red dragon. A Welsh king, attempting to build a new capital, was baffled by the disappearance during the night of each day's construction. Only the famous magician Merlin, then a young man, could explain how the stones were being displaced. Deep underground, Merlin said, were two fighting dragons, a red one and a white one. The red dragon was Cymry, the Welsh, and the white was the Saxons. They would continue to fight through the centuries, until finally the red dragon would prevail. The king moved his palace—and many Welsh still wait for the red dragon, now shown on the Welsh flag and other emblems, to win at last!

Literature. Before Geoffrey of Monmouth, Arthurian and other legends came from a body of tales called the *Mabinogion*. These old stories combined the exploits of historical or quasi-historical figures (such as Arthur) with material made up by the bards who composed them. Though the earliest written copies of the Mabinogion date from the 1300s, the stories are perhaps 1,000 (or more) years older. The bards (oral storytellers) come from a tradition that goes back to pre-Roman times, when they held an important place in Celtic society. Their prestige came from the ability with which they glorified the exploits of great warriors in battle.

The bards' poetic blood still flows strong in Welsh veins, and Wales boasts many fine poets. Most famous of all is Dylan Thomas (1914–1953). Aside from his poetry, he is remembered for works like *A Child's Christmas in Wales* and the radio-play *Under Milk Wood*. Other Welsh writers of this century include philosopher Bertrand Russell; T. E. Lawrence (Lawrence of Arabia), who describes in *The Seven Pillars of Wisdom* his World War I experiences in the Middle East; and travel writer Jan Morris, whose 1984 book *The Matter of Wales* gracefully and poetically describes her own land and people.

The arts. Among several well-known twentieth-century painters, foremost is Augustus John, whose portrait of Dylan Thomas hangs in Cardiff's National Museum. Wales' poetic language and traditions encourage vocal performance, as shown by a number of Welsh actors and singers. Richard Burton first made his mark in the plays of Shakespeare, later playing King Arthur in the Broadway musical *Camelot*. He also starred in movies such as *Becket* and *The Spy Who Came in from the Cold*. Ray Milland had a very successful Hollywood career; Emlyn Williams (a friend of Burton's), aside from acting, has written plays, including *The Corn Is Green*. Welsh singers known to the wider world include Tom Jones, Shirley Bassey, and opera star Margaret Price.

Eisteddfod. Welsh affection for poetry and music shows itself in the cultural institution of the *eisteddfod*. Hundreds of these folk festivals are held each year throughout Wales, featuring competitions in poetry, music, and folk dancing. An annual International Eisteddfod attracts participants from around the world. By far the most popular, however, is the yearly National Eisteddfod of Wales, whose site alternates between towns in North or South Wales each year. For the first week of each August, huge tents and pavilions house events and exhibitions; one may learn Welsh, buy a harp (the Welsh national instrument), and at week's end see the crowning of winning "bards" in the different poetic categories. The proceedings are run by officers modeled on those of the ancient Druid religion, which was overthrown in Wales by the Romans. The oldest recorded eisteddfod occurred in 1451, but the modern institution was begun as part of a resurgent interest in Celtic culture in the 1800s. For many in Britain and Europe, the National Eisteddfod is the most visible symbol of Welsh culture.

Language. *Cymraeg*, the Welsh language, visible in signs all over Wales, looks difficult to an outsider. It also sounds strange, with lilting, musical tones in which one word seems to slur into the next. And in a sense, it may—the first letter of a word may change depending on the word before it. This is called *treiglo*, and it achieves a smoothness treasured by the Welsh ear. Welsh also contains elusive sounds such as *ll* (in the name Llewellyn, for example), which is pronounced almost like a combination of *f, th* and *ch*, though not quite. Most English speakers don't attempt it. Complex as it is, Welsh can claim to be (in Jan Morris' words) "the oldest living literary language in Europe . . . .the truest badge of Welsh identity—*Yr Hen Iaith,* the Old Language of the country, as against *Yr Iaith Fain*, the Thin Language of the English" (Morris 1984, p. 158).

Food, clothing, and shelter. Welsh cuisine uses the basic ingredients of dairy products, eggs, seafood, lamb or beef, and simple vegetables such as potatoes, carrots and leeks. (A national symbol, leeks are waved at rugby football matches by Welsh fans. The leek—which resembles a thick, mild-tasting green onion—is Wales' most popular vegetable, being featured in soups and stews.) One favorite dish, Anglesey Eggs, includes leeks, cheese, and potatoes. Welsh Rabbit (often called Rarebit by the English) combines eggs, cheese, milk, Worcestershire sauce, and beer. The rich, melted mixture is poured over toast.

In the countryside, Welsh houses are most commonly built of stone, either bare or sometimes whitewashed. In industrial or mining areas, the people have often lived in cramped, drab row houses.

The Welsh dress much as Europeans and North Americans do, though perhaps a bit more formally than the latter. Among young people, however, jeans, a t-shirt and running shoes are as common in Wales as everywhere else. Traditional costumes, commonly worn at events such as an eisteddfod, feature colorful stripes and checks, with a wide-brimmed hat for women that looks like a witch's hat with the top half of the cone cut off.

For More Information

Morris, Jan. *The Matter of Wales.* Oxford: Oxford University Press, 1984.

Sutherland, Dorothy. *Enchantment of the World: Wales.* Chicago: Children's Press, 1987.

Tomes, John. *Blue Guide: Wales and the Marches.* London: Ernest Benn Ltd., 1979.

Williams, David. *A Short History of Modern Wales.* London: John Murray Ltd., 1961.

Williams, Glyn A. *When Was Wales?* London: Black Raven Press, 1985.

Glossary

Alans Iranian people who established themselves on land north of the Caspian Sea. From there they spread into the steppes of Russia and began (A.D. 1st century) to move into the Roman provinces along the Danube River and in the Carpathian Mountains. They were divided by the Huns into two groups: one traveled across Europe into Northern Africa; the other group retreated into the steppes, but were later forced to move to the Caucasus Mountains, where they became known as Osetes.

Althing A gathering of representatives from local governments (*things*) of Iceland and later Greenland for the purpose of establishing rules of government and hearing matters of law. The Althing, a Viking contribution to government, was the first example of parliamentary government in modern Europe (first formed in A.D. 930).

Carlists These followers of Carlos of Bourbon supported his claims and those of his ancestors to the Spanish throne. The Carlist stronghold was the Basque region of Spain, from which they launched several rebellions in the 1800s.

Carolingians (Carlovingians) The leaders of the Franks beginning with Charles Martel and ending with Louis V (d. 987). The Carolingians succeeded the Merovingians as rulers of the Franks and were themselves succeeded by the house of Hugh Capet. Charlemagne was one of the Carolingian rulers.

Corpus Christi This celebration was devised by the Catholic Church to follow immediately upon the end of Pentecost in honor of the Eucharist (a religious ceremony in which bread and wine are used symbolically in a reenactment of the Last Supper). This celebration was among the first to be abolished in Protestant churches that followed Martin Luther.

Dacia An ancient country in Central Europe bounded on the north by the Carpathian mountains and on the south and east by the Danube River. The country was conquered by the Roman Trajan and became a Roman province. Today, Romania is roughly the same as the old Dacia.

Dreyfus Affair An incidence of anti-Semitism in which certain French Army officers forged documents that convicted Alfred Dreyfus of treason in 1884—passing secret information to the Germans. Dreyfus was convicted and sent to Devil's Island for life. Two advocates for Dreyfus, Colonel Picquart and the famous author Emile Zola, were also imprisoned in the subsequent appeals (Zola for writing a castigation of the army management, "J'accuse"). Trials and accusations brought down the military establishment and caused a reorganization of the government before Dreyfus was pardoned by the president and restored to military duty in 1906.

Edict of Nantes In 1598, King Henry IV of France proclaimed religious tolerance of the Protestants in that country in the Edict of Nantes. Protestantism gained much ground in Europe as a result of this edict. However, in France, the Protestants used it to overwhelm the Catholics, confiscating Catholic properties and forming their own military organizations. The animosity that developed resulted in revocation of the edict in various stages until it was finally eliminated in 1685.

European Community Originally begun out of concern for common economic interests, the European Community has grown to include a common European court and a Common Market.

feudalism The condition in Europe between the ninth and fifteenth century under which land was owned by a few wealthy landowners and loaned by them to peasants who were then committed, as if they were slaves, to serve the owners.

fjord A long, narrow inlet of the sea bordered by steep cliffs and slopes. Fjords mark the coast of Norway and are found in Alaska.

futurism An art form that began in 1910 in Italy, which intended to capture the vibrance and motion of modern industry-driven society.

Grindadrap Faroe Islanders are dependent for some of their income on the hunting of whales. Pilot whales swim near the islands in groups. Faroe Islanders capture the whales by forcing them onshore in a hurried, inefficient method known as Grindadrap.

Habsburgs Popularly known as Hapsburgs, this family ruled Austro-Hungary. This royal family originated in Habaichtsburg, Switzerland, and ruled in Central Europe from the time of Werner II (1096) until World War I. Members of this family served at various times in the royalty of England, as emperors of Germany, as Holy Roman Emperor, and as rulers of Spain.

holocaust Originally a word that applied to great destruction by fire, holocaust came to signify any disaster of mass destruction, particularly of human life. Thus, Turkish destruction of the Armenians in the early 1900s may be termed a holocaust. At present, the word is most often used with a capital *H* to name the most disastrous of modern-day mass executions—the destroying of 6,000,000 Jews by Germany before and during World War II.

League of Nations An organization of many of the world's countries that attempted to establish worldwide laws and peace. The League of Nations was devised by American president Woodrow Wilson, but was rejected by the United States Congress. The United States never joined in this post-World War I effort at world unity.

lit de mort This term translates literally to "bed of death." It refers to the bed of a dead person while lying in state during a wake.

Mafia Probably initiated as the compani d'armi organized in Sicily to protect citizens against oppressive governments, the Mafia became a secret, militant organization dedicated to lawlessness and disdain for official court systems. It survives in a more moderate form today despite Garibaldi's declaring it illegal in 1890 and, later, Benito Mussolini's intense dedication to destroy it.

Minoans People of the island of Crete who, in the period of the discovery of bronze, had developed a kingdom centered at Knossos. Under King Minos, this society became powerful traders in the Aegean and Mediterranean seas. Elements of similar societies have been found on the Greek mainland at Athens and in Troy, for example.

Moesia An ancient country of southeast Europe between the Drinus River and the Black Sea and south of the Danube River. It was invaded by the Romans in 75 B.C. and fully conquered 45 years later. Moesia became two Roman provinces that later became Serbia and northern Bulgaria.

polder A polder is an area of land, once under water or boggy, that has been reclaimed by pumping and damming. Much of the Netherlands is formed of polders reclaimed from the sea.

reiks Rulers of the Goths.

Romansch One of a group (Raeto-Romance) of Romance language dialects, Romansch or Romansh is spoken in eastern Switzerland, parts of northern Italy, and the Tyrol.

Thing Before 930, the Thing was the gathering of local units in Iceland for the purpose of establishing rules of conduct and settling local legal issues. In 930, representatives of the various Things formed the first parliament, the Althing.

Thrace An area in southeast Europe drained by the Hebrus (Martisa) River, which included the Rhodope Mountains. The name came to include an expanded region taking in part of Greece and Turkey under Ottoman rule. Today, the original Thrace includes central and southern Bulgaria, northeast Greece, and the part of Turkey in Europe.

Union of Utrecht In 1543, Charles V separated 17 lowland provinces from the German Empire. Some of the southern provinces then united in the Union of Brussels (1577). In 1579, John of Nassau united seven northern Protestant provinces under the Union of Utrecht. This union is recognized as the beginning of the Dutch Republic, which preceded the Netherlands (1579-1814). The Union statement was the basis of Dutch law for 215 years.

United Nations Patterned after the League of Nations, this organization was formed after World War II as a means of communication among countries and an instrument to arbitrate world disputes and further education and health.

Bibliography

Ahmed, Aziz. *A History of Islamic Sicily*. Berkeley, California: University of California Press, 1979.

Ashton, Agnes. *Saints and Changelings: Folk-Tales of Brittany*. Glasgow: Blackie and Sons Limited, 1975.

Bailey, George. *Germans: The Biography of an Obsession*. New York: World Publishing, 1972.

Barzini, Luigi. *The Italians: A Full-length Portrait Featuring Their Manners and Morals*. New York: Atheneum, 1965.

Bradford, Sarah. *Portugal*. New York: Wather, 1973.

Brogger, Anton Wilhelm. *The Viking Ships*. New York: Twayne Publishers, 1971.

Bunge, Frederica M., editor. *Cyprus, A Country Study*. Washington, D.C.: American University, 1979.

Castro, Americo. *The Spaniards, An Introduction to Their History*. Translated by Willard F. King and Selma Margaretten. Berkeley, California: University of California Press, 1971.

Chibnall, Marjorie. *Anglo-Norman England 1066-1166*. Oxford: Basil Blackwell Limited, 1986.

Coburn, Oliver. *Sicily*. New York: Oxford University Press, 1968.

Davis, R. H. C. *The Normans and Their Myths*. London: Thames and Hudson, 1976.

de Figuarelo, Antonio. *Portugal: 50 Years of Dictatorship*. New York: Holmes and Weier, 1976.

de Gramont, Sanske. *The French: Portrait of a People*. New York: G. P. Putnam's Sons, 1969.

De Wolfe, Ivor. *The Italian Townscape.* London: Braziller, 1966.

Dodd, A. H. *Life in Wales.* London: B. T. Batsford, Ltd., 1972.

Edwards, Owen Dudley, ed. *Conor Cruise O'Brien Introduces Ireland.* New York: McGraw-Hill, 1969.

Fenton, Alexander and Hermann Pálsson, editors. *The Northern and Western Isles in the Viking* World. Edinburgh, Scotland: John Donald Publishers Ltd., 1984.

Fodor's Ireland 1989. New York: Fodor's Travel Publications, 1989.

Forgacs, David. *Italian Culture in the Industrial Era: 1880-1980.* Manchester, England: Manchester University Press, 1990.

Gantz, Jeffrey (trans.). *Mabinogion.* Harmondsworth, England: Penguin Books, 1976.

Gregory, Bishop of Tours. *History of the Franks.* New York: Columbia University Press, 1969.

Guin, Yamick. *Histoire de la Bretagne de 1789 a Nou Jours.* Paris: Librairie François Maspero, 1970.

Herr, Frederick. *Europe, Mother of Revolution.* New York: Frederick A. Praeger, 1972.

Hollister, C. Warren. *Monarchy, Magnates and Institutions in the Anglo-Norman World.* London: The Hambledon Press, 1986.

Ivanova, Anna. *The Dancing Spaniards.* London: John Baker, Publishers, Ltd., 1970.

Jackson, Hampden. *A Short History of France from Early Times to 1972.* London: Cambridge University Press, 1974.

Jewett, Sarah Orne. *The Story of the Normans.* New York: G. P. Putnam's Sons, 1986.

Jones, Gwyn. *A History of the Vikings.* London: Oxford University Press, 1968.

Kiray, Mübeccel, editor. *Structural Change in Turkish Society,* Bloomington, Indiana: Indiana University Turkish Studies, 1991.

Kohn, Hans. *The Mind of Germany: The Education of a Nation.* New York: Charles Scribner's Sons, 1960.

Llewellyn, Alun. *The Shell Guide to Wales.* London: Michael Joseph, 1969.

Lyon, Margot. *Belgium.* New York: Walker, 1971.

Machado, Dismantino P. *The Structure of Portuguese Society: The Failure of Facism.* New York: Frederick A. Praeger, 1991.

Markides, Kyriacos C. *The Rise and Fall of the Cyprus Republic.* New Haven: Yale University Press, 1977.

Meijer, Reinder P. *Literature of the Low Countries: A Short History of Dutch Literature in the Netherlands and Belgium.* New York: Irvington, 1978.

Nyrop, Richard F., editor. *Turkey, A Country Study.* Washington, D.C.: American University, 1979.

Payne, Stanley G. *Basque Nationalism.* Reno, Nevada: University of Nevada Press, 1975.

Peltenburg, Edgar, editor. *Early Societies in Cyprus.* Edinburgh: Edinburgh University Press, 1989.

Puzo, Mario. *The Sicilian.* Boston: G. K. Hale, 1985.

Read, Jan. *The Catalans,* London: Faber and Faber, 1978.

Salvadori, Nassimo. *A Pictorial History of the Italian People.* New York: Crown, 1972.

Schneider, Jane and Peter. *Culture and Politics in Western Sicily.* New York: Academic Press, 1976.

Sebilleau, Pierre. *Sicily.* New York: Oxford University Press, 1968.

Shinn, Rinn S., editor. *Italy: A Country Study.* Washington, D.C.: American University Press, 1987.

Smeets, Albert. *Flemish Art from Ensor to Permake.* Trelt, Belgium: Lannoo, 1972.

Volkan, Vamik D., M.D. *Cyprus—War and Adaptation.* Charlottesville: University Press of Virginia, 1979.

Wakelin, Martyn F. *English Dialects: An Introduction.* London: The Athlone Press of the University of London, 1977.

Wickham, Stephen B., editor. *Belgium, A Country Study.* Washington, D.C.: American University, 1985.

Willings, Heather. *A Village of the Cavennes.* Southampton: The Camelot Press Ltd., 1979.

Wilson, Epiphanius, editor. *Turkish Literature.* Freeport, New York: Books for Libraries Press, 1970.

Wulley, David. *Italians.* London: British Broadcasting Company, 1984.

Index